Studien zur Vergleichenden Berufspädagogik

Herausgegeben von der Deutschen Gesellschaft für
Technische Zusammenarbeit (GTZ) GmbH

Band 7

Cornelia Lohmar-Kuhnle

assisted by Christian Breustedt and
Ingrid Ceballos Müller

Occupation-oriented Training and Education for Target Groups from the Informal Sector

Translated by Mike Brookman and
Cornelia Lohmar-Kuhnle

 Nomos Verlagsgesellschaft
Baden-Baden

This study was drawn up as a research project on behalf of the Federal Ministry for Economic Cooperation and Development by GITEC CONSULT GMBH, Düsseldorf. The views expressed in the research reports of the Federal Ministry for Economic Cooperation and Development reflect the opinion of the author/authors.

Die Deutsche Bibliothek – CIP-Einheitsaufnahme

Lohmar-Kuhnle, Cornelia:
Occupation-oriented Training and Education for Target Groups from the Informal Sector / Cornelia Lohmar-Kuhnle. Assisted by Christian Breustedt and Ingrid Ceballos Müller. Transl. by Mike Brookman and Cornelia Lohmar-Kuhnle. – 1. Aufl. – Baden-Baden: Nomos Verl.-Ges., 1994
   (Studien zur Vergleichenden Berufspädagogik; Bd. 7)
   Einheitssacht.: Konzepte zur beschäftigungsorientierten Aus- und Fortbildung von Zielgruppen aus dem informellen Sektor <engl.>
   ISBN 3-7890-3530-0
NE: GT

© Federal Ministry for Economic Cooperation and Development, Bonn, Federal Republic of Germany
(Responsible: Dr. Frank Schwarzbeck, Werner Klein)
The German Version »Konzepte zur beschäftigungsorientierten Aus- und Fortbildung von Zielgruppen aus dem informellen Sektor« was published as Volume 100 of the Series »Research Reports of the Federal Ministry for Economic Cooperation (BMZ)« and can be obtained via the Weltforum Verlag, Marienburger Straße 22, D 50968 Köln / Germany.

1. Auflage Nomos Verlagsgesellschaft, Baden-Baden 1994. Printed in Germany. Alle Rechte, auch die des Nachdrucks von Auszügen, der photomechanischen Wiedergabe und der Übersetzung, vorbehalten.

This work is subject to copyright. All rights are reserved, whether the whole or part of the material is concerned, specifically those of translation, reprinting, re-use of illustrations, broadcasting, reproduction by photocopying machine or similar means, and storage in data banks. Under § 54 of the German Copyright Law where copies are made for other than private use a fee is payable to »Verwertungsgesellschaft Wort«, Munich.

Table of Contents

Abbreviations and Acronyms

Abstract.................................... 13

1. Introduction................................ 27
   1.1 Background and Scope of the Research Study .. 27
   1.2 Remarks on the Study's People-centred Perception............................. 29
   1.3 Clarification of Relevant Terms............. 33
2. Methodology 38
   2.1 Operationalization of the "Informal Sector" Concept.............................. 38
   2.2 Secondary Analysis of Concepts and Project Experience Relating to Occupation-oriented Training and Education................... 39
   2.3 Direct Information through Project Visits and Target Group Interviews in the Informal Sector 40
   2.4 Evaluation of Secondary Analysis and Direct Information........................... 46
3. The Informal Sector: Socio-economic Environment for the Economically and Socially Disadvantaged People 47
   3.1 Frame Conditions of Survival in the Market Economy and in the Subsistence Economy of the Informal Sector 48
   3.2 Economic Activities in the Urban and Rural Informal Sector 54
      3.2.1 Range of Economic Activities in the Informal Sector..................... 54
      3.2.2 Criteria for the Classification of Economic Activities as Informal Sector Activities... 57
      3.2.3 Interfaces between the Economies of the Informal Sector and the Modern Sector .. 59

	3.3	Some Critical Remarks as Regards the Reduction of the Informal Sector to Small and Micro-Enterprises under the Aspect of Economic Sector Promotion....................	61
4.	Multi-dimensional Identification of Target Groups from the Informal Sector		64
	4.1	"Rough Identification" of Target Groups Based on the Economic Activities Perceived	66
		4.1.1 Target Groups from the Urban Informal Sector	66
		4.1.2 Target Groups from the Rural Informal Sector	71
	4.2	"Specified Identification" of Target Groups with Regard to Learning Opportunities and Potentials...............................	74
		4.2.1 Determinants of Learning Opportunities and Potentials.....................	75
		4.2.2 Examples of Target Groups with Different Learning Opportunities and Potentials...	79
	4.3	"Status Identification" of Target Groups with Regard to Urban/Rural and Socialization-specific Integration.........................	82
	4.4	Summary of the Steps of a Multi-dimensional Identification of Target Groups from the Informal Sector	85
5.	Occupation-oriented Training and Education Needs of People from the Informal Sector		88
	5.1	Environment-determined Occupational Options as Determinants of Qualification Needs	89
	5.2	Essential Qualification Needs of People from the Informal Sector as Regards Training and Education	94
		5.2.1 Vocational Training with Regard to Realistic Occupational Options in the Modern or in the Informal Sector.......	95
		5.2.2 Strengthening of Self-help Potentials to Improve Living Conditions Through Subsistence Work	104
		5.2.3 Adequate Primary School and Adult Education for Better Vocational Training and Occupational Opportunities........	107

		5.2.4	Awareness Creation and Education on Health Care and Nutrition	111
		5.2.5	Social Education for the (Re)Integration of Rural and Socially Marginalized Target Groups	113
		5.2.6	Training and Education Measures Designed with Regard to Target Group-specific Learning Opportunities and Potentials	118
	5.3		Conclusions as to the Overall Objectives of Occupation-oriented Training and Education for Target Groups from the Informal Sector.......	121
6.			Approaches for the Occupation-oriented Training and Education of Target Groups from the Informal Sector	124
	6.1		Individual Qualification for a (Labour) Market-oriented Occupation and/or for Subsistence Work	126
		6.1.1	"Classic" Vocational Training and Education in (Partly) Government-run Training Centres	127
		6.1.2	Forms of Dual Vocational Training in Co-operation with Private (Small) Enterprises	138
		6.1.3	Informal Occupation-oriented Training ..	150
		6.1.4	Training and Education Related to the Environment-determined Occupational Options................................	161
		6.1.5	Vocational Training and Education with a Socio-pedagogical Approach in the Don Bosco Institutions...................	176
	6.2		Business Advice and Training for Small Enterprise Development and Self-employment Promotion	190
		6.2.1	Training for Small and Micro-Entrepreneurs "with Development Potential"	192
		6.2.2	Assistance for Small and Micro-Business Creation	199
	6.3		Complex Approaches to Occupation-oriented Training with Social Education for Rural Target Groups...............................	208
	6.4		Primary School Education as First Step Towards Occupation-oriented Training and Education ...	218

	6.4.1	Improved and Generally Accessible Primary School Education to Increase Occupation Opportunities............	219
	6.4.2	Environment-adapted Primary School Education Related to Realistic Occupation Opportunities	221
6.5		Synopsis of the Approaches Presented as Conceptual Modules	229
7. Recommendations for the Planning and Design of Vocational Training Assistance for People from the Informal Sector...............................			245
7.1		Towards a More Comprehensive Conceptual Perspective in (Bilateral) Vocational Training Assistance	246
7.2		Flexible and Dovetailed Planning and Implementation	253
	7.2.1	Participatory and Iterative Planning on Site	254
	7.2.2	Long-term Perspective, Continuity and Target Group Proximity..............	256
7.3		Suggestions as Regards the Conceptual and Institutional Design......................	258
	7.3.1	Suitable Approaches and Instruments ...	259
	7.3.2	Baseline and Tracer Studies	264
	7.3.3	Establishment of "Programme Offices" ..	265
7.4		Revised Self-perception and Qualification Profile for Development and Vocational Training Experts...............................	268
7.5		Remarks on the Financing of Occupation-oriented Training and Education for Poor Target Groups..........................	270
7.6		Conclusion.............................	273

Bibliography	277
Table of Contents.............................	279
Part I: Informal Sector.........................	280
Part II: Occupation-oriented Training and Education.	290

Abbreviations and Acronyms

AERDS	Agro Energy and Rural Development Society
AIT	Asian Institute of Technology
BGZ	Berliner Gesellschaft für deutsch-türkische wirtschaftliche Zusammenarbeit (Berlin Society for German-Turkish Economic Cooperation)
BMZ	Bundesministerium für Wirtschaftliche Zusammenarbeit (Federal Ministry for Economic Cooperation)
CDC	Community Development Cell
CDG	Carl-Duisberg-Gesellschaft e.V.
CDRT	Community Development and Rural Technology
CPY	Community Polytechnic Yellareddy
CREDA	Centre for Rural Education and Development Action
CSI	Church of South India
CTVT	Council for Technical and Vocational Training
DBISW	Don Bosco Institute of Social Work
DBSSC	Don Bosco Social Services Centre
DBTI	Don Bosco Technical Institute
DBTS	Don Bosco Technical School
DBYAC	Don Bosco Youth Animation Centre
DBYC	Don Bosco Youth Centre
DED	Deutscher Entwicklungsdienst (German Volunteer Service)
DESAP	Desarrollo de la Pequeña y (Micro-)Empresa
DOLA	Department of Local Administration
DOVE	Department of Vocational Education
DSE	Deutsche Stiftung für internationale Entwicklung
EZE	Evangelische Zentralstelle für Entwicklungshilfe
GO	Government Organization
GTZ	Deutsche Gesellschaft für Technische Zusammenarbeit GmbH (German Agency for Technical Coopertion)
GVS	German Volunteer Service
IERT	Institute for Engineering & Rural Technology
ILO	International Labor Organisation
INA	Instituto Nacional de Aprendizaje
INACAP	Instituto Nacional de Capacitación
INAFORP	Instituto Nacional de Cooperación Educativa
INFOP	Instituto Nacional de Formación Professional
INFOTEP	Instituto Nacional de Formación Técnico Professional

INSAFORP	Instituto Nacional Salvadoreño de Formación Professional
INTECAP	Instituto Nacional Técnico de Capacitación
IRDC	Integrated Rural Development Centre
ITC	Indian Training College
ITI	Indian Training Institute
KKU	Khon Kaen University
LTC	Lopburi Technical College
MEKSA	Foundation for the Promotion of Vocational Training and Small Industries (English Translation)
MES	Modules of Employable Skills
NFEC	Non-formal Education Centre
NGO	Non-Governmental Organisation
NOAS	National Open Apprenticeship Scheme
NRNFEC	Northern Region Non-formal Education Center
NRO	Nichtregierungsorganisation
NVTI	National Vocational Training Institute
PESP	Polytechnical Education Support Programme
PNFEC	Provincial Non-Formal Education Center
PPPR	Programa de Promoción Popular Rural
PPU	Programa de Promoción Popular Urbano
REAP	Rural Education and Agriculture Programme
SECAP	Servicio Ecuadoreano de Empleo y Capacitación
SENA	Servicio Nacional de Aprendizaje
SENAI	Servicio Nacional de Aprendiçao Industrial
SENAR	Servicio Nacional de Aprendiçao Rural
SENATI	Servicio Nacional de Aprendizaje para el Trabajo Industrial
SEP	Small Enterprise Promotion Project
SETCG	Self-employment Training Centre for Girls
SEWA	Self-employed Women's Association
SWRD	Small Water Resources Development Programme
TC	Technical College
THIRD	Thailand Institute for Rural Development
UNDP	United Nations Development Programme
UNESCO	United Nations Educational, Scientific and Cultural Organization
UNICEF	United Nations Children's Fund
ZGB	Zentralstelle für gewerbliche Berufsförderung (Industrial Occupations Promotion Centre)

It will be no possible solution to regard half of a population as a case for social welfare, without any significant economic development potential.

This would be beyond the economic capacity of even the richest welfare state. But what is more – it would mean to deny the dignity of millions of people who are willing to work hard to make a decent living.

Abstract

For most Third World countries it is true that in the foreseeable future the economic and technological development of their modern sector will be nowhere near able to provide adequate employment opportunities for all those willing to work. Therefore, a phenomenon called "the informal sector" will continue to grow in terms of both the number of people living there, and its economic and social relevance for the further development in those countries. Influencing and shaping this development of and within the informal sector towards the best possible utilization and mobilization of given resources and potentials must be regarded as one of the priority tasks of vocational training, too. As an occupation-oriented training and education for target groups from the informal sector it must contribute to the ultimate objective of development assistance, which is commonly understood to be the sustainable improvement of the living and working conditions of what is the majority of people. Against this background, the study explores what actually are the priority qualification needs of people from the informal sector, and how these needs could be met with target group-specific programmes and projects also within the framework of (bilateral) vocational training assistance.

As explained in greater detail in *Chapter 1*, the scope of the study has not been restricted to the "classic" formal and non-formal vocational training, but has taken into consideration various forms of directly and indirectly occupation-oriented training and education in a broader sense. It includes approaches which are (labour) market-oriented and more or less directly aimed at improving gainful wage- or self-employment opportunities, besides measures which are designed to provide a more subsistence-oriented occupational qualification enabling people to (better) secure a survival income and/or to improve their living conditions in self-help through subsistence work. Finally, some consideration is given to the occupational relevance of primary school education.

The study throughout follows a people-centred perception in which – different from a policy-centred approach – target groups are not regarded as somehow instrumental for the realization of primarily policy-determined objectives of development assistance, but as people in need of development assistance. The target groups themselves – i.e. certain social or economic group which have some basic features in common – and their needs, thus, are the reason for intended assistance measures, and the logics of planning with a people-centred perception accordingly is: Who should receive assistance for what reason, what are the priority needs and development options of the intended target group(s), and what would hence be an adequate objectives orientation and appropriate design for assistance measures which are meant to be target group-specific and needs-oriented. This puts social groups, people with their needs and potentials, first.

Chapter 2 outlines the research methodology applied. The study is based on an extensive secondary analysis of concepts and documented project experience in the field of occupation-oriented training and education as well as on direct information gathered through project visits and discussions with people from the urban and the rural informal sector during a reconnaissance mission to India and Thailand, and, finally, on own work experience especially with people from rural areas.

Without taking up in detail the extensive discussion within the professional community on the definition of the informal sector and the conditions of its evolution, *Chapter 3* characterizes the informal sector in Third World countries as the socio-economic environment in which millions of economically weak and socially disadvantaged people struggle to survive. The frame conditions for their survival in the market economy and in the subsistence economy of the informal sector, the economic activities in which they may be engaged, and, finally, the main interfaces between the informal sector and the modern sector are described to make aware of the economic and social factors which determine the conditions under which people from the informal sector live and work, and which influence their attitudes, needs, priorities and development options including the scope of their educational and occupational opportunities. Finally, some reservation is expressed against the widespread equation of the informal sector with the total of small and micro-enterprises under the aspect of economic sector promotion. This neither adequately reflects the phenomenon of the informal sector nor the situation and development options of the people living and working there.

The distinguishing feature of the informal sector against the modern sector is not seen in the illegality of economic activities, or in their missing or impossible statistical recording. A much more decisive polarity is in the living and working conditions. They differ for the economically weak and socially disadvantaged people of a society significantly from the norms and systems, the technologies, working conditions and life-styles of the urban-industrial culture which is worldwide labelled as "modern".

People who – for economic, social or personal reasons – are unable to settle or to remain in the economic and social systems of the modern sector, gather in the economic and social catchment area called "the informal sector". Living in the informal sector means having little or no access to formal education and vocational training, to reasonably paid employment, to development-relevant information, to credit at usual market terms, or to proper medical care, often not even enough food and (drinking) water – in short, being largely excluded from almost everything which could enable participation in the benefits of a society's modern economic and social development. The very fact that they cannot (any more) organize their lives along the norms, regulations and development perspectives prevailing in the modern sector, makes the living and working situation of countless people in Third World countries "informal". For most of them, this situation is marked by poverty in all its economic, social and psychological manifestations.

From this perspective, much more than only small and micro-entrepreneurs are discovered in a multi-dimensional identification of target groups from the urban and rural informal sector as carried out in *Chapter 4*. In various examples it is shown how people from the informal sector may be categorized in very different ways, if

– the economic activities – including subsistence work – to be observed, which give an idea not only of the people's economic and social situation, but also of their existing occupation-relevant knowledge, skills and experience, and of the scope of their development options ("rough identification");

– the individually and target group-specifically different learning opportunities and potentials, which include the factors objectively determining people's education and training possibilities as well as their subjective learning motivation and learning capacity ("specified identification");

– the urban/rural and socialization-specific integration of people in the economic and social framework of the informal sector, which essentially determines their scope of occupational opportunities and development options ("status identification"),

are taken into equal consideration. A fairly homogeneous target group then comprises people with basically similar features in all these three respects.

For any "Vocational Training Assistance for People from the

Informal Sector", such a multi-dimensional identification of possible target groups, should always be the first planning step. The purpose is to obtain – with reference to the respective circumstances – a picture as realistic as possible of the diversity of possible target groups for occupation-oriented training and education measures and their different "profiles" as regards priority qualification needs, development potentials and occupational options. Only this provides a basis sound enough for the conceptual and institutional design of assistance measures which are actually accessible and useful for the target group(s) addressed, and hence may contribute to a sustainable improvement in their living and working situation.

In the people-centred perception, the objective orientation as well as the concrete design of assistance measures are dependent on the target group-specific assistance needs. *Chapter 5*, thus, explores which are the major occupation-oriented training and education needs of people from the informal sector. Different from the notion usually underlying vocational training assistance, their priority qualification needs are altogether not primarily influenced by ideas of a "classic" vocational training. They rather relate to the most urgent needs in their respective living and working environment, and to the environment-determined occupational options realistically accessible to them.

The "environment-determined occupational options" of individuals or target groups are defined by the radius, time and scope of activities actually or potentially given to them for gainful wage- or self-employment, and/or for subsistence work and self-help activities. They are determined by the – locally effective – general economic, potential and social frame conditions, by the level of education and occupational skills, by social constraints and traditions, and by the nature of people's integration in the economic and social network of the informal sector and the intensity of their rural-urban "commuting".

Even though any kind of vocational training and education which promises to improve their income-earning and (self-)employment opportunities in the (labour) market of either the modern or the informal sector, is considered as a qualification need of top priority for people from the informal sector, it is by far not the only one. Many people would rather or in addition need – also in their own view – some basic yet broader artisanal skill training and a strengthening of their self-organizing abilities, which would enable them to improve their living conditions in self-help through subsistence work. A sound and actually accessible primary (school) education is another high priority need, since this essentially determines further education, vocational training and employment chances. Other urgent qualification needs relate to health education, in the urban squatter areas as much as in the villages. Furthermore, the need for social education cannot be emphasized enough – especially for rural target groups and marginalized social groups like, e.g., urban street children – for facilitating their social and occupational (re-)integration, and generally for the development of key qualifications such as the ability of theoretical learning, entrepreneurial skills, or an "intelligent handling" of innovative information. A need, finally, which is most emphatically articulated by people from the informal sector themselves, is that training and education measures addressed to them are in their design more realistically oriented to given learning opportunities and potentials.

While the details of the conceptual and institutional design of assistance measures for specific target groups ultimately vary from case to case depending on the general frame conditions, people's environment-determined occupational options, their learning opportunities and potentials, and their resultant qualification needs, the overall objectives orientation of an occupation-oriented training and education for people from the informal sector should – in a people-centred perception – invariably be

– to impart occupation-relevant knowledge, skills and abilities which would enable them to sustainably improve their living and working situation within the scope of occupational opportunities open to them, i.e. through a gainful wage- or self-employment in the informal or, if possible, even in the modern sector, or – at least partly – through subsistence work;

– to strengthen their "information processing capacity", their social competence, and their communication skills beyond the experience and abilities related to their immediate environment;

– to create more equal opportunities for them, especially as regards further education, vocational training and the chances of gainful (self-)employment;

– to strengthen the self-help potentials of the people in the villages and in the urban squatter areas.

Occupation-oriented training and education which is to have real relevance and sustainable benefits for people from the informal sector, must correspond to the scope of development options and occupational opportunities open to them. This, however, is hardly to be realized by just extending the formal vocational training and education system of a country to make it more accessible also for most target groups from the informal sector. The differences between people from the informal and from the "urbanized" modern sector – and within the informal sector itself – are too substantial as regards social and educational background, learning opportunities and potentials, priority qualification needs and occupational options. Therefore, also the elaboration of any one particular "standard concept" of occupation-oriented training and education for target groups from the informal sector makes little sense. Even if it were comprehensive to the utmost possible extent, it would still only inadequately reflect the heterogeneity of target group-specific conditions and qualification needs.

For these reasons, it was decided to present in *Chapter 6* a wider range of different approaches of various development agencies, institutions and NGOs engaged in the field of vocational training and education, mainly with reference to specific project examples. They are individually assessed as regards their suitability to actually reach target groups from the informal sector, and to respond to these people's specific qualification needs, given their own objectives orientation and their institution-specific instruments and scope of action. This allows to also conclude on their possible contribution towards improving the (self-)employment opportunities of people from the informal sector and their living and working situation, also in the subsistence economy. None of these – typologically partly extremely different – approaches is suggested to be the one best solution. They should be viewed altogether as "conceptual modules" to be taken into consideration when planning, designing and implementing measures of occupation-oriented training and education for target groups from the informal sector. Their particular suitability and the modifications required will have to be decided in each specific case depending on the circumstances.

The approaches presented and assessed refer to

– more "classic" vocational training as well as to forms of a broader occupation-oriented formal, non-formal or informal skill training, all aimed at either improving the chances of employment in the modern or in the informal sector, and/or increasing the possibilities and quality of subsistence work;

– business advice and training for (potential) small and micro-entrepreneurs and self-employed persons, aimed at strengthening existing small businesses and (self-)employment opportunities, or helping to create new ones;

– directly or indirectly occupation-oriented training and social

education within more integrated development strategies, especially for rural target groups;
- the relevance and possibilities of an environment-adapted primary school education as first step towards a better occupation-oriented training and education.

Beside two examples of formal and non-formal vocational training clearly oriented to industry-related vocational profiles and carried out in (partly) Government-run training centres, *Chapter 6.1* describes some approaches to dual vocational training, of which the "Cooperative Training Courses" at a non-formal vocational training centre in Thailand, and two very different types of informal dual occupation-oriented training – the "National Open Apprenticeship Scheme" (NOAS) in Nigeria and a local Workshop Centre in the Ivory Coast – appear to be particularly promising.

The many children and youngsters who have to contribute to the family income with their own work already from early childhood on, have the chance of a certain occupation-oriented skill training usually only in a kind of odd-job apprenticeship which allows them to also earn some money. The described form of informal vocational training is a by and large similar phenomenon in all Third World countries, with the peculiarity of an almost guild-like traditional apprenticeship in some West African countries. As a modern and apparently increasingly significant form of informal vocational training, the private commercial training institutes are also considered worth mentioning.

In view of the fact that in future, more than ever, not all job-seekers and not even all graduates will be able to find employment in the modern sector, broader occupation-oriented training and education approaches become increasingly relevant, which respond more to the environment-determined occupational options realistically given to the majority of the people, including work in the subsistence sector. One example are the so-called "public workshops" – "Talleres Públicos" – which have been established in Costa Rica to provide non-formal skill training opportunities for target groups from both the rural and the urban informal sector. The "Village Polytechnics" introduced in Kenya after dependence might have been unsuccessful at that time, yet are a still – or again – interesting concept. An almost exemplary model is the Community Polytechnic in Yellareddy in India, which provides an environment-adapted technical skill training combined with social education primarily for young rural people with little or no school education, most of whom will have to secure their living throughout their lives in a rural environment and at least partly through subsistence work.

Finally, the vocational training in the Don Bosco institutions, which is based on the social-pedagogical concept of "preventive education", must be regarded as a particularly suitable approach to a labour market-oriented vocational qualification of youngsters from the informal sector, despite the difficulties experienced in rural areas. A high-quality skill training in common artisanal trades embedded in a social education for "normal" social behaviour, self-esteem and a certain "work ethic", is considered the only possible way to compensate as much as possible for the social handicaps of children and young people from the informal sector, in order to increase their employment opportunities. Children from poor families normally receive free training and education. Particularly commendable is also the attempt for a social and occupational (re)integration of street children by setting up so-called "Anbu Illam" as contact points, homes, training centres and work places for them. An active and continuous social work, non-formal training and job counselling aims at putting them into a regular gainful (self-)employment.

Quite a lot of hope in development assistance is pinned on income generation and employment creation through the promotion of small enterprises and commercial self-employment. It should, however, be kept in mind that – at both the macro-economic and the individual level – the possibilities of earning a living through a small business (creation) and self-employment are limited by a region's overall economic situation just as much as the employment impacts of vocational training for wage-employment area. The first two approaches presented in *Chapter 6.2* are based on the assumption that by means of small business promotion significant (self-) employment impacts can be realized only, if the target group selection is strictly confined to small and micro-entrepreneurs and self-employed business (wo)men with an evident economic development potential. The small enterprise development programme of the Foundation Carvajal in Colombia may certainly serve as a model in this respect. The experience of two other approaches shows that with a thorough planning and adequate programme design, it is well possible to also create or stabilize self-employment and small businesses by promoting poor people who at first glance seem to have hardly any economic development potential. The "business consultant" concept as applied in Port Sudan deserves a special mention here.

Two comprehensive approaches to occupation-oriented training and social education of rural target groups at the village level are presented in *Chapter 6.3*, with reference to experiences in India. The work of the Centre for Rural Education and Development Action (CREDA), a local NGO, as well as the concept of the Integrated Rural Development Centres (IRDCs) are strongly related to the environment-determined occupational opportunities and development options given to rural people, including the subsistence economy and local provision of social services. Striking features in both approaches are that the poor rural target groups are really reached, that a long-term perspective is taken for an integrated planning and implementation of the assistance measures, and that beside a directly occupation-oriented training great importance is also attached to social education and a strengthening of the self-organizational abilities of the village people. The promotion of self-help potentials and community initiative is given a high priority in the belief that only by this way it may be possible for the majority of people from the informal sector to sustainably improve their living and working situation. In the IRDC concept, also the transfer of "appropriate technologies" is a major component of the development activities. Coherent social groups like, e.g., the subsistence farming family or the village community, are chosen as the smallest target group units, with which the development work then is carried out genuinely participatory.

For most people from the informal sector and especially for women, primary school education is the only education they may ever have the opportunity to attend. More than any other institution, the primary school, thus, possesses the potential to reach a large number of people – and this at their young, i.e. most educable, age. After some general remarks on the relevance of a good-quality primary school education for all as a first step towards improving the occupational opportunities of people from the informal sector, *Chapter 6.4* presents three project examples to point out how a primary school education which takes into account the environment-determined learning opportunities and potentials of village children and their future occupational options, can contribute to create for young people a life perspective with "farming as vocation". The "Escuela Nueva" in Columbia is finally mentioned as a possible approach towards primary school education for all also in sparsely populated and remote rural areas, which, in principle, is also not unsuitable for the incorporation of environment-adapted and occupation-oriented subjects into the curricula.

In *Chapter 6.5* the most important features of the approaches presented and their assessment are summarized again in a synoptic table. Some of them appear to have almost a model character, whereas from others just some elements might be taken into account when designing occupation-oriented training and education measures for target groups from the informal sector within the framework of (bilateral) vocational training assistance.

The comparative assessment of the various approaches shows that it is not so much the programmatic objectives or the target groups themselves which determine the suitability and the success or difficulties of a particular approach in terms reaching the target groups and achieving sustainable learning results and positive employment impacts. Much more decisive are the appropriateness of the design of the measures in detail, and the way in which they have been planned. The "suitability threshold" for occupation-oriented training and education of target groups from the informal sector, thereby, hardly runs along the formal – non-formal – informal line of demarcation. Furthermore, it may be seen that many of the approaches are not necessarily bound to one specific type of (counterpart) institution.

A critical assessment also reveals that success and sustainable – though not necessarily easily quantifiable – results seem to be achievable only, if
– the problem of availability, adequate professional and pedagogical qualification and motivation of – expatriate or local – teachers, instructors and other staff, and of intermediary target groups in the role of social multipliers is resolved;
– the planning takes place at least partly on site, with a knowledge as precise as possible of the target group-specific opportunities, and flexible adjustments in the concept, priorities, time schedule, or activities are made during implementation, whenever the need arises;
– there is a firmly established local (counterpart) institution to cooperate with, close enough to the target group in terms of both location and social access, working with a long-term perspective and exclusively for target groups from the informal sector;
– the occupation-oriented training and advisory services are not confined to a qualification in technical skills, but put equal emphasis on social and general education, to promote personality development, and to facilitate the social and occupational (re)integration of people from the informal sector;
– the training and education is (largely) free, except for advisory services and (advanced) training for small and micro-entrepreneurs, and also actively "propagated" among the target group(s).

A large number of unemployed and unskilled people constitute a social problem. A large number of unemployed yet skilled people, by contrast, are a potential. "Investing in people" with the aim of putting their labour and creativity to productive use for themselves and for society, therefore, is more than ever an essential requirement for a development in Third World countries, which will be to the benefit of the majority of people. With this understanding, the recommendations in *Chapter 7* outline the implications which – in a people-centred perception – should result for the planning and design of occupation-oriented training and education measures within the framework of a (bilateral) "Vocational Training Assistance for People from the Informal Sector".

These recommendations, first of all, relate to a more comprehensive conceptual perspective which extends beyond the conventional objectives orientation of the "classic" vocational training assistance. This would include not only technical skill training and social education to qualify (also) for subsistence work and self-help activities as an alternative option to a merely (labour) market-oriented vocational training, but also a greater emphasis on environment-adapted, innovative and integrated approaches to extend the scope of occupational options given to people from the informal sector, further more the realization of the importance of primary school education as the first step towards better occupation-oriented training and education, and finally specific training and education measures for women by taking into account their particular situation and needs.

Secondly, some major principles of a flexible and dovetailed planning and implementation of occupation-oriented training and education are formulated. They refer, in particular, to a participatory and iterative planning on site, which is mutually interlinked with the programme or project implementation, and to the requirements for a long-term perspective, institutional and staff continuity, and target group proximity throughout the implementation of this kind of assistance measures.

The suggestions for the conceptual design and the institutional set-up refer to the most suitable or promising approaches introduced as "conceptual modules" for the design of occupation-oriented training and education measures for target groups from the informal sector. Special attention is drawn to the idea of setting up some kind of local "Centres for Occupational Guidance and Training Advice". Also recommended is the use of existing non-formal vocational training centres or similar institutions for the (advanced) training of intermediary target groups which (could) assume the role of "social multipliers" in their villages and urban squatter communities, respectively, working there as instructors, teachers, social workers or technology advisers.

Furthermore, it is suggested to carry out some fundamental studies, namely a "Baseline Study on the Informal Sector" to learn more about the various forms and implications of poverty socialization in the urban slums and in rural areas, also a comparative "Tracer and Background Study on Trainees from the Informal Sector", and, finally, a "Cross-country Study on Private Commercial Training Institutes" to obtain detailed enough information to assess their (possible) role in the occupation-oriented training of some target groups from the informal sector.

The establishment of a countrywide or regionally operating "Programme Office" in areas where "Vocational Training Assistance for People from the Informal Sector" is (planned to be) one of a donor's priority fields of development assistance, would allow to realize the afore-mentioned principles of a flexible and dovetailed planning and implementation of occupation-oriented training and education measures, and to cooperate with different types of counterpart institutions also within the framework of a Government-support (bilateral) vocational training assistance, the effectiveness and sustainability of which would thereby probably be enhanced considerably. Furthermore, it would reflect – in the institutional framework of vocational training assistance – the understanding that target group-specific qualification needs cannot be determined in a separate planning phase on the basis of short-term visits of external experts, but must be identified in an iterative process on site, and that furthermore the success of training and education measures should be assessed not just output-, but process-oriented.

It is, in principle, well known that the "personality factor" is more decisive for the success of development assistance measures than commonly assumed. For measures in the field of training and education, however, it is the *key* factor. The advocated changes in the planning and implementation procedures, the character of the recommended approaches, and, last but not least, the nature of target groups from the informal sector must have implications also as regards the self-perception and the qualification profiles required for development planners, advisers, instructors and trainers. To plan and implement assistance measures with a people-centred perception requires that the experts involved – expatriates as well as locals – are personally capable and willing to also perceive their work from a people-centred perspective.

Finally, a few remarks are made on the financing of training and education measures for economically poor and socially disadvantaged target groups, in particular. With regard to the high portion of Government financing – and hence external financial assistance through development cooperation – inevitably required, it should be understood that education and training costs have, in fact, an investive character. They are an investment in the development of human resources, even though they are itemized in national budgets as running costs.

To a certain extent, a "Vocational Training Assistance for People from the Informal Sector" which is rooted in a people-centred perception, moves away – not only in its target group orientation, but particularly in its planning and implementation principles – from the idea(l)s of the "classic" vocational training assistance, mainly in that

– the starting-point for the planning and design of occupation-oriented training and education measures is not the definition of policy-centred development objectives, but the multi-dimensional identification of the target group(s) to be promoted;

– the objectives of assistance measures and their design in detail are derived in the first instance from the identified qualification needs of the respective target group(s), by taking into account their different learning opportunities and potentials and their environment-determined (potential) occupational options;

– the subjects of occupation-oriented training and education, accordingly, are related not only to the labour market and/or to business opportunities in the modern or the informal sector, but also to subsistence activities, altogether more adapted to the environment-determined actual and potential occupational options of the respective target group(s) than to "classic" vocational profiles clearly correlated to modern industrial and artisanal trades;

– occupation-oriented training and education more often than not has also a socio-pedagogical dimension in that not only technical knowledge and possibly entrepreneurial skills are imparted, but also social education and, if required, some basic primary-level education is carried out to facilitate social and occupational (re-)integration and promote key qualifications, such as "information processing capacity", creativity, self-reliance, self-organization ability, or a sense of work quality;

– the target groups are not merely viewed for a defined period as

simply receptive consumers of training, education or advisory services with a clearly specified content, but as actors shaping their own development and learning processes;
– training, education or advisory measures are not just "launched" and their mere existence then regarded as already sufficient announcement, but in particular target groups which are difficult to reach for training and education are actively approached and motivated to take up such an offer;
– the identification of the target groups as well as the conceptual and methodological design of assistance measures are not in advance binding determined in external planning, but are subject to a participatory process of dovetailed planning and implementation flexibly adjusted to changing conditions, to ensure that occupational options of the respective target group(s) and their related qualification needs are perceived as realistically as possible;
– the success of education training and advisory measures is defined and assessed not output- but process-oriented, and quantifiable results hence do not take priority over more qualitative criteria applied to assess learning success as indicator for the effectiveness and sustainability of a measure;
– finally, new demands are made on the technical competence, pedagogical skills, "social intelligence" and personality traits – i.e. the qualification profile – and on the motivation of local as well as expatriate experts, who should as instructors also be educators, as advisers also sincere counsellors, and as planners also observers and partners in discussion.

In order to realize a "Vocational Training Assistance for People from the Informal Sector" in this sense, a rethinking and revised (self-)perception is required in the minds of all those involved in the planning and implementation of occupation-oriented training and education measures for these target groups. In the interest of the people from the informal sector it can only be hoped that this will not be postponed to some time or other.

1. Introduction

The introductory chapter includes a brief description of the background and scope of this research study, and a few comments on the basic approach to the subject-matter. Furthermore, some relevant conceptual terms are clarified in order to avoid misunderstandings at a later stage.

1.1 Background and Scope of the Research Study

Since the informal sector as a conceptual term first appeared in the international discussion on development policies in the early seventies[1], subsequently becoming the focus of numerous studies[2], a closer look has been taken at the need and the scope for promoting its economic potential. The development interest in this particular part of Third World societies and – especially – economies has been growing as it became more and more obvious that, for various reasons, in future the economic absorptive capacity of the modern sector in these countries will also be nowhere near able to provide adequate employment opportunities for all those willing to work, even though more people than in the past will have better qualifications.

For a large number of people it will thus prove impossible to secure an acceptable standard of living, even at the subsistence level, through wage-earning employment, and they will have no option but to come to terms with a lifetime in the informal sector. For a tremendously large number of young people, even with secondary-school qualification, for many women, and for all underprivileged and poor who otherwise will be entirely excluded from any career and employment opportunities, not to mention social acceptance, chances to improve their living conditions, and to develop prospects for a better future, if any, will be found only in the informal sector.

Whether the informal sector in Third World countries should be promoted at all, in order, for example, to cushion some of the economic and social structural problems inevitably emerging in the

1 The term was introduced with reference to the urban informal sector in Africa by *HART* (1973).
2 In particular, the ILO carried out numerous studies on the structure of the informal sector in large urban areas of the Third World, especially in Africa and Latin America; cf. Part I of the bibliography.

process of modern sector development, is a futile discussion in view of the realities. The informal sector does exist as an economic factor and as a social phenomenon, and it will continue to grow – externally promoted or not – both in terms of the number of people living there, and in its economic and social relevance for the further development in the Third World countries. Furthermore, the informal sector is much more than just a synonym for low-level economic activities – it is people struggling for better opportunities, more decent living conditions, or for their mere survival.

Therefore, every effort should be made to direct and support the further development within the informal sector towards the greatest possible mobilization and utilization of existing development potentials, in order to achieve sustainable improvements in the living and working conditions of what is the majority of the people.

Against this background, this research study was undertaken to explore

– what actually are the priority needs of different target groups from the informal sector as regards occupation-oriented training and education;

– what – and with which overall objectives – various approaches or projects of different donors, training institutions or NGOs (may) contribute towards meeting these target group-specific qualification needs;

– what kind of institutional set-ups would be more suitable than others for the planning and implementation of measures for occupation-oriented training and education, for target groups from the informal sector, in particular.

In accordance with the BMZ, the scope of this study as regards the identification of suitable approaches for vocational training and education for different target groups from the informal sector, was deliberately not restricted to formal and non-formal approaches of vocational training in the "classic" sense, but also takes into consideration various promising approaches for a broader directly and indirectly occupation-oriented training and education[3].

3 This reflects arguments and lessons learnt from the controversy over the future orientation of German bilateral vocational training assistance to Third World countries, which flared up in 1986 after the presentation of a new "Sectoral Concept for Development Cooperation in Technical Vocational Training". The main bone of contention was the continued biased focus merely on by vocational training for "the occupations in modern industries (and) the development of a mid-level technical and management staff" in order to "counter the mass problem of a lack of qualified vocational training", preferably by introducing the German model of the so-called "dual system" of vocational training; cf. *BMZ* (1986), p. 43, also pp. 44 ff. (translated by the author); in addition, cf. Part II.1 of the bibliography.

Considered as occupation-oriented are all those training and education measures which are
- (labour) market-oriented, and intended to directly create employment and/or income opportunities by trying to qualify target groups from the informal sector for a reasonable paid and fairly permanent wage-employment in the modern and/or informal sector, or for self-employment including commercial home production;
- subsistence-oriented, and aimed at the application of the imported knowledge and skills (also) in activities which would secure a subsistence income, and/or in subsistence or community work to improve living conditions such as the housing environment, or the nutritional situation;
- oriented towards an environment-adapted primary education and social education for children, youngsters and adults, contributing to better occupational and income opportunities indirectly by improving individual or target group-specific learning potentials, and directly by inducing a considerable demand for local teachers, instructors, social workers and other social intermediaries from within the informal sector.

1.2 Remarks on the Study's People-centred Perception

Before suitable concepts and strategies for "Occupation-oriented Training and Education for Target Groups from the Informal Sector" can be elaborated, the general intention of respective assistance measures needs to be clarified. This can be done from two perceptions which, at first glance, appear to be fairly similar, but lead to different perspectives and conclusions, namely from
- a policy-centred perception, or
- a people-centred perception.

In the policy-centred perception of development assistance, which still prevails in development planning, the initial question is: "What targets are to be achieved through the measures to be undertaken, and where should, therefore, be started, involving whom?" The starting point, thus, is the question for the priority policy objectives and related output targets, which then determine the kind and direction of any subsequent questions. The logical perception in such a project planning process may be described as follows:

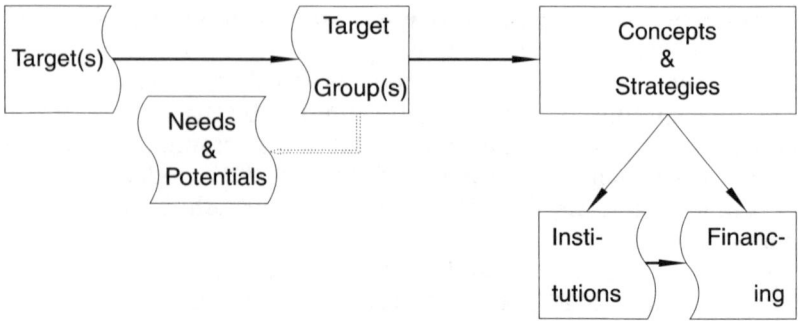

The initial question in a people-centred perception, on the contrary, will rather be: "Who should for what reason receive assistance, and which objectives could, therefore, be considered as meaningful and realistic?" This puts people first, and the needs and potentials of social groups will determine the kind and direction of subsequent questions in a different way as compared to the policy-centred approach. Accordingly, the logical perception in the initial steps of a planning process is reversed in the following manner:

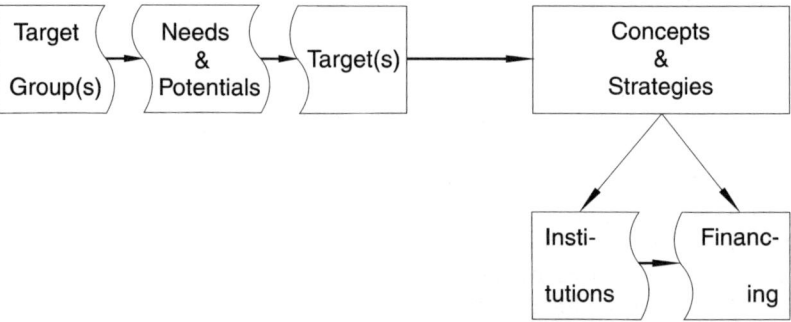

In a policy-centred approach, concepts and strategies, thus, are developed basically with regard to policy objectives or technical targets, initially fairly irrespective of any particular target group. The subsequent target-related identification of the target groups has a mainly instrumental character in this context. In a people-centred approach, on the other hand, the starting point of any further considerations are one or more social groups as possible target groups. The objectives and targets of an assistance measure will then be determined with regard to their specific needs, potentials and expectations as identified in a dialogue with them or their competent representatives.

Deciding which of these essentially different perceptions to choose at the initial stages of project planning, is far from being mere logical hair-splitting. It has far-reaching implications not only for the assessment of what should be considered as suitable concept or strategy in a given context, but also for the formulation of questions and for the awareness of problems in the process of project planning and preparation, and hence for the project design. The following considerations may further clarify the difference.

(1) Policy-centred Planning and Design of Measures for Occupation-oriented Training and Education

Regardless of controversies over details, the current policy-centred discussion on strategies for the promotion of "the informal sector" is fairly unanimous on the *general objective* of stimulating the economic development and stabilizing the social situation in Third World countries, by significantly increasing employment and income opportunities. Therefore, the economic potential of the informal sector which is perceived and defined almost exclusively in terms of economic features, must be promoted. Accordingly, small and micro-enterprises "with development potential", and also women – which in most countries are the backbone of a mainly informally organized private sector, but still far from being adequately integrated in the commercial market systems – are identified as priority *target groups* with an as yet untapped development potential, since their as efficient as possible participation in the monetarized economy still is impeded by numerous factors.

As far as these impediments directly concern the production factor labour, the analysis describes the full range of lacking technical and entrepreneurial skills, including a normally underdeveloped entrepreneur personality. Assuming that, in principle, such deficiencies can be reduced by a trade- and labour market-oriented vocational training and education, *strategies* of "human resource development" have been elaborated. With special regard to target groups from the informal sector the concept of "environment-adapted occupation-oriented training", centres or mobile units for non-formal vocational training, or small business creation and small enterprise development programmes emerged.

All these policy-centred concepts and strategies undoubtedly incorporate a great deal of expertise and often apply highly sophisticated training methods. Normally, however, they suffer from one shortcoming which is serious enough to substantially impair the efficiency and sustainability of such measures: They mainly focus on imparting technical or entrepreneurial skills – often in very short courses – without adequately taking into account the social context and learning capacities of the target group(s), not to mention the relevance of education and vocational training for building up social values, personality development and social awareness creation. Even the postulate of self-help promotion in reality often tends to be taken as an excuse for project managers and instructors to shift the responsibility for the application of the imparted skills one-sidedly to the target group(s), instead of actively assisting them in strengthening their self-help potentials and "information processing capacity".

(2) People-centred Planning and Design of Measures for Occupation-oriented Education and Training

In a people-centred perception, the identification of suitable strategies of vocational training assistance to the informal sector first of all requires a redefinition of what is "the informal sector". Leaving aside the academic discussion of its emergence, significance and potentials, the informal sector in Third World countries is seen as that part of society where the economically weak and socially disadvantaged people are found. Here they look for niches to survive in a society which excludes most of them from formal education and vocational training, from the labour market, the business and credit systems of the modern sector, and from political participation, anyway, for either formal or social reasons. These people are small or micro-entrepreneurs, mostly in a family business, self-employed business(wo)men, unskilled labourers, exploited factory and construction workers, families engaged in subsistence farming or landless labourers, (young) people without (adequate) education and employment, street children, prostitutes, or domestic servants, in all groups both men and women.

For these (*target*) *groups*, gainful employment often is not an end in itself, but a meagre cash income is needed to ensure survival, often enough possible only through (additional) subsistence work. While their dreams may be stimulated by the mass media and the cliches of the modern consumer society, their pragmatic aims primarily reflect their immediate needs for improved living conditions. Their *potentials* for self-help and development are manifold, but largely untapped or suppressed. Their missing or completely inadequate primary school education and their social background alone more often than not already determine their lifelong stay in the informal sector – because they cannot gain access to or get through the formal education and vocational training system, find no longer-term and reasonably gainful employment, have their self-reliance, assertiveness and initiative fading away, and never had a chance to develop creativity and autonomous learning abilities.

Perceiving the informal sector from such a people-centred perspective, the search for suitable concepts for a needs-oriented vocational training assistance begins with the identification of those social groups whose living conditions and employment prospects could and should be sustainably improved with priority, followed by a realistic assessment of their learning opportunities and potentials, the (potential) scope of their occupational options and their resulting qualification needs. Desirable and feasible *objectives* of the assistance is then formulated on this basis. Suitable *strategies*, i.e. the conceptual and methodological design of occupation-oriented training and education measures, are those which respond to these target group-specific qualification needs, and are most likely to activate existing learning and self-help potentials.

The sincerely open-minded search in this study for occupation-oriented training and education concepts able to meet the actual qualification needs of the various (target) groups from the informal sector and help activating their endogenous development potentials, was essentially carried out with this people-centred perception which, however, by no means meant to disregard the macro-economic dimension. After all, it is a country's level of economic and technological development, the economic frame conditions, and the "position" of a target group within the economic system which ultimately determine the feasibility, effectiveness and sustainability of results also for assistance measures with objectives derived from target group specific qualification needs and potentials.

1.3 *Clarification of Relevant Terms*

To avoid a later lack of clarity it appears useful at this stage to explain for some particularly relevant terms why and with which interpretation they are employed in this study.

(1) Informal and Modern Sector
When the economic significance of the value added from services was realized, but could not be attributed to either of the two classic productive sectors "agriculture" and "industrial and artisanal

manufacturing", all services were classed as a "tertiary sector". Any more precise definition was infeasible in view of the large variety of this type of economic activities.

In a similar way, the "*informal sector*" emerged as a residual category for all those economically obviously relevant activities of small enterprises and self-employed business(wo)men marginalized by modern development, which can hardly be classified in one of the ordinary economic categories. Their common features are that they are almost impossible to be statistically recorded in a sufficiently systematic way and, thus, disregarded in the gross domestic product, mostly not legally registered, and apparently operating in rather "arche-capitalist" ways, yet without any significant distinction between the business and private spheres. For all these reasons they do not fit in with the economic profile of the modern sector.

With this type of economic activities in artisanal and agricultural production as well as in many services, the informal sector is a cross-section of the three modern economic sectors, though at lowest economic, technological and organizational level, lacking linkages with or access to established credit, marketing, information or political decision-making systems – a "quaternary" sector, so to speak, with own economic potential for value added production.

In Third World countries, this informal sector is a refuge primarily for the economically and socially poor people who – for formal reasons or de facto – have (almost) no access to the formal(ized) systems of the modern sector[4].

In this study, the informal sector explicitly is *not* regarded as the total of illegal economic activities and non-registered enterprises[5].

Likewise, it is not equated with the traditional sector, even though, in fact, both may be fairly identical in some urban areas, especially in Africa. In most conurbations, however, the informal sector often encompasses much more "modern" than traditional economic activities. Examples are refuse-collecting street children, roadside secretaries, or backyard repair workshops for radios, refrigerators or television sets. On the other hand, there are still rural areas where the local or even the regional markets are exclusively supplied by traditional farmers and crafts workshops, a segmentation into a

---

4 For details on this aspect, cf. Chapters 3 and 4.
5 Anyone earning a good money as, say, agent of a "car dismantling" gang selling components of stolen cars as spare parts, as real estate broker trading plots of illegally occupied land, as producer and/or distributor of pirate EDP software or music cassettes, or as pimp would, no doubt, be regarded as belonging to the informal sector under the aspect of illegality. However, insofar as this would be the decisive criterion for affiliation, he would be disregarded in this context.

modern and an informal sector, thus, has not yet taken place. The same applies even to the urban areas in countries where a world market-oriented industrial production has hardly developed yet, like, for example, in Indochina.

As regards the *modern sector* in contrast to the informal sector, preference is given to this term rather than to the linguistically closer term of "formal sector", especially because neither illegality nor non-registration and difficult or impossible statistical recording of economic activities were considered essential criteria. The decisive polarity is in the living and working conditions which for economically and socially disadvantaged people differ in some specific aspects significantly from the structures, mechanisms and norms of the urban-industrial culture, technology, work organization and life-style, described worldwide as "modern".

(2) Subsistence Economy, Subsistence Work and Subsistence Income

Subsistence economy is the (largely) non-monetarized part of the economy where productive activities and social services serve directly and indispensably to secure a person's or family's livelihood, or to fulfil – in cash or in kind – social or religious commitments within the community.

In the subsistence economy, products and services are not really marketed. Nevertheless, there are both monetary and non-monetary activities in the subsistence economy. The latter include farming for own consumption, household activities, care for children and elderly family members, the production of utility goods required to satisfy basic needs, and other – also communal – work carried out to meet personal, family or community needs. These productive activities and social services are called *subsistence work*.

In many rural areas the subsistence economy still functions to a great extent without money, even though hardly anywhere entirely. In urban areas, on the contrary, a minimum of cash incomes is indispensable for survival. Neither subsistence work nor barter trade can substitute for various essential cash expenses like, for example, patronage fees or tenancy rates for a commercial plot or rent for a dwelling, municipal charges for electricity or land use, the costs of staple foods, clothing and medical care. Activities which merely serve to gain this *survival income* or *subsistence income* are also regarded as subsistence work.

Home production – normally a domain of women – has a subsistence character, if it either is for direct personal or family consumption, or for sale to secure the subsistence income. By contrast, from commercial home production or home-based yet paid services, a more or less modest surplus income may be gained.

(3) Formal, Non-formal and Informal Vocational Training and Education

With regard to occupation-oriented training and education for target groups from the informal sector, the distinction between formal and non-formal training is hardly of any fundamental significance, the more as the antagonisms commonly used may be applicable in a specific context, but cannot be generalized[6]. For people from the informal sector, training and education opportunities do not depend only on formal admission requirements in terms of age, primary school graduation, sex or social background, but just as much on the time schedule, location, training objectives, and level of the training. Also for non-formal training courses these factors can be so adverse to the learning opportunities and potentials of someone from the informal sector that a course attendance is virtually impossible or unattractive. On the other hand, a training which in various respects could well be classified as non-formal, can be quite formalized or extensive, and may even end with a certificate, as is the case in some of the Don Bosco Technical Schools.

In this study, the classification, wherever relevant, of occupation-oriented programmes and projects is made according to the differentiation in the GTZ-Guidelines on "Promotion of Regional Rural Development through Formal and Non-formal Vocational Training and Education" insofar as *formal training and education* is roughly equated with education within the formal public educational system, whereas non-formal education takes place outside this system. The formal educational system may also include certain other types of organized and institutionalized education[7] at primary school level as well as in polytechnics or other secondary technical schools. In this study, however, this applies only as far as they are carried out under Government responsibility, or in officially recognized institutions. Also the Government–regulated forms of dual vocational training in cooperation with enterprises are regarded

---

6 One example is the differentiation between the formal education and vocational training system in general and the non-formal training at the "Integrated Rural Development Centres" (IRDCs) in northern India; ref. *REHLING* (1988), pp. 173–177.
7 Ref. *GTZ* (1986), pp. 16–19, esp. p. 16 and 17 (title of the publication translated by the author); this also corresponds with the definition in the 1984 UNESCO Glossary, cf. *KRÖNNER* (1989), pp. 27 f.

rather as formal vocational training, since the fact that part of the training takes place in a private workshop or factor, hardly alters its generally formal structure.

Non-formal training and education comprises a broad range of measures. Contrary to the GTZ Guidelines, this is not only taken to include the out-of-school youth and adult education relating to (back-up) literacy programmes, advisory services and training for community development and in health care[8], but more extensively
– any kind of systematic and structured occupation-oriented training and education outside of the graded and formal public education and vocational training system, and
– the primary education of children outside of Government (-recognized) schools, as carried out by many NGOs, especially in rural areas, as a separate measure or as part of more integrated occupation-oriented training and education programmes.

A clear distinction should be made between non-formal training and education, though this also – and primarily – takes place outside of the public education and vocational training system, but follows established curricula developed by the respective institutions, and forms of *informal training and education*[9]. The latter normally takes place exclusively in the private sector and under private initiative. The training content is determined, unaffected by any official curricula regulations, by the master craftsman. A modern form of informal training is carried out – mainly for occupations in the modern service sector – by the private commercial training institutes which have been mushrooming over the past few years in many big cities.

Not meant here is the informal education within the family and in social communities. Although it still plays a key role, especially in rural areas, in imparting general knowledge as well as agricultural and other practical skills to the younger generation, it is such an intrinsic part of unstructured family education that it should not be defined as just another form of occupation-oriented training and education.

---

8 Cf. *GTZ* (1986), pp. 49 and 52.
9 Cf. with a similar distinction *HERSCHBACH* (1989), p. 8 with further bibliographic references.

2. Methodology

From a methodological point of view, the study comprises the following steps:
– Operationalization of the "informal sector" concept;
– Secondary analysis of concepts and documented project experience in the field of vocational training and education with regard to their relevance for target groups from the informal sector;
– Direct information through project visits and discussions on site with project staff and vocational training experts on the planning and implementation of occupation-oriented training and education measures, and through interviews among various target groups from the urban and the rural informal sector;
– Evaluation of secondary analysis and direct information to formulate recommendations for the planning and design of the occupation-oriented training and education measures for target groups from the informal sector, in particular.

2.1 Operationalization of the "Informal Sector" Concept

In professional discussions on Third World development there is normally some vague consensus on what is meant with the term "informal sector", at least as long as it is used to describe a phenomenon understood as predominantly economic in nature. Opinions differ, however, when attempts are made to find an analytically precise and comprehensive definition of the informal sector, and to explain its emergence and its significance. All efforts made hitherto on such a definition have shortcomings in that they either are too vague, too stereotypical, or too schematic, or perceive and discuss only a very few aspects of the phenomenon.
This study does not intend taking up this theoretical discussion to eventually merely add yet another variant to the existing definitions[10]. Instead, an attempt was made to operationalize the concept of the informal sector in Third World countries in a way that
– first of all, the living conditions and constraints may be better

---

10 The literature consulted during secondary analysis provides a comprehensive review of the latest state of the art in this discussion with reference to Latin American, African and Asian experience; cf. Part I of the bibliography.

comprehended under which millions of people struggle every day to survive in the economic and social environment called "the informal sector", and also the wide range of their economic activities and the main interfaces between the informal and the modern sector are seen (*Chapter 3*);
– the diversity within the informal sector is shown in a multidimensional identification of possible target groups for occupation-oriented training and education measures in the urban and in the rural informal sector, with reference to their economic activities, their different learning opportunities and potentials, and their "status" in the informal sector (*Chapter 4*).
Both the selection and evaluation of the literature and project experience consulted in secondary analysis, and the approach for the direct information collection are essentially based on a perception of the informal sector operationalized along these aspects.

2.2 Secondary Analysis of Concepts and Project Experience Relating to Occupation-oriented Training and Education

Beside own work experience and the direct information gained during a reconnaissance mission to Thailand and India, secondary analysis of various approaches and documented project experience in the field of vocational training and education provided the basis for the identification of the priority qualification needs of different target groups from the informal sector as well as for the assessment of different kinds of approaches as regards their suitability for occupation-oriented training and education of these target groups, in particular.

The secondary analysis consisted of a comprehensive consultation of literature which, however, was not restricted to projects or concepts of "classic" vocational training. Apart from general literature on the informal sector and on small enterprise promotion, especially approaches for a broader occupation-oriented training and education – including functional adult education – seeming particularly suitable for target groups from the informal sector, were taken into consideration as well as concepts and experiences relating to women's development, self-help promotion, or employment and income generation in the subsistence economy. This includes also various integrated development approaches for community development, for appropriate technology transfer, and for the incorporation of social education, youth work or recreation pedagogics in measures for vocational training and education. Last but not least, special attention was given to approaches and experiences in the field of training of trainers, teachers, social workers and other social intermediaries. Finally, it was tried to give fairly equal consideration to concepts and experiences from Latin America and from African and Asian countries, respectively, and to include countries representing different socio-cultural structures and levels of development. Furthermore, a distinction was made between the urban and the rural informal sector, in view of their significant differences as regards economic and social structures and development potentials, and the mentality of urban and rural people.

In addition to the consultation of literature selected under the aforementioned aspects, several interviews and discussions were conducted with representatives from different development agencies involved in bilateral technical and financial cooperation as well as from church-related and other non-governmental organizations (NGOs) engaged in vocational training and education, mostly prior to the reconnaissance trip. The purpose was to obtain supplementary information on specific projects and vocational training institutions, and/or to discuss possibly up-coming new approaches or project plannings for the promotion of target group from the informal sector through occupation-oriented training and education.

2.3 Direct Information through Project Visits and Target Group Interviews in the Informal Sector

Apart from secondary analysis, a reconnaissance mission was undertaken to obtain direct information through project visits and on-site discussions with experts and trainers on the (conditions of) success and the problems in the planning and implementation of measures for vocational training and education of target groups from the urban and the rural informal sector, respectively. This allowed to take into consideration for the study also the experience, views and suggestions of local experts, especially in NGOs. In addition, interviews were carried out with quite a few people from the informal sector to get an exemplary direct view of their own ideas on their assistance needs as regards training and education.

Basically, only those projects or institutions were selected, which from the relevant literature or discussions appeared likely to provide useful additional information during a visit, because

– they have already several years of experience in the implementation of occupation-oriented training and education for target groups from the informal sector;
– they are pursuing particularly promising approaches, the positive development, achievements, general framework and/or difficulties of which seem worth being assessed in the sense of "lessons to be learnt", and/or
– their approach appears to contain elements which may be suitable, in principle, for interregional and intercultural transfer.

Altogether, the visited projects and institutions should represent as wide a scope as possible of different project types and approaches in the field of occupation-oriented training and education. Therefore, it was decided to choose Thailand and India for the reconnaissance mission, since in these two countries a variety of projects and experience in this field is found, and a rather well-developed infrastructure allows to reach also rural locations within reasonable time. Moreover, knowledge of the Thai language and previously established contacts enabled direct target group interviews in the urban and the rural informal sector in Thailand.

Apart from these more practical aspects, the criteria for selection related to
– different types of target groups;
– approaches with different conceptual orientations, and locations in urban or rural areas, respectively;
– varying strategies for the design and the implementation of occupation-oriented training and education measures;
– different types of institutional set-ups as regards the (project) executing (counterpart) institutions.

The interlocutors for the target group interviews were selected in such a way as to provide insights into the specific living conditions, and information on the education and training opportunities, the employment situation, and the resulting different qualification needs and development prospects of
– people socialized and living in the urban informal sector;
– people still firmly rooted in a village community, including the social intermediaries living there;
– rural-urban migrants forced by poverty to seek (self-)employment in town, either temporarily or for a longer stay.

From Table 1 overleaf, it may be seen which criteria were decisive for the selection of the respective projects and institutions actually visited and the target groups interviewed, and which criteria proved only

Table 1: Criteria for the Selection of Institutions Visited and Target Groups Interviewed During the Reconnaissance Mission to Thailand and India

Institution/ Target Group Selection Criteria	(1) SWRD (CDG)	(2) Metal Work Lampang (GVS)	(3) DBTS Bangkok (Salesians)	(4) TC Lopburi (Gov.)	(5) ILO Bangkok (Donor)	(6) THIRD Bangkok (NGO)	(7) Rural Migrants (Target Group)	(8) Slum Dwellers (Target Group)	(9) Micro-entrepren. (Target Group)	(10) Villagers (Target Group)
				[2]		[3]	[3]	[3]	[3]	
1. TARGET GROUP(S)										
1.1 Villagers/Village Families	(O)					●				●
1.2 Youth/Children		O	O	O	O					O
1.3 Women						O	●	●		O
1.4 Micro-/Family Enterprises					●	O	●	●	●	
1.5 Trainers and Social Multipliers	● [1]				O	●				
2. CONCEPTUAL TARGETS AND REGIONAL ASPECTS										
2.1 Urban Centres/Slum Areas			●	(O)				●	O	
2.2 Rural Areas	O	●		●		●	●			●
2.3 Market Integration/Business Creation		O	O	●	O	O	●			
2.4 Subsistence/Training for Subsistence Work						●				
2.5 Integration into the Modern Sector	n.a.	O	O	O	●	O	●			
2.6 Remaining in Informal Sector	n.a.	(O)				●		●		

3.	**STRATEGIES**						
3.1	Purely Vocational Training/Ed.		●		○		
3.2	Vocational Train. as Comp. of Dev. Strat.	(○)					○
3.3	Formal Training/Education			○	○		○
3.4	Non-formal Training/Education	○	●		○		○
3.5	(Non-)formal Primary Education/Pre-School						○
3.6	Social Education/Value Teaching			●			
3.7	Consideration of Soc./Mental Factors						○
3.8	Linkage Training and Appropr. Techn.			○		(○)	○
3.9	Decentr./Mobile/Vill.-Based Training	●					●
3.10	Training of Teachers and Multipliers	●[1]			○		●
4.	**PROJECT COUNTERPART INSTITUTION**						
4.1	(Semi-)Govt./International Institutions		○	●	○		
4.2	Church-rel./Church-affiliated institutions			○			
4.3	Local NGOs or Similar Institutions	○					●

Table 1: Continued

Institution/Target Group Selection Criteria	(11) St. Joseph's (Salesians)	(12) Beatitudes Madras (Salesians)	(13) DBYAC Ennore (Salesians)	(14) Joseph's Home Katpadi (Salesians)	(15) Agro Tech Polur (Salesians)	(16) Anbu Illam Madras (Salesians)	(17) Polytechnic Yellareddy (CSI–CTVT)	(18) SETCG Wadiarum (CSI–CTVT)	(19) IERT Allahabad (priv. Inst.)	(20) CREDA Mirzapur NGO
1. TARGET GROUP(S)										
1.1 Villagers/Village Families					(O)		●		●	O
1.2 Youth/Children	O	O	O	O	●	●	O	O		●
1.3 Women		●	O				(O)	●	●	●
1.4 Micro-/Family Enterprises				O						
1.5 Trainers and Social Multipliers			●					●	●	●
2. CONCEPTUAL TARGETS AND REGIONAL ASPECTS										
2.1 Urban Centres/Slum Areas	●	●	O			●				
2.2 Rural Areas			O	●	●		●	O	●	●
2.3 Market Integration/Business Creation	O	O	n.a.	●	●	O	●		●	(O)
2.4 Subsistence/Training for Subsistence Work		O	n.a.		●	O	●	●	O	●
2.5 Integration into the Modern Sector	O	O	n.a.	O	O					
2.6 Remaining in Informal Sector		●	n.a.	(O)	O	●	O	O	O	O

44

STRATEGIES

	C1	C2	C3	C4	C5	C6	C7	C8
3.1 Purely Vocational Training/Ed.	○	●		○	○			
3.2 Vocational Train. as Comp. of Dev. Strat.					●	●	○	●
3.3 Formal Training/Education	○	●						○
3.4 Non-formal Training/Education	○	●	○	●	○	●	○	○
3.5 (Non-)formal Primary Education/Pre-School		○		○	○	○	○	○
3.6 Social Education/Value Teaching	●	●	●	○	○	●	○	
3.7 Consideration of Soc./Mental Factors	●	●	○	○	●	○	(○)	●
3.8 Linkage Training and Appropr. Techn.		n.a.				(○)	(○)	(○)
3.9 Decentr./Mobile/Vill.-Based Training					(○)		●	●
3.10 Training of Teachers and Multipliers	(○)		●				○	●

4. PROJECT COUNTERPART INSTITUTION

	C1	C2	C3	C4	C5	C6	C7	C8
4.1 (Semi-)Govt./International Institutions								
4.2 Church-rel./Church-affiliated institutions	●	○	○	○	●			
4.3 Local NGOs or Similar Institutions						● [4]	○ [4]	●

Legend: ●, Major selection criterion for visit; ○, Citation of subordinate relevance, or only identified during visit; (○), Criterion applies with reservations; n.a., not applicable. [1] The core target of the training project is strengthening of the planning and decision-making competence in the counterpart institution as well as within the target groups. [2] Indications given refer to conceptual ideas within the ILO only; respective projects have not yet been implemented. [3] Marks given do only describe the type of target groups. [4] Strictly speaking, this is a church-related institution with funding from church-affiliated institutions (CSI–CTVT and EZE). Programme implementation, however, by and large is under similar conditions as for local NGOs, especially as regards aspects of funding and personnel.

during the visits and interviews to be applicable in addition, or, on the contrary, to a limited extent only[11].

2.4 *Evaluation of Secondary Analysis and Direct Information*

On the basis of the secondary analysis and the direct information and impressions gained from the project visits and the target group interviews – supported by own working experience especially in rural areas – the priority qualification needs of various target groups from the informal sector were identified. As a conclusion, then some overall objectives were formulated, which should generally guide assistance measures for the occupation-oriented training and education for such target groups (*Chapter 5*).

Subsequently, various approaches in this field were assessed – mainly with reference to specific projects as "samples" – as regards the extent to which they (could) actually – with their objectives orientation and training and education measures, and with the scope of action and instruments at disposal of the respective executing institutions – reach target groups from the informal sector at all, and contribute to improve their (self-)employment and income opportunities and their living and working conditions, also in the subsistence economy (*Chapter 6*).

Finally, the resulting implications – also as regards the "personality factor" and the financing of assistance measures for poor target groups – and the recommendations concluded for the planning and design of occupation-oriented training and education measures for target groups from the informal sector are presented, with special respect to their possible realization within the framework of Government-executed (bilateral) vocational training assistance (*Chapter 7*).

---

11 The full names of the institutions mentioned in Table 1 only with their abbreviations may be taken from the list of abbreviations and acronyms.

3. The Informal Sector: Socio-economic Environment for the Economically and Socially Disadvantaged People

The informal sector in Third World countries is neither sociologically nor economically a homogeneous phenomenon, not even within one country. This makes its operationalization extremely difficult. The literature available on this subject has also been found to be unable to describe or even define its complexity and multi-faceted character in a convincing and appropriate way.

How is the informal sector normally perceived when viewed analytically and descriptively? The prevailing perception in development theory and practice is that of a primarily economic phenomenon, by and large identical with small and micro-enterprises which have certain common features[12]. Economically and socially deprived groups which are not visibly active and difficult to motivate, are only marginally perceived and rather as a socio-political phenomenon which, however, is not associated with the informal sector. Even subsistence work in agriculture or in the home environment, especially the work done by women, is not taken into consideration to the extent it would deserve already because of its economic significance.

This narrow perception of the informal sector from the classic economic perspective draws a dividing line which does not exist in reality, between those who clearly (could) act (labour-)market-oriented[13], even though at lowest level and often with extreme difficulties, and those who help secure their own and their family's survival in the subsistence economy. In many cases, in fact, an individual or a family can be found on both sides of the line at the same time or changes sides more or less frequently. This is one of the secrets of survival in the informal sector, on the functioning mechanisms we still have no more than superficial knowledge, let alone a true understanding.

---

12 Numerous studies provide quite detailed descriptions of the economic activities and the operational structure of small and micro-enterprises, especially in the *urban* informal sector in Latin America, Africa and Asia; cf. Part I of the bibliography.

13 This one-sided orientation to the (labour) market can also be found in all contributions to the anthology "Training for Work in the Informal Sector" published by the ILO; cf. *FLUITMAN* (1989).

As already mentioned, this study refrains from taking up the discussion on the definition of the informal sector and the conditions of its evolution. Instead, an attempt is made – with the people-centred perception outlined above – to characterize the phenomenon of the informal sector as a socio-economic environment where the economically weak and socially disadvantaged people who in most Third World societies represent a growing share of the population, organize their survival.

– The description of the frame conditions of survival in the market economy and in the subsistence economy of the informal sector,
– a brief description of the type of economic activities observed in the urban and the rural informal sector and its main interfaces with the modern sector, and
– some critical remarks on the widespread equation of the informal sector with small and micro-enterprises under the aspect of economic sector promotion

are to provide the background for the subsequent identification of possible target groups for occupation-oriented training and education in both the urban and rural informal sector.

3.1 *Frame Conditions of Survival in the Market Economy and in the Subsistence Economy of the Informal Sector*

The informal sector is made up of people who – for economic, social or personal reasons – are unable to gain a foothold or to remain in the economic and social system of the modern sector, or who cannot gain access to it at all. In this sense, the informal sector is the economic and social "catchment area" for all those who cannot (any longer) organize their living in accordance with the norms, regulations, social rules and development perspectives prevailing in the modern sector. This very fact renders the living and working situation of millions of people in developing countries "informal".

Despite the variety of income-earning activities and all the differences in background and social status of individual people from the informal sector, the majority of them experience quite similar general living and working conditions. These are marked by poverty in all its economic, social and psychological manifestations. Hunger, malnutrition and illness without access to medical care are conditions which already have irreversible adverse effects on the development prospects of rising generations. Humiliating and often also uncertain housing conditions and the daily worries about food, water supply and a sufficient day income, the risk of being driven away from a sales location, or the fear that unavoidable costs may occur – all this fosters an attitude towards life in which planning and expectations, irrespective of dreams of a better future, only develop from one day to the next, and all opportunities whose benefit is not clearly to be seen, are normally regarded as unattainable and virtually irrelevant.

Moving beyond the wide variety of possible classifications, it is tried with the following description of the general frame conditions of survival in the informal sector to explain, with reference to as few characteristics as possible, which economic and social factors determine – although to a varying degree – the living and working conditions of people from the informal sector, and hence their attitudes, priorities, and realistic opportunities and options. To mention are:

(1) Economic Poverty

In most cases, the income gained from the accessible, often changing, brief or uncertain occupations of all working members of a family together is hardly enough to live on. Often it is not even enough to satisfy basic needs, let alone to consider education for the children, or to participate in the positive aspects of economic development. Housing conditions are basic to very poor, often uncertain, and disastrous in terms of hygiene and health aspects, especially in the urban slums and squatter areas.

(2) Almost no Chance to Accumulate Savings and Social Security only through the Family

It is almost or entirely impossible to accumulate savings for investments, education of the children or as a buffer for crisis situations. In the case of a loss of income resulting from illness, accidents or unemployment, or any resultant additional financial burden, there is no other social security than the support within the family. This situation is accompanied by social hardship and the constant risk of financial crises, rendering it virtually impossible to make plans on the use of a possible income surplus.

(3) High Work and Time Input for Low Income

For an income which often is below the statutory minimum wage, small and micro-entrepreneurs, self-employed business(wo)men and wage-earners alike have to work hard and excessive hours per day, generally without paid days off and in many cases under health-hazardous conditions. The same applies to the subsistence work carried out mainly by women and children in the agricultural sector and in the household. In many families, two or more sources of income or one source of cash income plus subsistence work are required to enable a minimum standard of living. In the urban informal sector, in particular, but also in subsistence farming, survival or a modest living is generally only possible by sacrificing personal and social needs. As long as there is any work possible to do, leisure time is regarded as a luxury, which again is particularly true for women and girls.

(4) Extreme Dependence on Market Fluctuations
Whether small and micro-enterprises, family enterprises, subsistence farmers, wage-earners or odd-job apprentices in the urban or rural informal sector, or women engaged in marketable home production – all of them are extremely dependent on the fluctuations of prices and other relevant factors on the sales and procurement markets and on the labour market. This means often unpredictable hardships and loss of income, and it requires a tremendous flexibility towards changing situations or new opportunities, in order to ensure survival in the face of often extreme competition from the modern and/or within the informal sector.

(5) Difficult or No Access to Credits at Market Conditions
High credit costs reduce the already low incomes and profits. For manufacturing small and micro-entrepreneurs the difficult and expensive access to credits also makes (cost-saving) stock-keeping and profitable purchasing impossible, and often necessitates the use of inferior-quality production means and materials, resulting in poor product quality. Smallholder families and self-employed business(wo)men like, for example street vendors, are often extremely dependent on moneylenders, pawnbrokers, supplier loans at exorbitant interest rates, or rich farmers who grant loans against a farmland "mortgage" generally impossible to be extinguished again. Such credits which often may exceed by far the repayment capability of the family, however, are also raised in emergency situations to satisfy daily basic needs, for "prestige purchases', or in certain events of social commitment.

(6) No (Adequate) Access to Education and Vocational Training
More often than not formal, social, distance or time reasons do not allow a vocation-related (advanced) training or education which could help to maintain the present employment or to find a new

one, or to improve the chances for a successful business creation. For the same reasons and at least just as frequently, basic education cannot be started or not completed, or does finish with results not good enough to allow a further education or vocational training.
Consequently, the formal requirements and/or skills for a reasonably gainful employment are missing, which makes existing social barriers higher again. Even with a vocational training or some work experience, first-time employment, or a necessary vocational reorientation are often virtually impossible due to disparities between existing and required skills and working experience and no retraining possibilities available. Training offers for a subsistence-oriented qualification are rare, anyway, which again hits particularly hard on women and girls.

(7) Lack of Experience in Acquiring and Applying Innovative Ideas and Relevant Information

Knowledge of innovative techniques or equipment which could be applied under the given conditions and with already given knowledge and skills to improve work quality, generate more income, facilitate (subsistence) work, or save time, which, in other words, are appropriate for the local conditions and needs, is generally no more but vague, if there is any, at all. Such information is not only difficult to obtain, but often its availability is simply unknown, even though it might, in principle, be there in the country. The lack of experience in independently acquiring and applying necessary or useful information – i.e. a hardly developed "information processing capacity" – also jeopardizes any incline towards an innovative behaviour or interest in new "appropriate technologies".

(8) Trespassing of Legal Regulations and Social Norms to Secure a Living

Restricted access to employment and income opportunities in the modern sector force many people – permanently or temporarily – to take on economic activities which are (almost) illegal, to secure their survival. This includes not registering a business, evading taxes and other fiscal charges, prostitution, stealing, poaching or illegal slash and burn in forest areas. Yet, in most cases it would be wrong to assume that villagers or small and micro-entrepreneurs have no consciousness of guilt or of environmental problems. They simply have no choice, which also explains why poverty-induced damages of the environment are so difficult to stop, certainly not through "environmental education" alone.

(9) Social or Mental Detachment from "Outside" Developments

Life under poverty and the almost daily struggle for survival in the informal sector – aggravated in villages by the monotony of everyday life and the "distance to progress" in all respects – shape a person's social behaviour and mental disposition. This may be reflected in an under-developed or destroyed sense of self-confidence, especially when confronted with "modern" phenomena, in a low level of creativity and innovative behaviour, and in problematic social behavioural patterns, especially among urban youth.

In the atmosphere of a routine everyday life or extreme stress, the relevance of learning or of any occupation-oriented training is either not even realized, or this realization cannot be translated into action. Furthermore, learning itself has to be learnt, too, but it normally is hardly taught at school – if there is school attendance, at all. As a result, the ability of theoretical learning as well as the ability to comprehend, independently assess and apply information which does not evidently fit into the frame of previous experience and the familiar environment, is not too well developed, in the villages even less than in urban areas where a certain mental confrontation with innovation, a flood of information and rapid social change does inevitably take place.

(10) Economic and Social Solidarity within the Family and Neighbourhood

Despite, or probably precisely because of the tremendously difficult living conditions in the informal sector, the majority of people there are still integrated into the social security systems of the (extended) family, the neighbourhood, or the village community. These social networks generally provide economic and also – at least towards outsiders – human solidarity, easing the individual hardships of the struggle for survival which takes place in tough competition with countless other people finding themselves in the same hopeless situation. What makes the situation of many street children in the big cities so disastrous, is that they very often do not even have this social network to comfort them.

The other side of this social integration are the accompanying social and financial commitments, for which a sense of responsibility is still, by and large, intact among the people in most African and Asian societies, even in urban areas.

Someone who has received financial or other support – which may include renouncing due proceeds – from the (extended) family, whether for training or education, for setting up a small business, or simply for a ticket to the next city where then paid employment was found, usually is obliged – and generally willing – to share even small incomes gained. This is to maintain or improve the own position within the family and/or the status of the family as a social value in itself[14]. But it is also necessary to maintain the entitlement to financial and social support in future case of emergency. This not only includes financial assistance or simply payments requested within the family, or bringing back "appropriate" presents from a trip to town, but also donations or offerings on the occasion of community celebrations or religious ceremonies.

Numerous experiences gathered by local NGOs as well as own working experience – the latter mainly in Asia – have repeated shown that this "code" of financial and social responsibility of individuals towards their social communities – which even those can hardly evade who want to do so when realizing that they have to in order to save their own advancement – substantially influences and sometimes jeopardizes assistance measures, especially in the field of vocational training and small business promotion.

To sum up, living in the informal sector means having difficult access to reasonably gainful employment, proper education, credit, development-relevant information and medical care – in short, being largely excluded from almost everything which could enable participation in a society's economic and social progress, and contribute to improve the living conditions.

For most people from the informal sector, this is an everyday experience in some way or other. For outsiders, it is much more difficult to see, and even more so to comprehend the less obvious impacts, such as the paralysing effects of hopelessness which sometimes makes it impossible for people to really think about ways out to improve their living conditions, let alone to take the necessary steps. At the same time, however, this situation fosters a tenacious will to survive, resourcefulness and persistence, which all is reflected, for example, in the extremely wide variety of economic activities which an average family from the informal sector pursues to secure a living.

---

14 The social mechanisms in communities in which ensuring "prestige" has a high economic as well as social and psychological value for the individual, are described quite vividly in *LÖWE* (1987) with reference to the example of the Senegalese "mécanicien" Cheikh.

3.2 Economic Activities in the Urban and Rural Informal Sector

In many respects, the informal sector is an autonomous social and economic system with a number of specific features required for it to function. Yet there are also numerous interfaces with the modern sector which is both a supplier and a market for the informal sector whose emergence and growing significance in many Third World countries is in turn both a condition for, and a result of the development of a modern industrial sector oriented towards international markets, standards and values. The informal sector also appears to be growing most rapidly in regions where the modern sector is most closely interlinked with the international economy.

3.2.1 Range of Economic Activities in the Informal Sector

The only almost generally applicable features of the economy of the informal sector are the limited radius of the economic activities and the small size of the enterprises operating there. Beyond that, diversity and heterogeneity begins.

Typical manifestations of the productive economy of the informal sector are the small workshop which often also serves as home of the entire family, commercial home production, and the subsistence work carried out mainly by women and children in the household and in agriculture, or as self-help activities for housing or road construction for family or community use. Artisanal production modes are predominantly found, using mostly relatively basic tools, equipment and techniques. Apart from traditional local products, like, for example, conventional farming tools and implements, charcoal stoves, all kinds of carts or clothing, also basic goods for a more modern demand are produced, such as matches, plastic slippers, or furniture.

Services including repair are offered as well to meet both the traditional demands and those of modern life, coming up with the increasingly widespread use of electrical appliances and motorized vehicles, a growing building and road infrastructure, or middle-class consumer desires such as beauty care or fresh flowers. With the further development of an urban middle class in which also married women seek gainful employment, there is also an increasing demand for all kinds of domestic servants.

Examples for the range of economic activities in the fields of commerce, transportation and other services in the informal sector start with the retail trade in village shops or with sales carts, the roadside foodstalls or sewing services, the secretarial or hair-dresser services offered under the shade of a big tree, go on to local trade intermediaries and black marketeers, the transport of passengers and goods with private vehicles of all kinds in rural and in urban areas to supplement or compensate an inadequate public transportation system, and are still far from ending with the refuse disposal and recycling carried out by street children beside, in competition or instead of a municipal service, or the "cachuelero" who, with a brilliant talent for improvisation, tries to earn a sufficient daily income through a variety of jobs from street hawker to odd-job worker in the same day.

Straight and one-dimensional careers are extremely rare in the informal sector. In the lives of most people, a range of economic activities form to a heterogeneous and varied picture of working life, during which as many sources as possible are tapped to support the family at a minimum or, if possible, little higher level. This is important to realize, since the needs, potentials and development options of people are not necessarily evident only from their current (un)employment situation, but may be determined as much – or even more – by their previous work experiences and social background, or by the confinement to their home places and the limited occupational opportunities existing there to secure a living.

Basically, three types of economic activities may be observed in the informal sector:

(1) Market-oriented Small Business and Self-employment

In the numerous small and micro-enterprises with only a few informally employed workers, the family and one-person businesses for artisanal production and small trade, the smallholder and subsistence farms, and in local transportation and other basic services, the economic activities of the informal sector are most easily visible. Quite a few of these businesses operate fairly profitably, though at the lowest level of technology and with minimum capital investment. At least just as many, however, especially the one-person businesses, earn no more than a subsistence income, and often have only a short life. Small and micro-enterprises which are already on the threshold to the modern sector may also be found, in rare cases even among one-person businesses. The overwhelming majority of them, however, will probably secure their economic survival only by deliberately remaining within the informal sector economy.

Looking from the outside, the development potential of many

self-employment activities tends to be overrated, because they are usually perceived as *enterprise* activities, even though they essentially are *individual*, often only temporary activities, with all the resultant limitations.

In many cases decisive for the set-up of small and micro-enterprises and for their economic viability in the informal sector is the unpaid work contributed by family members, often also by one or more younger children. In particular, the business administration of small enterprises – not only in the informal sector – very often is the domain of a female family member, which normally remains unperceived and hence underestimated from the outside.

(2) Wage Employment, Often Alternating with Unemployment

The majority of men and boys of working age – and also many women and girls – have to, or want to earn some cash income. By far not all of them, however, are able or willing to do so in self-employment, not even as completely informally operating self-employed persons. Most of them try for wage-employment which they may easiest obtain as – generally poorly paid – casual or day labourers, either in small and micro-enterprises in the informal sector itself, or in various fields of the modern sector, e.g. in the construction industry, in factories, in industrial estates on the outskirts of urban areas, or in the tourism trade.

Most people from the informal sector are repeatedly – often for longer periods – without (adequately) paid employment, because they

– are unable to find a (suitable) job, not even in the informal sector, because of the overall labour market situation, or a lack of required skills or formal qualification;

– were unsuccessful in self-employment or as small entrepreneurs due to competition, financial trouble or lack of entrepreneurial skills, or – as farmers – lost (too much of) their farmland for cash crops;

– lost their jobs in the civil service in the wake of structural adjustment programmes, perhaps with a financial compensation meant to help them setting up their own business which, however, is rarely realized despite a reasonable formal qualification and professional experience, since this money is normally rapid put to consumptive use by the whole family, and former civil servants usually lack innovative and risk-conscious "entrepreneurial behaviour" and often also the willingness to work hard, at least initially;

– only recently moved from the rural areas to town in search of some kind of – perhaps only temporary – employment which they either cannot find at all, or in which their previous work experience and skills are of little or no use.

(3) Permanent and Exclusive Occupation in the Subsistence Economy

Many if not the larger part of the economic activities in the informal sector happen in the subsistence economy where, in particular, women and children are engaged to an extraordinary extent in unpaid labour in order to make a living for themselves and their families. They struggle to survive without any great prospect of change, and with very little time left for any training which could possibly help to improve their situation.

This subsistence work is mainly carried out by
– women engaged in all kinds of domestic work – including home gardening and small livestock raising – who often are more or less tied to their homes or village, because of their responsibility for bringing up the children and/or for traditional social reasons;
– subsistence farming families of which often only women, old people and children still remain in the villages, but in which women generally carry the main burden of the subsistence work;
– children and youngsters as unpaid – in some regions like, for example, in the north-east of India even bonded – labour in domestic work, in agriculture, or in (carpet) manufacturing, or as "self-employed" street children in the big cities.

3.2.2 *Criteria for the Classification of Economic Activities as Informal Sector Activities*

The question according to which criteria smaller *enterprises* may be classified as belonging to the modern sector or the informal sector, respectively, was subject of numerous discussions in the specialized literature. If, however, not illegality because of non-registration or non-payment of taxes and fees, but rather economic, technological and sociological factors are to be the main criteria, the lines of distinction will remain vague in many cases. Schematic classification criteria, thus, will hardly be of great help.

Indications for a classification may instead be obtained, with reference to a specific region or situation, from answers to the following questions:
– At what technological level does the enterprise produce or

operate, including the technical qualification and skills of the owner and the workers, if any?
– According to which criteria are the investment decisions taken?
– What is produced or traded to supply which group(s) of customers, and why just those products or services, respectively, and those customers?
– Which factors determine the volume and schedule of production or trading, and is there any business planning and/or stock-keeping, and if not, for what reason?
– From within which radius, through which channels, and on what terms procurement and sales are carried out, involving which kind of suppliers and clients, and why just those?
– To what extent is the enterprise innovative as regards the acquisition and application of – hitherto unknown – new technologies?
– How often and how long does the enterprise need to take a credit, for what purposes, and which credit sources are available on what lending terms?
– How stable is of the enterprise in terms of capital resources, demand, and tenancy or ownership rights for the business site?
– Is there a distinction (possible) in accounting and/or in practice between private and business use of returns, savings, investment and consumption?
– To what extent does the business rely on the unpaid labour of family members?

In reality, it will depend on the specific conditions whether a small or micro-enterprise rather belongs to the informal or the modern sector. What may rank as a small or micro-enterprise of the informal sector in one place or area, may in another context with a generally lower level of development or different economic structure be regarded (still) as a normal traditional small enterprise.

The other question of how far *wage-earners and job-seekers* should be classified as belonging to the informal sector, will have to be judged mainly from
– their own and their family's social and economic living conditions in general;
– the type of enterprise in which they work and/or the type of occupation they are (normally) engaged in;
– the type of social security provision, if any, in the case of illness and accidents, or the leave entitlement resulting from an employment;
– their education and (formal) qualification from vocational training as well as – in most cases – their social background;

- the quality and scope of their occupation-relevant knowledge and skills.

3.2.3 Interfaces between the Economies of the Informal Sector and the Modern Sector

The interfaces between the economies of the informal sector and the modern sector are numerous and complex in most conurbations. The market economy of the informal sector is based on the supply of cheap goods and services for the majority of the people who have only a limited purchasing power in both the modern and the informal sector. Especially in the urban informal sector, many economic activities are only possible because of such a demand also from the modern sector. On the supply side, production, trade and consumption in the informal sector largely depend on the availability of cheap goods from industrial mass-production, and from the waste produced by the throw-away-minded upper-class consumers from the modern sector. In many urban areas, this provides the basis for recycling businesses in the informal sector, for many other small workshops and service businesses, and for the employment of countless day labourers, odd-job workers and domestic staff.

In rural areas, on the other hand, there is (still) only little economic and social interference between the modern and the informal sector. Strange enough, however, it is more difficult here than for the urban areas – in theoretical discussion as well as in reality – to clearly distinguish both. By no means the entire agricultural sector, not even the entire smallholder agriculture, can be regarded in all countries per se as informal sector. In many regions, modern agriculture, forestry, livestock raising, or irrigated farming exist integrated in the monetarized market economy, also including quite a few smallholders. At the same time, there is the marginal agriculture of the – normally larger – informal sector where subsistence farmers are predominant, with women often in the majority, especially in Africa. Other groups in the rural informal sector are the families of landless labourers, the artisanal workshops with only sideline or seasonal activities, and the many women and children who substantially contribute to their families' survival through subsistence work in the household, with a small home-based production or service, or as unpaid helper in a family sideline business.

Generally, interfaces between the informal and the modern sector do not only exist for enterprises and farms, or in the flow of goods, but also at the individual level, for example, where families from the urban informal sector have a small income also from employment in the modern sector, at least temporarily. But also more and more families from the urban middle class are forced to earn an additional income through (self-)employment in the informal sector, the father, for example, being a civil servant, with a sideline business as cobbler or tailor, or a supplementary informal income as a driver, or the mother operating a roadside foodstall.

Altogether, the interfaces between the modern and the informal sector are less extensive and less significant in rural areas as compared to urban areas, yet similar in their structure. The subsistence agriculture, however, exists fairly separately, indeed. As far as there are interfaces, they appear, in particular, in

– the procurement of raw materials and other production supplies, such as cheap industrial goods or waste products from industrial production and consumption in the modern sector, for recycling or direct productive or consumptive use in the informal sector;

– the supply of cheap products and (repair) services from small and micro-enterprises from the informal sector for middle-class consumers with only moderate purchasing power as well as for enterprises in the modern sector, thus keeping wages there at a lower level;

– the (partial) rendering of – in principle – municipal services like refuse disposal or urban mass transportation, which the responsible Government authorities are not able or not willing to provide, by people from the informal sector;

– the cheap labour from the host of poorly educated and landless people gathering in the informal sector, thanks to which costs and prices in industrial production, in the construction business, for private and public services, in commercial trade and tourism, and also in modern agriculture are kept at a level which is still competitive on the world market, and moderate with regard to the normally rather weak domestic purchasing power, hence conducive to the further development of the "urbanized" modern sector.

In economic terms, the interfaces between the informal and the modern sector, thus, are varied, especially in urban areas, and the "permeability" for goods and services, and for cheap labour is comparatively high. As soon as it comes, however, to the genuine "ingredients" of development such as education, access to information and credit, technology, political and social participation, the informal sector and the modern sector exist as almost separate societies, the latter at the expense of and thanks to the former.

3.3 Some Critical Remarks as Regards the Reduction of the Informal Sector to Small and Micro-Enterprises under the Aspect of Economic Sector Promotion

In the relevant literature, the informal sector normally is considered as the total of small and micro-enterprises and low-income self-employment, not more and not less. Most employment promotion programmes for the informal sector follow the same perception. Their target groups hence are (potential) small and micro-enterprises and individual self-employed business(wo)men with an evident economic development potential.
For their definition and distinction from small enterprises and self-employment in the modern sector, more than one classification scheme has been developed. All of them face the same dilemma that many of these business units – under legal, technological, financial and/or business administration aspects – often operate well below the threshold beyond which economists would consider them as belonging to the modern sector, yet undisputedly are integrated somehow in the economic system of the modern sector.
Programmes for small and micro-enterprise promotion – and for the promotion of the informal sector in this definition – are basically regarded as policy instruments for the economic promotion of this sector. Consequently, vocational training and education, especially in (partly) Government-run vocational training institutes, are also seen and applied in this sense. The (potential) owners and employees of small and micro-enterprises as well as the low-income self-employed business(wo)men with an acknowledged development potential are thus – along the policy-centred logics – a "derived" target group whose vocational training and education is an instrument in sector promotion.
Advocates of this strategy and perception should, however, take into consideration that
– especially if the promotion of small and micro-enterprises is to be effected through vocational training programmes, the criteria for the categorization of small and micro-enterprises and self-employed business(wo)men should find a basis which is more meaningful than the stereotype antipodes of "informal" versus "modern", the more so

as quite a few small and micro-entrepreneurs regard their "marginalization" into the informal sector as unjustified and even discriminatory[15] and may, therefore, react with ignorance to training and advisory offers labelled as "for the informal sector";
– there are a tremendously large number of people whose living and working conditions in no way correspond to the structures, norms and development options within the modern sector, which for them are neither applicable nor accessible, but whose economic activities for income generation and satisfaction of basic needs are not carried out in small or micro-enterprises or in gainful self-employment;
– every kind of vocational training and education in the first instance aims at enabling *people* to earn a living up to the possible best of their abilities and their occupational options, not to mention the intrinsic value of training and education and its relevance for personality development;
– vocational training measures, thus, should not one-sidedly or even exclusively be designed to meet the labour demands of modern enterprises, but take into due consideration also the qualification needs and the learning opportunities and potentials of the people (potentially) working in these enterprises, and also the occupation opportunities of the many others who will never have the chance of getting one of these rare jobs.

With respect to these considerations, the informal sector should not be regarded as just a residual "quaternary" sector of Third World economies, whose contribution to the value added is difficult to estimate, and which consists of a certain type of small and micro-enterprises. Instead, it should be perceived and promoted as the socio-economic environment of a growing number of economically weak and socially disadvantaged people who, by no means, all (can) earn their living from (self-)employment in a small and micro-enterprise, but who, nevertheless, want to survive and to improve their living and working conditions by any possible means.

In this study, the identification of possible target groups for a (bilateral) vocational training assistance which aims at promoting

---

15 Past own experiences in this respect in Southeast Asia, similar remarks in the target group interviews carried out in Thailand, and comments by NGO workers from Colombia and Peru make it clear that many small and micro-entrepreneurs who according to generally accepted criteria belong to the informal sector, may well agree to have more problems than larger and more modern enterprises, yet by no means therefore consider themselves as belonging to a basically different, namely "informal" category of small and micro-entrepreneurs.

"the informal sector", consequently is not restricted to small and micro-enterprises and self-employed business(wo)men. The following considerations are meant to contribute to the development of concepts and strategies for the *occupation-oriented training and education of people* from the informal sector, *not* towards concepts for a merely *economic sector promotion* by means of training.

4. Multi-dimensional Identification of Target Groups from the Informal Sector

In accordance with the people-centred approach on which this study is based, considerations on suitable concepts for "Occupation-oriented Training and Education for Target Groups from the Informal Sector" start with the identification of these target groups. Efforts to find a corresponding realistic and operational categorization of people from the informal sector, however, run into considerable difficulties. Every attempt to identify target groups in an "easy-to-handle" and thus necessarily one-dimensional way is doomed to failure to the extent to which it tries to adequately take into account the heterogeneity and complexity of the economic and social phenomena in this field.

When projects are planned on the basis of the policy-centred approach, the target groups are usually identified with regard to the envisaged project objective, i.e. the selection of the target group(s) has a mainly instrumental character. Since the informal sector is above all, as a rule, viewed under the aspect of its possible contribution to a country's economic development, the identification of possible target groups for assistance benefiting the informal sector is primarily oriented to the economic activities which can be observed there. The assessment of the relevance of correspondingly categorized target groups and of the extent to which they should be promoted thus depends implicitly or explicitly on the assessment of the development potential of precisely these economic activities, not so much on the assessment of the development potential of the people in the respective target groups (at the time of identification).

But what is actually behind the term "target group"? Apart from the fact that members of the same target group have certain living and/or working conditions in common, it normally consists of people with often extremely varying backgrounds and interests, possibly a different type of integration into the economic and social framework of the informal sector, above all with often extremely varying learning potentials. People in rural areas, for example, especially if they have always lived there, react in a different way to anything "new" and have a different perception of "learning" than someone influenced by a more urban environment, even if both are subsumed under the target group category "small and micro-entrepreneurs", "unemployed youngsters", or "economically active women". A corresponding variety of actual qualification needs can be the result, even within the same target group identified solely under economic aspects, in a policy-centred approach.

With regard to the formulation of training and education measures which are appropriate for target groups, i.e. which are accessible, needs-oriented and beneficial from the viewpoint of the target group(s), this means that it cannot be sufficient to categorize the people living in the informal sector, merely based on the economic activities actually or potentially carried out there, in economically more or less relevant target groups.

Such a step is important – and is often also the only possible initial approach to the informal sector – for the tentative determination of the objective of an assistance measure and the decision in which of its segments the informal sector should be supported. Furthermore, this may help to find out whether and to what extent occupation-oriented training and education can serve, under the respectively given conditions, as a suitable instrument to assist the envisaged target group(s).

For their proper design, i.e. the determination of learning content and teaching methods and an adequate implementation strategy, as well as for a more precise definition of attainable objectives for such measures, however, sufficient reference points can only be obtained via a multi-dimensional identification of potential target groups, taking into account

– initially, the various observable or possible economic activities in the informal sector, which not only determine the economic and social situation of the people there, but also give planners a certain idea about the already existing occupation-relevant knowledge, skills and experience and about the possibilities for further development;

– as a key aspect, the different learning opportunities and potentials of individuals and specific target groups, which relate to the objectively (not) given possibilities for education and training as well as to the subjective learning motivation and learning capacity of individuals or specific target groups;

– finally, the character of their spatial and socialization-specific integration into the economic and social framework of the informal sector, which, to a large extent, decides on the actual and potential occupation opportunities and options.

In the following multi-dimensional identification – with regard to these three aspects – of possible target groups of occupation-oriented training and education measures, only those people from the informal sector are considered who are actually able and basically willing to work. Elderly and sick people whose support must be regarded as a task for the families or for public and private social welfare, are not taken into consideration.

4.1 "Rough Identification" of Target Groups Based on the Economic Activities Perceived

The various economic and subsistence activities which people from the informal sector in urban as well as rural areas are found to carry out in order to earn a living, give first ideas and indications for a rough identification of possible target groups. At the same time, they provide a fairly comprehensive and differentiating picture of the variety and scope of the economic and social living conditions in the informal sector. Since individuals, quite often, have several occupations simultaneously or in frequent alternation, in order to gain a sufficient income for themselves and the family members to be supported by them, they can possibly be related to different categories of target groups identified on this basis, depending on the activity carried out at the time of observation.

All groups described below can be found in Third World countries – although to a varying extent and significance in different regions – and can, in principle, be viewed as possible target groups for development measures for the informal sector. In what way occupation-oriented training and education, in particular, could be suitable instruments to improve the living and working conditions of the respective target groups is furthermore determined by their qualification needs and development options.

All of the following categories of target groups include women, generally in large numbers. Only in the group of small and micro-entrepreneurs with additional employees, i.e. as employers, women are clearly a minority[16].

4.1.1 Target Groups from the Urban Informal Sector

In the informal sector of larger urban areas and their catchment areas, ten possible target group categories were identified based on the observable economic activities:

---

16 However, some West African countries are an exception here; especially in Ghana, where a female hereditary line has also traditionally existed, women owners of small and micro-enterprises are a common phenomenon.

(1) Small and Micro-Entrepreneurs with Few Informal Employees
This category includes already active as well as potential small and micro-entrepreneurs, who are both employers and, quite often, also masters, while owning small enterprises in artisanal production, in the field of services and repair, in the transport sector or in commerce. They employ – exclusively or partly – members of their families[17], more or less qualified wage labourers or young helpers as a kind of apprentices. As production enterprises they can either be sub-contractors tied to one supplier and one buyer only, or enterprises which procure their raw materials, intermediate products and equipment independently and choose their (varying) buyers themselves. They generally operate independently, but occasionally, especially in Latin America, also in mergers, in which each merger participant is responsible for a part of the same production.

As already mentioned, women are rarely represented in this group, and if they are, there is no major difference between a female and a male enterprise owner. As small and micro-entrepreneurs, both have basically the same problems and orientations.

(2) Self-Employed Persons
(Women) Owners of small stationary or mobile production, repair, service or vending businesses try to create employment and generate income for themselves by setting up or leasing a one-person business. This applies, for example, to street traders, food stall owners, roadside secretaries or women contributing towards the family income through home production, for example by sewing. Many of them are relatively "established" with a business they have been operating already for a long time. Many others, however, are only temporarily occupied as self-employed persons until they find other employment or because they run into problems. Some, like the "cachueleros" in Lima mentioned earlier, are double, triple or multiple self-employed entrepreneurs.

This category also includes many sideline job income earners, members of the urban middle class, and often public service employees whose principal income from employment in the modern sector can (still) only insufficiently meet the costs of what is regarded to be a reasonable standard of living. The income earned through a side-line activity as self-employed – or the sideline job income earned by wives

---

17 This can be "genuine", i. e. productive workers, for which a replacement has to be found in case they leave, as well as family members who help out in the business for lack of other work opportunities, but whose leaving would not have a negative effect.

in the informal sector – is quite often even higher than the principal income[18].

(3) Wage Workers and Trainees in Small and Micro-Enterprises of the Informal Sector

These are usually members of the informal sector who are unable to find employment or (as school-leavers) a training vacancy because of lack of (formal) training requirements, due to their social background and/or simply because of the shortage of jobs in the modern sector. They normally work for an extremely low remuneration, generally without any social security, as trainees generally only in return for free lodging and/or board. Many are employed on a contract-only or seasonal basis. Their knowledge and technical skills differ substantially and are by no means inadequate in every case. Many of them are temporary migrants from rural areas, who cannot earn an adequate living in the agricultural sector.

(4) Lowest-Income Workers in Industrial, Construction or Service Enterprises in the Modern Sector

This category includes construction and factory workers as well as employees in restaurants, in tourism or in municipal services such as street cleaning, who often have been working in the modern sector since long, but for a very low income – in many cases lower than the statutory minimum wage – and without any social security in case of accidents, illness or dismissal. Some come from rural areas, but the majority of them seems to belong to the second generation of rural-urban migrants, born or, at least, grown up in one of the urban squatter areas. In Southeast Asian countries, many of them are women. As a rule, these workers are poorly trained or untrained, but may have gained in their jobs certain skills and working experience qualifying them to a limited extent.

(5) Odd-Job Workers, Day Labourers and Casual Labourers

This group is very similar to the one described under (4). Among the odd-job workers, day labourers and causal labourers, however, there are more often temporary or permanently settled first-generation migrants. They hardly stand a chance of learning much through such activities, since the work is strenuous and usually full-time but technically, organizationally and mentally pretty undemanding. For

---

18 The term "sideline job income" thus refers not so much to the level of income, but rather to the working time devoted.

many of them, such kind of activities in alternation with unemployment is a permanent situation. Some only work temporarily as day labourers or casual labourers, for example, to finance training and education, or to pull through a situation of dire economic need.

(6) Street Children

Street children are a particularly inaccessible group. They mainly live in the big urban areas, among them more boys than girls. In some respects, they are identical with (5), but much younger, the youngest not more than 5 years old. Many have no permanent home and often lack any family. The majority have only been out on the streets for 3 years, but roughly a quarter already for 10 years or more. Most of them have (almost) no primary school education, but nevertheless still hope to get a "proper" job. Almost all street boys work, generally to earn a living for themselves but partly for the family as well, quite a few working more than 10 hours a day, mainly as "autonomous" rag-pickers, load carriers, some as messengers, often enough out of poverty as "professional beggars", and some as professional thieves. Most of them manage to get enough to eat through their work. Yet they rarely have a permanent place to stay or more than the set of clothes they wear.

The situation for girls is generally even tougher for boys. They also have more difficulties to find an income-generating activity, apart from prostitution[19]. Above all in the big cities of Latin America the economic and social conditions make boys more susceptible to crime and drug abuse. Many are unable, in the long term, to escape the influence of gangs and cliques.

(7) Prostitutes

In the metropolitan areas of almost all countries, to a lesser extent in rural towns, prostitution is clearly a job market for young women, and an indirect, often vital source of income for numerous rural families. They either receive transfer payments from daughters working as a prostitute, or they have sold them to an agent for an amount of money urgently needed at some stage. Like street children, prostitutes are a target group which is not easily accessible, although adequate training and education could open up, especially for the younger women, alternative occupational opportunities. At the same

---

19 This description of the situation is based on the findings of two sociological studies carried out by the Bosco Institute of Social Work in Tirupattur/India about street children in Madras and – only in 1990 – in Salem; cf. *BOSCO INSTITUTE* (no year of publication) and *ibid.* (1990).

time, they could function, under certain circumstances, as change agents in their native rural environment they originate from.

(8) Domestic Staff
People in this category normally also never had the chance of proper education or training. Many of them did not even finish primary school. Through their work they make – often since early childhood – sometimes decisive contributions to their families' income, or even make training and/or education possible for one of their brothers. In some countries, domestic jobs are a women's, in others a men's domain. Job security can be relatively high in this field, provided the work is done reliably, since domestic employers are not interested in a high fluctuation among their staff. However, there are normally no social security provisions in the event of illness or old age, often not even holidays.

(9) Unemployed Persons Able and Willing to Work
This group including people of all age, is by definition not economically active in a true sense. It is, however, an integral and significant part of the economic reality in the informal sector. Most people living there are at some stage unwillingly unemployed, many of them repeatedly and for longer periods. Distinction, however, has to be made as regards social background, duration and reasons for unemployment. Many of those who are frequently unemployed have a low education, and many are (almost) illiterate.
Increasingly, however, this group also comprises young people who completed secondary or even technical school education, but are unable to find employment in the modern sector because of a general shortage of jobs there. For those who did not already grow up in the informal sector, but are children of a middle class family, it is also hard to find employment in the informal sector instead, and they are particularly afraid to "fall down" the social ladder. Secondary-school leavers in general tend – at least initially – to not be interested in employment in the informal sector, since they had high hopes of getting a job in the modern sector through that education, and do not or cannot simply drop this idea.
In growing numbers also civil servants dismissed in the wake of structural adjustment measures are found in longer-term unemployment. Their chances for reemployment depend on whether they acquired some other skills through a sideline activity in a private business or job in the informal sector while still working in the civil service. Prospects are dim for those who – precisely because of their

position in an administration – have neither the experience or qualification nor the attitude required for starting a business or taking up a job in the private modern or informal sector.

(10) Subsistence Workers

These are above all women and children, who struggle to support their families through – usually regular – subsistence work, therefore often refraining from taking on paid employment elsewhere. Apart from the regular household work and child care, their activities mostly focus on securing basis needs for food, water and firewood. But they also include re-construction or maintenance work on their own housing, sorting out refuse for further use in the home or for sale, or subsistence work on the family farm.

4.1.2   *Target Groups from the Rural Informal Sector*

It should be emphasized again that not the entire rural economy can be regarded as belonging to the informal sector, even where the level of agricultural production is, altogether, comparatively modest. In the many villages and small rural towns, there are farmers and artisanal enterprises which, through regular sales of their products and services on the market, certainly secure a sufficient income to support the family.

Nevertheless, it still will be true for most countries that the economic activities in rural areas are predominantly in the informal sector which largely, though not exclusively, consists of subsistence farming. Basically, the following categories of possible target groups can be identified with regard to the economic activities in the rural informal sector:

(1) Subsistence Farming Families

These smallholder families are owners or leaseholders of land, on which they can grow a certain amount of food for subsistence or sale. The proceeds, however, are just about enough in good years at most to provide the food they need, but even then are hardly sufficient to finance other living costs, the farm inputs needed for the following year, or even school attendance for their children. Most subsistence farming families of which – especially in Africa – often only women and children live in the villages following migration of the men, suffer at least temporarily from hunger, water shortage and disease. In many areas they are already so heavily indebted, often forced to "pawn" parts of their farmland or their own labour and that of their children, that a complete repayment of the credits is nearly impossible. The migration rates are correspondingly high, especially among young people, and – at least in Southeast Asia – the suicide rates, too, especially among older farmers. Wherever possible, at least some family members seeks seasonal sources of sideline activity income in nearby areas, as agricultural workers in areas with several harvests per year, or through temporary migration to urban areas. Many subsistence farming families could not even survive without at least occasional financial support of a family member working in urban areas.

(2) Owners and Employees of Small and Micro-Enterprises

Insofar as they can be classified as belonging to the informal sector, these are either sideline activity enterprises or impoverished traditional artisanal enterprises whose products are increasingly displaced from the rural market by cheap mass-produced industrial goods because of inferior quality, higher prices, or the "modernized" preferences of customers. They are generally one-person operations or small and micro-enterprises with helping family members and/or 1–2 younger helpers as trainees.

Enterprises which should actually not be seen as belonging to the informal sector, comprise the traditional rural crafts, such as blacksmiths, potters or carpenters, which produce, by and large without competition, to satisfy basic local needs with one or more qualified craftsmen on the basis of know-how which has often been handed down for generations, using simple technologies. These enterprises – at least still – have a market which gives them a comparatively decent income. Just as little to be seen as part of the informal sector are modern small and micro-enterprises which are located in rural areas and meet the needs of a certain market with adequate profits.

Another question is to what extent they could and should, nevertheless, be included in training and education for rural target groups with regard to the promotion of occupational opportunities in rural areas outside of the agricultural sector.

(3) Women and Children in Domestic Subsistence Work

In particular women and children are the cornerstones of the subsistence economy and, thus, for the survival of entire families, just as in the urban informal sector. Their work comprises all kinds of domestic activities to meet the family's subsistence needs, including small husbandry or horticulture, if possible also simple home production or preparation of meals for sale to contribute to the family's subsistence income required to buy essential items. Women's interest, however, is often less on *cash* income sources, but on any opportunity to support with their labour – paid or unpaid – their families, i.e. in the first instance parents and children. Often the women are the ones who work hard and make savings in order to allow a proper education for at least one of their children.

(4) Unemployed or Underemployed Youngsters

A growing number of young people in rural areas are faced by the situation of neither being able to work at present in their family's farm or artisanal enterprise, nor having the perspective of taking over, at a later date, this enterprise, or a part of it which is sufficiently large to make a living. They have to, at the latest when they intend marrying and having a family, seek an independent source of income outside of the agricultural sector, or independent of their parent's enterprise, which they are often unable to find at all in rural areas and only temporarily by migrating to an urban centre. Even there, their chances of finding employment in the modern sector, let alone on a regular basis, are slim, with their level of education being poor, their social background forming an obstacle, and their numbers being large. They will either find themselves in groups (2), (3), (5), (8) or (9) of the urban informal sector, or return to the villages into the same, unchanged situation.

(5) Landless Agricultural Workers

Their attributes resemble those mentioned under (4) insofar as they do not (any more) have an independent economic basis of their livelihood in the agricultural sector. However, there are two essential differences: they can be found in all age-groups, and very often they have a family to support. Many of them were once independent farmers who lost their farm land through heavy indebtedness or acquisition by the state (e.g. for road construction), but who still have agricultural know-how and skills.

(6) Middle Class Families with Insufficient Income

As in the urban areas, the small and medium-size rural towns also have a middle class in the modern sector. It comprises mainly civil servants such as teachers, police officers, administrative staff or extension workers. Their income from these jobs is normally too low to fully support the families. They, thus, have to rely on a sideline income from at least one activity in the informal sector. This may be in domestic horticulture or small livestock raising for own consumption and/or sale, but also taking on all kinds of casual work, or running a small tailoring, cobbler's or hair-dressing business, generally in the town where they live.

To improve the living and working conditions of these various target groups from the urban and rural informal sector, or to enhance their development options in general, different objectives are conceivable and realizable, whether through training and education or through other types of assistance. The possible scope of any promotion measure, especially if designed to improve the *economic* situation of a target group, is all the more difficult to determine, and its success is the more difficult to predict, the less the target group acts, or is able to act in a (labour) market-conscious way. Chances may be best for the target group of already active small and micro-entrepreneurs, but even in this case not always as certain as assumed, with more difficulties in rural than in urbanized areas, and here again easier in places like Bogotà or Bangkok as compared to Bangui or Hanoi.

4.2 *"Specified Identification" of Target Groups with Regard to Learning Opportunities and Potentials*

As already pointed out, the initial "rough identification" of target groups under the aspect of economic activities provides a basis to determine the priority area and orientation of the intended assistance, e.g. as a programme for the promotion of small enterprises, for women's development, for the qualification of unemployed youth, or for rural community development. When it comes to elaborating attainable objectives especially for measures in the field of vocational training and education, however, it is too unspecified for both, the identification of qualification needs as well as the determination of the target group-specific training objectives, curriculum development and teaching methods adequate for the respective target group(s) – in other words the actual design of occupation-oriented training and education programmes for people from the informal sector.

A key question is what – apart from the general economic conditions and development options – actually determines qualification needs, a person's expectations and interest in training or advice, and, finally, the learning success. From the background of own work experience with people from the informal sector and on the basis of various observations and discussions during the reconnaissance mission, a few factors are considered as – target group-specifically and individually varying – learning opportunities and potentials, which crucially determine chances, success and difficulties of learning – and hence also the impact and success of occupation-oriented training and education measures.

Some examples of target groups categorized under the aspect of learning opportunities and potentials may show that there are people with substantially varying training and education options, learning motivation and learning capacity in the urban as well as in the informal sector. The target groups considered similar or comparable under this aspect, however, need not at all to be identical with the target groups identified with regard to the economic activities observed in the informal sector.

4.2.1 *Determinants of Learning Opportunities and Potentials*

Irrespective of the objectives of a training measure and the related expectations of an individual or a target group, any individual learning success and thus, finally, the suitability and sustainability of occupation-oriented training and education measures as such will largely depend on the extent to which they have been designed by taking into consideration the varying learning opportunities and potentials of people, as described below.

(1) Non-personal Factors Determining Learning Opportunities

The possibility for target groups or individuals to respond to occupation-oriented education, training or advisory offers addressed to them, is determined by quite a few factors which are largely beyond their influence. These non-personal factors exert a pre-selective effect already on the decision whether or not to apply for participation, which cannot be rated highly enough.

Among the non-personal factors which essentially determine learning opportunities are, in particular,
– how easily the training location can be reached, considering the availability of transport, travel costs, familiarity with the training location, permission to leave home, and the like (spatial factor);
– the possibility to take sufficient time off from other commitments at home or at work, and/or to interrupt it without major difficulties to participate in a training or education (time factor);
– savings or a sufficient family income so as not to have to earn money beside the training, at least not to an extent which could

jeopardize the training success, and to be able to meet the direct and indirect costs of training insofar as this does not offer associated income earning opportunities (financial factor);
– the social status influencing the ability and possibility to assert an interest in occupation-oriented training and education, an extremely relevant – and often restrictive – aspect especially for girls and women (socio-cultural factor);
– available information on education or training opportunities, presented in a way that it can be understood and allows to assess the relevance of the training offer with regard to one's own situation (cognitive factor);
– the existence of training and education institutions without restrictive admission requirements of a formal or social nature (institutional factor).

(2) Motivation to Learn and Interest in Advice
The motivation of a target group or an individual to seek occupation-oriented qualification through education, training or advice, to support an also vocation-oriented primary school education of the children, varies considerably not only on the individual level, but also for or among a social group, and often also with different regions.
It depends to a substantial degree on
– the subjective perception and assessment of the non-personal factors determining the learning opportunities;
– the subjective assessment of the relevance of the training on offer as regards the applicability and usefulness of the knowledge and skills to be learnt for improving employment and income-earning prospects or the living conditions in general;
– finally, the individual and group-specific social values and priorities, influenced by socio-cultural traditions as well as by the general living and working conditions prevailing in the informal sector, as described above.
In view of its significance which too often tends to be underestimated, a closer look is taken at that last aspect. People from the informal sector live – especially in urban areas – in arrow spatial and social environments, in the villages to a great extent in monotony and seclusion, constantly confronted by all forms of poverty, hopelessness, and the struggle for survival. Most of them experience themselves as marginalized members of society, not recognized socially, exploited economically, whose dignity is repeatedly violated, whose needs are not perceived or are misunderstood, and who are administered as a mass social phenomenon which has to be

kept as quiet as possible. Especially in the older generation, however, traditional values still dominate, in rural more than in urban areas, although they are being eroded in the younger generations without being replaced by other guiding values or acceptable models and ideals. Whereas older people tend to simply accept the often hopeless situation they have to struggle through every day, although not always without complaining, this situation, among younger people, turns to a growing extent into frustration, escapism, aggression, or an uncompromising desire for social advancement.

This situation supports the emergence of a certain type of attitudes and orientations for individual and group behaviour, which is somehow typical for people from the informal sector, although there are, of course, considerable differences between and even within specific target groups, and sometimes even contradictory attitudes. Altogether, they may be described as follows:

– a basically conservative attitude and scepticism towards all changes affecting personal and social habits, for fear of unpredictable risk or inexperience in dealing with new situations and options, especially in the villages;

– a day-to-day perspective in view of the difficulties and uncertainties of the everyday struggle for survival, and a way of thinking rooted in the traditional social patterns of family, neighbourhood and village structure, and oriented to avoiding conflicts and to social conformity;

– a lack of self-confidence, especially when confronted with the unfamiliar, as well as with people from the urban environment or a different social class, and at the same time little confidence in people outside the own social group of reference;

– either the desire for the best possible education for one's children, at least for one or two of the sons ("training disease") as the only hope for better prospects in life for them and thus for the family, or, on the contrary, a denial of the chances related to primary school education or vocational training in a feeling of resignation, or because of a lack of information on, and/or imagination of the resulting options;

– the desire, especially among young people, to copy modern urban lifestyle, including its status symbols and customs;

– in the case of the overwhelming majority of people, the determination of self-help, but also – especially where "project experience" has already been gained – a tendency to wait for external assistance.

Such attitudes and maxims for behavior are by and large typical for people from the informal sector, although to a varying extent in individual cases, depending on cultural factors and specific regional features. They influence strongly and in a subtle way the attitude towards training, education and learning, and thus, the learning motivation, as regards both the own participation in training and education as well as the willingness to support or tolerate the training and education desires of sons and daughters.

(3) Individual and Group-specific Learning Capability

Learning itself and the ability to apply what has been taught also have to be learnt, as well as appropriate social behaviour and self-assertion have to be learnt in the process of social education. The more this is recognized as an essential prerequisite for the success of any training programme, the more the limitations of target group identification for occupation-oriented training and education measures merely under economic aspects become apparent. The learning capability which varies depending on the social, cultural and regional background, needs to be taken into account.

Learning capability includes

– the ability to make an "intelligent use" of information and new skills, i.e. acquire, comprehend and critically digest both, independently assess their relevance for the own purpose, and adapt newly imparted skills and information which extends beyond the immediate sphere of hitherto experience to one's own requirements and possibilities;

– the way of dealing with change and "news" in general, and with new subject matters introduced through education or training courses in particular;

– the mental aptitudes for theoretical and systematic learning, for dealing with so far unknown techniques, and for the acquisition of practical skills.

Learning capability is influenced by the background of individual and – as far as social groups are concerned – collective experience, which is determined by

– previous work and life experience (primarily) in either an urban or a rural living environment, including the extent of exposure to modern ways of life and technology, rapid social change, "urban" norms, the experience of time as a structuring factor in life, and the like;

– given learning experience as regards education at school, in the family and in the social community, but also occupation-oriented training and education of any kind.

Learning capability develops by no means regardless of the economic and social conditions in the family and in the community of social reference, which also have far-reaching implications for the development of the individual mental predisposition for learning. All too often, even if this predisposition is positive, the learning capability then is negatively influenced – by inadequate demands regarding systematic learning and/or the psychological and physical strains of poverty, or nutritional deficiencies and diseases already during childhood. As a result, not only adults, but also older children and youth in the informal sector often find learning a particularly difficult task.

4.2.2 *Examples of Target Groups with Different Learning Opportunities and Potentials*

In the second step of "specified identification" of target groups for occupation-oriented training and education measures, the people from the informal sector are not primarily or even one-sidedly categorized with regard to their main or recent economic activities, but rather with regard to similar learning opportunities and potentials, stemming from similar social and/or economic situations or a comparable background of experience.

Under this aspect, *among others* the following possible target groups can be identified, for occupation-oriented training and education measures for people from the informal sector:

(1) (Potential) Small and Micro-Entrepreneurs and Self-Employed Persons with Basic or Vocational Training and Work Experience[20]

whose training needs, if any, are primarily business-oriented with regard to their own enterprises, and who are mainly to be found in or near urban areas where they

– already operate reasonably successfully their own business which, however, could be expanded or strengthened with the help

---

20 In the identification of target groups, this group should be distinguished from those small and micro-entrepreneurs and self-employed persons, who, in principle, have a basis in private business which they master "technically", and whose development bottlenecks hence do not primarily result from the lack of know-how, but, for example, from problems of access to credit, uncertainty about the permanence of their business site, or the inadequate purchasing power of their customers. These small and micro-enterprises and self-employed persons which also include numerous street traders, are hardly a target group for occupation-oriented training and education measures, as long as they simply want to continue their activities. Insofar as they want to improve their qualification for better occupation opportunities, they belong to the first group described under category (3) below.

of some technical and/or business administration training, or specific advisory assistance;
– through suitable technical and/or business administration training, could be encouraged and qualified for a new business creation, possibly with some financial support in addition;

(2) Smallholder and Subsistence Farming Families with a (still) Existing Agricultural Basis of Livelihood,

who can be helped through on-site practical training adapted to their local opportunities, and/or a regular agricultural advisory service on appropriate technical implements and techniques to increase their yields, to find additional sources of income from non-farming sideline activities, to reduce the burden of subsistence work, and/or to improve the village infrastructure through qualified community work;

(3) Men and Women with Basic or Vocational Training and/or Work Experience, but without a Long-term Basis of Livelihood,

who generally need a specific training rather than a (renewed) basic education or a comprehensive vocational training, with the required scope and content of the training depending on the reasons for their – despite basic education and previous work experience – weak economic situation, for example whether
– their own business just cannot earn them a sufficient income, as in the case of many subsistence farming families, street vendors or other one-person businesses, and numerous women engaged in poorly paid home production;
– they are unable to generate sufficient income in wage-earning activities accessible to them, or their jobs are not secured, which both applies to many workers in small and micro-enterprises in the informal sector as well as to the lowest-income workers in modern sector enterprises;
– they can find or take on only casual or seasonal work, as landless farm labourers or as poorly paid day labourers or helpers without any social security;
– have lost an economic basis they once had, for example because of squatter resettlement, the loss of (mortgaged) farm land, or the dismissal from work;

(4) Young People without (Adequate) Basic or Vocational Training and Only Negligible Work Experience,
who, in growing numbers, can be found in urban as well as rural areas, without any own basis of livelihood, as underemployed casual labourers and helpers, or unemployed persons without prospects of a better future and often with a problematic social behaviour, including a particularly large number of young women whose underemployment in income-generating activities is largely hidden in their often hard and time-consuming subsistence work in the household and/or in agriculture;

(5) Adult Illiterates with (Subsistence) Work Experience,
who do have practical skills, but often lack a secure basis of livelihood, and who can be mainly found in groups (2) and (7), with the ability to read and write being much more urgently needed by those living in and near urban areas, their illiteracy not only being a severe handicap with regard to employment opportunities, but often to the development of their personality and self-confidence, all the more so, the more inevitable their contact with the modern sector becomes;

(6) Children with Inadequate or No Primary Education,
who have hardly any chance of a proper occupation-oriented training or a fairly gainful employment, which applies to boys and girls to almost the same extent, and in urban areas primarily to the children – especially the daughters – of first-generation migrants with a still weak basis of livelihood in the family – this resulting in many of them hanging around at home or on the streets, some susceptible even to drug addiction, apathetic or aggressive; but also found in large numbers as cheap (sometimes bonded) labour in the agricultural sector, in factories or service enterprises, as odd-job workers on construction sites, as prostitutes or as "self-employed" street children, with – thanks to their young age – nevertheless still slightly better chances for their social (re-)integration and occupation-oriented qualification than in most cases of older youngsters or adults in a similar situation;

(7) Immobile Groups without (Adequate) Education, but Considerable Subsistence Work Experience,
which include, in particular, women and girls who are restricted in their activities to the close proximity of their homes because of numerous responsibilities in the household and for subsistence

agriculture, or because of socio-cultural tradition, generally more so in rural than in urban areas, and whose education and training as well as employment opportunities depend first and foremost – regardless of all other factors – on the proximity to their homes;

(8) Social Intermediaries and Animators with a Sound General Education and Possibly Vocational Training,

relating in particular to trainers, village school teachers or local community workers from the immediate environment of the target group, who – with regard to the required target group proximity, long-term nature, continuity and, finally, the sustainability of occupation-oriented training and education measures for people from the informal sector – should be trained and motivated in sufficient numbers and to adequate, though not too high standards.

In each of these eight exemplary target groups, the last one being somehow special, the learning opportunities and potentials of the people are different, because of the differences in their economic situation *and* in their education background and work experience. Accordingly, qualification needs and options for occupation – and hence what can be considered as a suitable occupation-oriented training approach for the respective target group – are different in each of these eight target groups.

A more specifically target group-oriented planning and design of occupation-oriented training and education measures, which takes into particular account the varying learning opportunities and potentials, could substantially improve the chances for many people from the informal sector to make use of such offers.

4.3 *"Status Identification" of Target Groups with Regard to Urban/Rural and Socialization-specific Integration*

The qualification needs of people from the informal sector and hence the scope of possible assistance are essentially determined by the type and scope of occupation-relevant opportunities and options open to them in principle. For both individuals and social groups, these opportunities and options are – apart from the general frame conditions dealt with in greater detail in the following chapter – very much a result from the nature, duration and stability of their integration in a certain economic and social environment in the urban or rural informal sector and the degree of rural-urban "commuting", respectively.

Within a multi-dimensional identification of possible target groups for occupation-oriented training and education measures, therefore, the people from the informal sector can and should also be categorized under the aspect of their "location" in its economic and social framework and their thereby influenced socialization. This would enable an easier and more precise identification of development options and hence the occupation-oriented opportunities of different target groups, to be taken into consideration in the planning of promotion measures. From this "status"-based point of view, three major categories of target groups with various sub-groups may be identified:

(1) The People "At Home" in the Urban Informal Sector
are firmly rooted in the urban environment as regards their social integration and their orientation for occupation and education. For this type of urbanized rural people, a permanent return to their home village is basically out of the question.
Sub-groups are
– the "established" first-generation of rural-urban migrants who have been able since a longer period already to settle and to somehow make a living in the city;
– rural-urban migrants who have no other choice than to stay in the city despite a shaky or bad basis of livelihood there, because they cannot return to their home villages either for social reasons – which, for example, applies to many street children and young prostitutes – or because there is no (longer an) economic basis there for them, or – especially in the case of many women – because they want an urban school education for their children;
– most children of the second and third generations of rural-urban migrants, who have already grown up and been socialized in the milieu of the urban informal sector and hence see themselves entirely as towns (wo)men, often even unable to master village life as many of them discover when they visit their (grand)parents' villages;
– youngsters from the a.m. group with a secondary-school certificate with which they hoped to get access to employment in the modern sector, but failed because of the general lack of jobs there, a poor school-leaving certificate and/or their "inferior" social background;
– urban dwellers from the modern sector with a fairly regular sideline income from an activity in the informal sector, required to secure the standard of living regarded as desirable.

(2) The "Commuters" and "Newcomers" in the Urban Informal Sector

come partly – and up to now predominantly – from rural areas, and partly – but to a growing extent – from the modern sector, especially in the big cities. Needless to say that both groups are from completely different socialization backgrounds. There are following major sub-groups:

– rural-urban migrants who only recently arrived in the urban area – voluntarily or out of necessity – with the intention to stay, but with no secure basis of livelihood (yet);

– regular, often seasonal rural-urban commuters who came to town in search of temporary employment, but who still have their social basis and, so to speak, their "main place of residence" in the rural community where many of them also would like to stay permanently, if only they could earn a sufficient living there, and see any chances for themselves and/or their children to get access to training and education;

– members of urban society with education and professional experience in the modern sector, who have "fallen down" the social ladder either because they lost their job there, and/or have been increasingly unable to maintain their standard of living due to inflation, and who have to look for a housing, often also for (sideline) income in the informal sector, depending on the family situation finally ending up there permanently;

– urban middle-class women who suddenly find themselves in the position of "head of the household" with the necessity to earn a living for themselves and their children, which in view of their often insufficient or lacking education means to take on a job in the informal sector;

– more and more youngsters from middle-class families, who despite secondary or even technical school certificates have little chance to find employment in the modern sector because of the lack of jobs there and who, at the same time, also have no experience or any contacts in the informal sector.

(3) The People "At Home" in the Rural Informal Sector

are either so closely attached to their rural communities that even temporary migration to an urban area is no option to them, or they cannot do so because of personal reasons or the great distance of the next urban area and/or the high travel costs involved. This category includes, in particular,

– the almost immobile villagers exclusively or primarily occupied in

subsistence farming, many of whom have never left the rural area or not even their village and, thus, have rarely come into contact with modern technology and modern "urban" development;
– the seasonal migrants within the rural areas, especially subsistence farmers (mainly male) and landless (male or female) labourers, who try to find temporary employment in areas with different or more frequent harvest seasons, or, during the agricultural "slack period", as casual workers in one of the few rural enterprises, or with lack of alternatives simply stay unemployed in their villages.

People's basic preference, compulsion or chance for a life either in an urban area even with humblest housing conditions, or in the rural areas, if at least a survival at subsistence level is possible, gives them completely dissimilar options and development perspectives with often essentially different income and occupation opportunities and hence qualification needs.
As compared to these vary clearly either urban- or rural-rooted groups, many of the temporary rural-urban commuters often have – at least for a while – a basis or development perspective in both environments, and thus to a certain extent broader options. Their priority qualification needs will depend on their long-term preferential place to stay. Here, target group-specifically designed occupation-oriented training and education measures with a clear focus on the applicability of imparted skills and knowledge within the rural environment, would presumably well contribute to reduce rural-urban migration.
Very specific employment opportunities and hence assistance needs have those people who come involuntarily and rather abruptly from the modern to the informal sector. With their "modern-urban" socialization and their education, many of them could be the prototype of a small entrepreneur "with development potential". On the other hand, it is precisely their lack of socialization and experience in the informal sector, which makes it particularly difficult for them to settle down there.

4.4 Summary of the Steps of a Multi-dimensional Identification of Target Groups from the Informal Sector

The design of any concept for occupation-oriented training and education of target groups from the informal sector first of all requires to have a reasonably precise idea about their profiles and about who should receive assistance for which purpose. Therefore, the importance of a multi-dimensional identification of possible target groups of respective measures – especially in a people-centred approach – is emphasized again.

As already pointed out, meaningful and sustainable measures for occupation-oriented training and education for people from the informal sector must reflect their actual qualification needs. In view of their heterogeneity, it is necessary – in the planning process – to initially identify as precisely as possible the various possible target groups and their specific qualification needs.

The profile of a target group is *equally* characterized by the economic activities the people carry out, by their learning opportunities and potentials, and by their "status" in the informal sector. Depending on how people from the informal sector are categorized with regard to all three aspects, their development potentials, occupation opportunities and options are different. Accordingly, they form different target groups with respectively different qualification needs as well as different possibilities of assistance.

This is fairly evident when considering such different groups like, for example, existing small and micro-entrepreneurs in the urban informal sector, women street vendors, subsistence farmers, unemployed youth in rural areas, or street children in big cities – they all have obviously fundamentally different development options, occupation opportunities and experience. And what may superficially appear to be the same situation, normally is different again for women and men. A similar degree of differences, however, exists, for example, between a self-employed person having lived for years in a stable economic and social network in the urban informal sector, and a self-employed person in a rural area. In either case, it makes a further difference whether the person is illiterate or at least has basic education, whether it is a man or a woman, and to what extent he or she is engaged in subsistence work and hence restricted in mobility. Similarly, someone who stays only temporarily in an urban area or has been there only for a short time, is in a fundamentally different situation as compared to someone who has lived in an urban slum since long, even if both have no school education and work on the same construction site as day labourers. With a basic or even technical training, or any relevant work experience, their opportunities and options differ yet again.

All these people have different qualification needs due to their varied working and living situation. The economic activities pursued are a prime indicator for target group identification, since they are relatively easy to identify, but they can also be misleading. Equally

significant are the learning opportunities and potentials and people's "status" in the economic and social framework of the informal sector. Therefore, a multi-dimensional identification of target groups is recommended, which at the same time *and* to an equal extent takes into account
– the actual or possible economic activities – including subsistence work – which occur in the informal sector, to identify tentatively the overall objectives of the intended assistance and the segment of the informal sector to be promoted with priority
→ "Rough Identification" of Target Groups;
– the individually and (target) group-specifically different learning opportunities and potentials of people, to adequately design the concept and methods of intended training and education measures
→ "Specified Identification" of Target Groups;
– the urban/rural and socialization-specific integration of people in the economic and social framework of the informal sector, to understand and assess the occupation-relevant opportunities and options realistically accessible to them, and to correspondingly define the objectives and targets of intended measures and their design more precisely
→ "Status Identification" of Target Groups.

The purpose of such a multi-dimensional identification of target groups is to obtain a picture as realistic as possible of the profiles and the diversity of possible target groups for occupation-oriented training and education, which adequately reflects the complexity of their respective living and working situations in the informal sector. Only on this basis, a differentiated identification of the respective target group-specific qualification needs and development options will be possible.

5. Occupation-oriented Training and Education Needs of People from the Informal Sector

In the perception of the people-centred approach, the objectives orientation as well as the design of development measures are essentially determined by the specific assistance needs of the respective target groups. It is crucially important, therefore, that these needs are identified as realistically and as precisely as possible. Both the subjectively felt and the objective assistance needs of people from the informal sector are influenced, in particular, by the environment-determined occupational opportunities and development options open to them.

In view of the employment situation actually prevailing in Third World countries, their assistance needs as regards occupation-oriented training and education have – contrary to the notion usually underlying vocational training assistance – since long diverted from the "classic" artisanal occupations, such as fitter, welder, carpenter or joiner – if this ever was the main orientation for the majority of people from the informal sector, at all.

Their primary qualification needs rather related to the acquisition – in whatever way possible – of know-how and skills enabling them to satisfy their basic needs as regards, for example, reasonably dry and stable housing, (drinking) water, fuelwood and food, at as low a cost as possible. Or they require better skills and information to satisfy other essential needs, such as small-scale irrigation, protection against the erosion of their farmland, road construction or transportation means to places where markets, schools and health stations are located; since many of such needs will be satisfied only, if at all, through their own (or communal) initiative and subsistence work.

Insofar as a craftsman – usually someone in the family or neighbourhood – is needed then only to help solve the problem at as low a cost as possible, for example (helping) to build a house or repair a vehicle. A bricklayer or electrician with a specialist technical training is usually both over- and underqualified for this task, since he is unable to work with wood or metal on a relatively broad basis and with a talent for improvisation, but merely masters a partial qualification "too well" – and is thus generally also too expensive.

Also on labour market of the modern sector, most job opportunities are available for relatively cheap labour with a sound but not too high level of qualification and a broad allocation spectrum.

The actual qualification needs of the various target groups from the urban and rural informal sectors, therefore, are mostly not determined by ideas on "classic" vocational training, but primarily by the problems and needs in their immediate living and working environment and their maximum scope of environment-determined occupational options[21].

Accordingly, alongside the multi-dimensional identification of possible target groups also their respective environment-determined occupational options must be assessed as realistically as possible in the planning stage of any occupation-oriented training and education project as a prerequisite for the identification of the target group-specific qualification needs.

5.1 Environment-determined Occupational Options as Determinants of Qualification Needs

In this study, "environment-determined occupational options" or – used rather synonymously – "environment-adapted occupation opportunities" define the radius, time and activity scope which basically exist – or might be extended through suitable assistance measures – for gainful (self-)employment and/or subsistence work and self-help activities of individuals or a target group. They are determined by the prevailing local living and working conditions, by the accessible occupational and training/education possibilities, and by social constraints and traditions, or any other particular area-specific development options.

The kind and diversity of the maximum spectrum of environment-determined options open to a target group does not only influence the assistance needs, but also determines which kind of assistance measures would – under the given circumstances – be of most occupational relevance for that target group. A clear assessment of the specific environment-determined options of a target group, thus, helps to realize which objectives orientation would be most meaningful and possible for the intended assistance measure, and where the target group-specific limits to development assistance lie.

What actually are the (potential) environment-determined options of

---

21 A similar view is also taken by *SCHLEICH* (1987), pp. 363 ff. or *MÖLLER/ SCHLEGEL* (1987), p. 373, although the concept of the "environment-determined option" ("Handlungsfeld") is hardly operationalized.

various target groups, and how occupation-oriented training and education can best contribute under the given circumstances to improve their living and working conditions, depends – apart from specific cultural and regional factors – on
– the respectively concrete manifestation of this individual and (target) group-specific working and living situation;
– the correspondingly relevant general economic, political and social frame conditions.

As regards the *individual and (target) group-specific working and living situations* of people from the informal sector, they are
– reflected to a substantial degree in the economic activities which they (may) carry out to support themselves and/or their families;
– closely related to the target group-specific learning opportunities and potentials insofar as the scope of environment-determined occupational options is wider or narrower depending on people's education and occupational skills;
– substantially and directly determined by people's "status", i.e. their rural/urban and socialization-specific integration in the economic and social network of the informal sector.

This is why the categorization of people from the informal sector into various target groups, as presented in the previous chapter using the multi-dimensional identification of target groups, is based on the consideration and assessment of these factors, which have also been explained in detail in this context.

A more detailed look should be taken at this stage, however, at some of the main *general* economic, political and social *frame conditions*, which – to varying degrees – also influence the occupationally relevant environment-determined options for people from the informal sector.

(1) The general economic and technological level of development of a country or a region

determines the significance of the industrial-modern sector for the economy as a whole including its influence on social norms and standards, and thus also the environment-determined options in the informal sector, especially with regard to
– the lifestyle viewed in urban and rural areas as desirable and the type and significance of material status symbols, which influence both the structure of demand for goods and services as well as the need for money income;
– the importance of the subsistence economy in the informal sector of large urban areas and in the rural area both as a (re)productive

sphere of economic activity and as a "pool" for involuntarily unemployed and underemployed people;
– the local purchasing power of urban and rural markets and the structure of existing goods, money and job markets and their accessibility for (a growing number of) people from the informal sector;
– dependent on this factor, the private willingness and ability to invest, also in rural areas, and in particular of (potential) small and micro-entrepreneurs and self-employed;
– the level of income, basic education and vocational training required for economic and social integration into or to be able to remain in the modern sector;
– the level of imported and endogenous technological development, which co-determines the quality standards of products as regards their saleability and the qualification needs of the work force as well as the need and scope for the use of locally produced or developed appropriate technologies.

(2) The local availability of utilizable resources or waste products which can be recycled
decides on potentials for the development, production or application of technologies appropriate for target group-specific needs and living conditions, and thus on both the possibilities to establish a viable rural small-scale industry structure and to guarantee a sufficient food base in the subsistence farming. Even a modest small-holder surplus production can become the basis for a local processing industry, just as the availability of waste products in larger quantities can lead to the creation of small and micro-enterprises for recycling, provided that low-cost and easily applicable techniques and equipment are known and available.
The type and the prevailing level of technologies accessible and basically known to a target group, therefore, substantially determines both their occupation-oriented training and education needs as well as the possibilities or scope for creating innovative or extended environment-determined options through correspondingly suitable development measures[22].

(3) The infrastructural and economic development of rural areas is normally accompanied by the modernization of part of the

---

22 This correlation is explained very well by Rehling (1989).

agricultural sector and at the same time by the destruction of numerous small and subsistence farming enterprises, caused by the loss of farm land as a result of indebtedness and/or competition with modern producers, which in turn contributes towards an erosion of traditional economic (subsistence economy) and social systems in rural areas which had previously functioned quite well. In some cases, this has irreversible effects on
– migration from rural to urban areas, which is additionally encouraged by the improvements of the transport infrastructure which often accompanies rural development and at the same time leads to a further neglect of the extension of the rural social infrastructure of schools and health stations;
– the advent of the money economy, wage labour, technological and social change, and a "modern" consumer-mindedness in rural areas, especially among younger families, without this development towards monetarization and the growing need for *money* income there being completed by an economic and technological development which can generate the corresponding income and employment.

(4) The structure and growth of the population,
including the attitude of women *and* men to family planning, determines to an increasing extent the longer-term development prospects, the continuation of existing, and the creation of additional viable environment-determined options. More and more frequently, the rapidly growing number of people from the informal sector, who compete for a by far inadequate number of employment opportunities and living (survival) environments, itself threatens to again ruin the success of development efforts within a short period or prevents them in the first place despite an assistance strategy which is basically suitable; after all, every system – whether agricultural enterprises or residential areas, training and education institutions or health stations – can only absorb a finite number of people and only cope with a limited expansion without adverse effects on its efficiency and viability.

(5) The social status of women and girls
determines – more often than not very restrictively – their environment-determined options, especially as regards their rights and possibilities to take up occupation-oriented training and education

offers, at the latest when it comes to taking up appropriately paid employment. This applies particularly in rural areas – unless the girls are sent to urban areas to earn an income, which tends to result from sheer economic necessity rather than from an understanding for equal rights. At the same time, the economic significance of the work they usually carry out without payment in the subsistence economy or to guarantee a mere survival income as street traders or as producers in the agricultural sector and/or in the domestic environment is generally underrated, not to mention any social recognition derived from such activities.

(6) The legal and institutional frame conditions
finally – this is the basic feature of the informal sector – influence the environment-determined options of the people living there and their development potentials in almost every area of life and work in an extremely restrictive way. From any participation in political decision-making processes they are by and large excluded. Even the organization of groups representing their interests is often prohibited by law, impeded or at least subtly made ineffective. In many cases, access to formal – public or private – training and education institutions, to entire segments of the employment market, and to sufficient farm and grazing land is also formally and almost always de facto denied.

However, not only legal regulations but also the nature and the political interests of government institutions, the social background and the priorities of the officials working there, and the constellation of the interests of industry and the modern agricultural sector – given preferential treatment by the state – and of the large wholesale, retail and marketing organisations, which is one-sidedly oriented towards a modern economic-technological development, constantly have detrimental effects on the environment-determined options of the people living in the informal sector.

Before describing the basic qualification needs of the various target groups identified in the informal sector in the field of occupation-oriented training and education, the following chart presents *in summary form* the connection between the respectively accessible environment-determined options, the resultant qualification needs and the objectives orientation and design of the corresponding promotion measures elaborated on this basis:

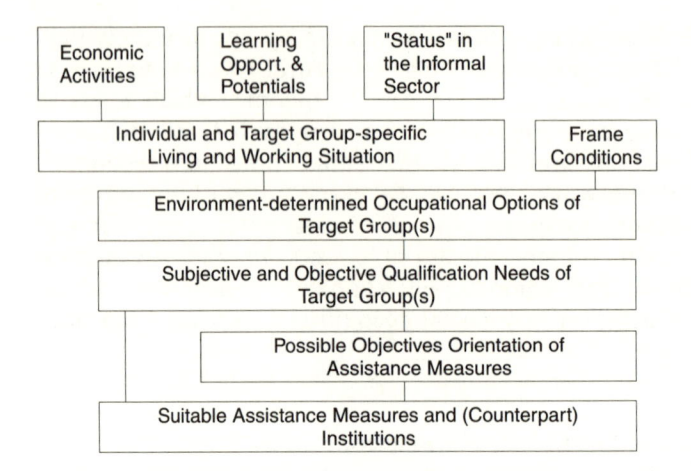

```
┌──────────┐  ┌──────────┐  ┌──────────┐
│ Economic │  │ Learning │  │ "Status" in│
│Activities│  │ Opport. &│  │the Informal│
│          │  │Potentials│  │  Sector   │
└──────────┘  └──────────┘  └──────────┘
┌─────────────────────────────────┐  ┌──────────┐
│ Individual and Target Group-specific │  │  Frame   │
│   Living and Working Situation  │  │Conditions│
└─────────────────────────────────┘  └──────────┘
      ┌──────────────────────────────────────┐
      │ Environment-determined Occupational Options of │
      │            Target Group(s)           │
      └──────────────────────────────────────┘
      ┌──────────────────────────────────────┐
      │ Subjective and Objective Qualification Needs of │
      │            Target Group(s)           │
      └──────────────────────────────────────┘
          ┌──────────────────────────────┐
          │ Possible Objectives Orientation of │
          │       Assistance Measures    │
          └──────────────────────────────┘
      ┌──────────────────────────────────────┐
      │ Suitable Assistance Measures and (Counterpart) │
      │              Institutions            │
      └──────────────────────────────────────┘
```

5.2 Essential Qualification Needs of People from the Informal Sector as Regards Training and Education

What the qualification needs of people from the informal sector as regards occupation-oriented training and education for themselves and/or for their children, in view of their actual and potential environment-determined occupational options? An attempt was made to answer this question by combining the objectified perspective of an external analyst with the subjective perspective of target groups, on the basis of a secondary analysis of the relevant literature, personal practical group interviews during the reconnaissance trip to Thailand and India.

The identified essential training and education needs of target groups from the informal sector exist in some cases as extremely different levels, but are all more or less directly occupation-oriented and/or -relevant[23].

They relate to

- a vocational training improving income-earning opportunities in the (labour) market, either in the form of reasonably paid wage-employment, self-employment, or through small business creation in the modern or in the informal sector;

---

23 Individual qualification needs, of course, can only be identified in relation to a specific situation. The aim here, therefore, is not a comprehensive needs analyses for each informal sector target group. The description concentrates on *essential* needs and shows how even these fundamental needs can vary within one and the same target group category defined according to economic activities when also learning opportunities and potentials and actually given occupation oppotunities and options are taken into account.

- a qualification in artisanal technical skills and a strengthening of self-help potentials for improving the living conditions through subsistence work;
- a sound and actually accessible general education for all with an adequate enough standard to allow a further occupation-oriented, maybe even a full-fledged vocational training, and/or a reasonably paid (self-)employment;
- awareness creation and education in the field of health care and nutrition, in the villages as well as in urban squatter areas;
- social education to facilitate social and occupational integration, especially important for rural target groups and for social groups which are difficult to reach, such as street children and young prostitutes;
- a methodological and didactical design of training and education measures which adequately reflects the specific learning opportunities and potentials of the different target groups from the informal sector.

5.2.1 Vocational Training with Regard to Realistic Occupational Options in the Modern or in the Informal Sector

The most urgent problem for the people from the informal sector is to secure the economic basis for their survival, which particularly in urban areas requires to earn a minimum of cash income for food purchases and housing. The modern sector does by far not provide enough jobs for all, especially since more and more young people are pushing into the employment market as a result of the population growth. With the disadvantages of a weak social background and poor education, anyone coming from the informal sector normally has little chance to successfully compete for the in relative (and sometimes even absolute) terms decreasing number of jobs in the modern sector.

One of the central needs of most people in the informal sector is an improvement of this situation. Hence, they are interested in a vocational or generally occupation-oriented training which takes into realistic consideration the environment-determined options of the respective target groups for gainful occupation and their actual learning opportunities and potentials in such a way that it will enable them to secure an adequate income for themselves or their families through reasonably paid wage employment in the modern or in the informal sector or through self-employment as small or micro-entrepreneurs or subsistence farmers.

Most members of the younger generation living in the urban informal sector – especially young men – as well as rural youths keen on improving their situation seem to prefer a wage-earning job, if possible for a (semi-)governmental employer because of the social security benefits which generally go with the job or in a modern sector enterprise. They generally realize themselves that only a minority will be able to achieve this "dream goal". Some aim at setting up their own business – if possible after several years of job experience or a kind of apprenticeship – either as a makeshift solution and hesitantly in view of the hardly predictable risks and their inexperience in entrepreneurial skills, which cannot normally be learnt anywhere, or because at least one parent is already a street vendor or the like.

As for the large number of those who, for whatever reason, do not or cannot decide to become a small or micro-entrepreneur or self-employed and for whom an occupation in subsistence farming does not represent a realistic option, they can only choose between wage-earning employment in the modern or informal sector or unemployment.

(1) Underemployed persons or job-seekers with work experience and a certain basic or vocational education

could possible be helped in this situation by

– qualified technical training possible also beside a job to extend – also qualitywise – their existing know-how and skills and/or to specialize in a certain field, also with regard to the growing importance of quality standards and standardization in export-oriented production;

– training in innovative technical fields for which there is still a lack of skilled workers due to new qualification requirements, for example, in the fields of recycling techniques, cost-saving building construction, ecological and resource-saving production and packaging techniques;

– a good non-formal training in a relatively broad range of skills and oriented towards quality consciousness at work as fairly versatile semi-skilled workers, especially in regions with a relatively labour-intensive industrial-technological development;

– providing regularly available occupational guidance services where they can find information about training and, at the same time, seek individual advice on occupation-oriented training possibilities which would suit their personal opportunities and options.

(2) Youngsters with inadequate (primary) education and (almost) no job experience

need, in principle, a qualification with a similar orientation, but with a training standard suitable to give them a realistic chance on the job market. In view of their poor or (almost) non-existent school education and their social background this means that
- apart from a sound technical training,
- beforehand or at the same time a (consolidating) general basic education is required,
- for which, in any case, admission must be non-formal,
- and, in addition, some social and value education as regards reliability, quality consciousness and diligence at work, personal behaviour as well as the development of a positive self-esteem.

As school-leavers and "job beginners" young people from the informal sector, who normally have hardly any access to information outside of the informal communication network of their more immediate social environment, urgently require
- guidance and individual advice on occupation-oriented training and education alternatives which are suitable for them and realistic in terms of employment opportunities, also and especially in the field of non-formal or informal vocational training[24].

One possibility in this context would be to set up – perhaps mobile – "training and vocational guidance centres" in urban slum areas and/or in small rural towns, with special advice offered to girls and young women.

(3) Small and micro-entrepreneurs and the majority of established self-employed business(wo)men

have, in some respect, extremely different qualification needs, which is hardly surprising in view of the heterogeneity of their activities and concrete additions. One thing they all have in *common*, is that any technical advice or training on a once-only basis, which fails to take into account the specific problems of the respective enterprise, and often are too short, anyhow, are generally of little use, since their content cannot properly be understood. This becomes evident at the latest when the newly imparted skills or know-how is to be practically applied. What they need – also in their own opinion – is above all
- access to a firmly established advisory service – in the sense of reliably available, but not necessarily in a permanent location – with

---

[24] This special need for advice on training and education opportunities was also recognized by *OXENHAM* (1984); cf. esp. p. 198 f.

someone easily accessible and competent for technical and/or commercial advice, whom they can consult whenever need arises;
– advise on and training in how to deal properly with authorities, banks, traders and – once business is extended beyond the familiar clientele – with clients too[25] as well as information on potentially useful regulations and business promotion laws;
– support and advice to strengthen the organizational abilities of businesses in the informal sector, which should, however, be differentiated for small and micro-entrepreneurs on the one hand, and self-employed business(wo)men, especially street vendors, on the other hand.

Furthermore, both small and micro-entrepreneurs and self-employed persons often feel that all they need is credit and financing assistance, even though the need for qualification in the commercial and/or technical field is in fact often just as great if they intend asserting their positions on the market over a longer period, opening up new markets, or making better use of market niches. As long as many of them only take part in further training measures if this is a requirement for granting[26] credit, the sustained success of learning can be expected to be correspondingly poor, since they merely "sit out" the training course. It is important here to prepare advice and training offers in such a way that the target group(s) can perceive its/their overall benefit – not just the credit assistance aspect.

Especially for the small and micro-enterprises in the informal sector, advisory and training needs are determined by conflicting necessities: while business survival is absolutely impossible without flexibility and improvization, on the one hand, a certain systematic approach in business organization – for procurement, production and marketing – would, on the other hand, increase the chances for the business to stay in the market, through improved efficiency – and thus profit, too – and/or reduced need for credit.

(a) In sofar as urban small and micro-enterprises in the production or service sector are concerned, which are already on the threshold or closely linked to the modern sector,
– advisory and training needs are usually less oriented towards personal qualification as to specific business requirements, to improve business organization, sales opportunities, product design

---

25 This applies much more for small and micro-entrepreneurs than for the self-employed whose contacts beyond the familiar social and economic environment are comparatively limited.
26 This was confirmed by *GRAF* (1989) in the case of small and micro-entrepreneurs in Latin America; cf. pp. 213 and 261.

and diversification, or to introduce a basic accounting system with cost and investment calculation;
- technical/artisanal training still tends to be of no more than secondary importance to the owners as well as to the workers.

(b) Many "basic" micro-enterprises, on the other hand, which (almost) only provide the comparatively simply structured markets in the informal sector with low-cost goods or services for general and everyday consumption often exist precisely *because* of their basic business structure, not only because of their therefore extremely low production costs, but above all because of the "manageability of the business and the only limited outside customer contacts required. Most are pure family enterprises, or they (additionally) employ, often just for certain contracts, one or two young helpers. Many of their owners and the majority of the people employed there, are (at best) semi-literates, often unfamiliar with even simple mathematics, and their felt learning needs in this respect are generally strictly purpose-oriented. Training and education measures addressed to this target group, therefore, should

- principally not be designed as mere business advice, but rather as individual, though clearly business-related qualification for their owners;
- if possible, also include all the (longer-term) employees, which especially for business administration training often means to include the owner's wife and/or one of the daughters.

From the content, the training and advisory needs in this target group primarily relate to
- increase their level of business-relevant information and their ability to acquire and "intelligently handle" information available and relevant to them, which for production enterprises also includes the understanding and practical application of technical blueprints;
- information, ideas and, if necessary, skill training for the production of good quality products for the local market, such as improved agricultural implements, low-cost transportation means, energy-saving stoves, or the like, which can be built with the technical equipment at their disposal;
- skills in the maintenance and repair of machinery and electrical appliances already in local use;
- the identification of (additional) local or possibly also regional or national sales markets, and to risk assessment;
- acquire sufficient knowledge in simple cost calculation and accounting, to be able to present clear business data to a creditor – training in accounting, thus, to increase the credit-worthiness.

(c) Self-employed business(wo)men in the urban informal sector, who want to continue with their present business as their principal occupation[27], certainly will appreciate the availability of a regular business advisory service at local level, provided it corresponds to their needs. Beyond this,
– any general statement on their training and education needs is hardly possible, since their occupation opportunities and options vary substantially depending on the business sector, the location and the general level of economic development in the respective area.

In countries or regions, even urban areas, with a less complex economic structure, in which modern enterprises either hardly exist or produce (almost) exclusively for exports, in other words only operate to a negligible extent as competitors for the limited local mass purchasing power, self-employed persons – and also small enterprises – still play an important role as suppliers. Correspondingly, their economic situation is comparatively more stable than, for example, the large urban areas in newly industrializing countries, where they not only have to compete fiercely and in growing numbers with each other at a lower technological-economic level but also with modern industrial enterprises for a clientele which is also increasing in size but whose purchasing power is tending to decline in many countries.

What is valid for the "basic" small and micro-entrepreneurs, applies to them to an even greater extent: they exist (survive) precisely because of their confined context, and they have only been able to establish and assert themselves *because* they already mastered their respective activities or needed no special previous experience to run their business. Almost most of them have little or no training and often hardly any specific technical skills. Though, they generally feel that their major problems and development bottlenecks result from uncertainty over their business location or the financial dependence on private money-lenders rather than from their only poor education, especially if they have already gathered many years of self-employment experience[28].

To what extent additional skills or advice on product diversification or new market potentials could actually contribute to expand or stabilize their business, depends on the concrete situation. Some

---

27 Insofar as they do not want to do this, they are covered by other target group categories, for example, misallocated employees or job-seekers with job experience, or women in the subsistence sector.

28 Reasonably successful street vendors, by the way, rarely have training and education ambitions for themselves, but tend to focus their expectations on their children's education for which they often work hard to pay for it.

people in this group would definitely – like the small and micro-entrepreneurs – like to learn some basic accounting in order to enhance the soundness of their business in the eyes of creditors – not necessarily banks – and thus to be able to negotiate better terms.

(d) In rural areas the situation is often completely different, since both small and micro-entrepreneurs and the self-employed here are normally cut off from information on technical possibilities and development to a much greater extent, not to mention their basically much more limited realistic opportunities and options. What is more, their level of education is generally lower, and because of the mentality of rural people they generally find it more difficult to identify market opportunities and even more so to seize them.

As a rule, therefore, the rural small and micro-entrepreneurs have quite extensive education, training and advisory needs, similar to the "basic" urban micro-entrepreneur, which are aimed at stabilizing their existence in view of the limited rural purchasing power and – in more developed areas – also in the face of competition from cheap and "more modern" mass-produced industrial goods.

In this respect, it should be taken into account that

– often also technical training and advice, but in any case a training in even the most elementary accounting or the like, is hardly possible without an accompanying basic education in reading, writing and – especially – basic mathematics;

– economically active women, especially in regions where they are traditionally responsible for the family's "finances" – including the family enterprise's – should as much as possible be explicitly addressed with training courses in business administration.

(e) For self-employed business(wo)men in rural areas applies, in principle, the same as for those in urban areas. For many of them, however, self-employment in a small business, such as selling food at lunchtime in front of schools or seasonal home production for fruit or vegetable processing, is only a temporary and often a sideline activity. The question whether especially the women in this group want and can extend such activities into a full-fledged and economically viable business, depends on the local purchasing power of their (potential) clients as much as on their other workload in (subsistence) farming and/or in the household. In particular women who are more or less tied to their home places, but are, at the same time, (co-)responsible for the economic survival of their families, are often very interested in establishing or extending a home-based income-earning business.

(4) Potential business(wo)men
have training and advisory needs which are, in many respects, similar to those in already existing small and micro-enterprises or in self-employment. In this group, too, a distinction must be made between those who plan to set up a small or micro-enterprise with – at least initially – the unpaid help of one or two family members, and those who want or have to consider self-employment for the first time.

A common feature of both groups is that they generally have no significant business experience. In this respect, regardless of varying skill training and other assistance needs, the provision of a minimum know-how in business administration – taking into account their given educational background – can be very useful for them.

(a) Among the potential small and micro-entrepreneurs there are especially those who
– already have some sound but often rather narrow technical skills which they acquired through longer-term or repeated employment as lowest-income workers in an enterprise in the modern or informal sector, but who lack any form of entrepreneurial experience;
– are basically able to run a small or micro-enterprise due to a relatively long work experience, though not necessarily in one specific occupation, and a certain business talent, but who must, however, train these abilities, and also normally require a further qualifying skill training;
– receive(d) informal training already at young age through observation and helping out in a family business, but whose entrepreneurial and technical skills could and should be improved by means of additional vocational training and/or some general education;
– have a secondary or even technical school education, but (almost) no work experience, and hence need entrepreneurial as well as technical skill training to be able to set up their own business.

(b) Potentially self-employed persons will generally have a poorer education and work experience, and are more often illiterate. Furthermore, their plans for self-employment are more often than not an expression of their economic plight rather than the result of an entrepreneurial decision, and for many this would also not be their only economic activity. At least most of the women who want to increase the family income through self-employment, generally already have various subsistence work tasks which they have to continue to fulfil.

Their qualification needs with regard to self-employment can hardly – as in the case of the already active self-employed – be defined in general terms. Training and education will – and can – only play a part insofar as the time required can be made available, and an interest in a technical skill training does exist, at all. Information and advisory programmes on the radio or television can here sometimes be a meaningful way of (initially) addressing this target group.

On the whole, however, it should not be overlooked that many people from the informal sector take up self-employment, especially as street vendors or home producers, because they must or want to earn some money as fast and cheap as possible with their given abilities, i.e. *without* having to invest time or money in any kind of training or education.

(5) Smallholders and subsistence farmers
naturally have a differently structured, though a similarly extensive need for advice and training as industrial, artisanal or service enterprises in the informal sector. It should be realized, however, that a village is far from being economically homogeneous, with all families living in more or less the same conditions. Even among poor families qualification needs and development opportunities are not necessarily the same.

In order to exploit their potentials more effectively – including own processing of part of their crops – and to come to a level of subsistence farming which actually satisfies the basic needs and perhaps even produces modest surplus, they above all require

– agricultural advisory services with strong reference to local conditions, resources and potentials to extend their know-how beyond traditional growing techniques and products to diversify agricultural production in an ecologically and environmentally balanced way for a better food supply, farming cost savings and/or increase of cash crops, and to introduce improved agricultural implements at costs the farmers can afford;

– training and advice as regards the storage and processing of locally grown fruit and vegetables for improved own supply, sale and/or as basis for a commercial home production;

– longer-term and patient advice on how to identify and make use of market opportunities for their products;

– at the same time, information and training on techniques to improve their housing, or for better supply or saving of (drinking) water and fuelwood, since in a subsistence farming situation, efforts to increase yields and to improve the general living conditions through subsistence work cannot be viewed separately and are equally important;

– training and (social) education to promote their learning capability, especially with regard to their ability to understand, critically assess, select and apply information received through training or in the media, as far as relevant to their needs and options, and to acquire required information on their own;

– generally an application-oriented basic education in the fundamental skills of reading, writing and mathematics, especially an understanding of what is "per cent" and "interest".

Even more so than in other businesses, advisory and training measures meant to assist subsistence farming families must not address individuals or narrow "functional" groups only, but must perceive the entire village in its socio-economic complexity as, so to say, one target group with sub-groups. This also means that not just one or two village groups – for example, only subsistence farmers or farmers "with development potential" or only "the" women – should be addressed on the basis of economic or gender criteria. Instead, the *entire farm family* as living in a household should be considered as the smallest unit for assistance, in principle.

Impact, acceptance and sustainability of all occupation-oriented training and related advisory assistance will increase with the extent to which each participant is given the opportunity to contribute and apply already existing knowledge, skills and work experience. In this context, it may well prove meaningful or even necessary not to just offer advisory services or training courses according to "functions", but gender-unspecific – at least partially – separately for men and for women.

Meeting the outlined needs for vocational training with respect to income-earning activities oriented to the (labour) market of either the modern or the informal sector is undoubtedly of central importance for the improvement of the living and working conditions of the people from the informal sector. There are, however, for objective reasons as well as from the subjective perspective of various target groups other occupation-related qualification needs.

5.2.2 *Strengthening of Self-help Potentials to Improve Living Conditions Through Subsistence Work*

In its largest part, the subsistence economy of the urban informal sector comprises activities in the domestic environment, including the repair of dilapidated or provisional housing, very often fetching (drinking) water, but also marginal income-generating activities outside to earn (a part of) the subsistence income. In the rural areas it comprises part or all of the agricultural production and animal husbandry, with often much less cash flow involved than in town. If case is needed which can neither be sent by a member of the family working in urban areas nor borrowed in anticipation of the next harvest, (staple) food originally produced and stored for own consumption, has to be sold.

Without the unpaid subsistence work carried out every day mainly by women and children – generally at the lowest possible technological level and with a maximum input of time and labour – to economically and socially support their families, hundreds of thousands of people in the urban and rural informal sector would be unable to survive. Without subsistence work the extent and economic relevance of which is hard to quantify, but beyond any doubt substantial, the economy of the informal sector would be unimaginable – and consequently, also the economic development seen in the modern sector would also be impossible. In the subsistence economy, people do not only work and produce to meet their own basic needs, but here almost all necessary welfare services and missing public services such as water supply are compensated by subsistence work.

At the same time, the conditions for survival in the rural subsistence economy – especially but not only in Africa – are becoming increasingly different. Since the smallholder and subsistence agriculture, for various known reasons, fails to provide the steadily increasing number of rural people with enough food, younger people and men, in particular, decide to migrate. Not only are they driven to town by the increasing need for cash income in the villages – for electricity, agricultural inputs, water fees, school fees, clothing, supplementary food purchases or just the "modern" consumer wants – but also by a desire to catch up with urban civilization. The result is that even subsistence farming is becoming increasingly difficult, and children have become an irreplaceable, even though only "half strong" part of the farm labour force. For the women, the days during the sowing and harvest periods are too short to extract even the small maximum possible yield.

Under these circumstances there is neither time, definitely no longer uninterrupted periods, nor money and often no understanding for a participation in any regular vocational training – generally carried out over a longer period and almost always too far away from home – or even for the school education for the children.

Even though life in many rural regions has thus turned into a nightmare, those who want to voluntarily exchange rural life for urban life *on a permanent basis* are not in a majority. Most of the adult generation would rather like to stay, provided that they can satisfy their basic needs there in a humane way and can see some prospect of gradual improvement of their living conditions.

Especially in rural areas from where already a considerable migration to urban areas has occurred in the past and/or where are critically reporting mass media, a gradual change of attitude can be observed also among younger people. Reports on the dark sides of urban life, and the often negative urban experience of villagers show that survival in the large urban squatter areas is generally at least just as hard as in the rural areas, that living conditions there are often humiliating, that children are much more exposed to the danger of drug addiction and gang crime, and that yet the economic situation of the families have not really improved substantially. The more this is realized among the rural population, the more there is a growing conviction among many young people that rural life might perhaps still be the better choice as long as they have a place to live and a small plot of own land[29].

Against this background, there is a tremendous need for assistance to strengthen self-help potentials – both at individual and community level, in villages as well as in urban squatter areas – also through occupation-oriented training for (more efficient) subsistence work and to support people's self-organization efforts.

This need is normally stronger articulated by women, even more often in rural than in urban areas – probably because women there are more tied to their domestic environment, also in their income-generating activities. Especially following marriage they often have no option but to make the immediate living environment as attractive as possible and to do subsistence work for their families.

As regards, in particular, rural target groups – with their more limited occupation opportunities and options and a generally lower level of education – there is a need to also provide subsistence-oriented development perspectives. In addition to the qualification needs already outlined for smallholders and subsistence farmers[30], this means a need for

---

29 Reports by NGO workers in Thailand and India as well as own observations and talks with many people in rural areas in Asian and African countries have, during recent years, contributed to this impression. According to experts who worked with NGOs there, it also tallies with observations in Latin American countries.
30 Cf. in the previous section 5.2.1, point (5).

– information and training, especially for women, on the use of labour-facilitating, cost- and/or time-saving equipment or techniques, especially in the household, in agriculture and for local transportation;
– artisanal-technical training, especially for youngsters under-employed in agriculture and for village craftsmen, for example, in production and repair of simple agricultural equipment or household appliances, construction and maintenance of weather-proof and stable houses, storage facilities, water-tanks or village lanes at a low cost, or small irrigation systems;
– an application-oriented basic education, for – more or less concealed – illiterates of all ages, to improve their general education, their ability to acquire and assimilate new information, and their social competence;
– assistance in developing a strong ability for self-organization for local community action so as to jointly improve the living environment and provide community-based social services – such as pre-schools – which can hardly be expected from other sources, or to become better able to negotiate with authorities, traders or "projects".

Of course, such subsistence-oriented occupation-related training and advisory needs exist among the urban just as much as among the rural population, although there are different points of emphasis. In urban areas, for example, there is less need for the self-organized construction of roads or storage facilities, whereas here a strengthening of self-organization skills is particularly important with regard to the special problems of life and survival in an urban (squatter) area.

The specific subsistence-oriented assistance needs as regards a strengthening of self-help potentials will always depend on the local conditions. In most cases, they will not be met through occupation-oriented training and education measures and social education alone, but will require integrated measures to create development perspectives which the people from the informal sector can perceive as a chance to substantially improve their living conditions through subsistence work and self-help.

5.2.3 *Adequate Primary School and Adult Education for Better Vocational Training and Occupational Opportunities*

In the "World Charter on Education for All" adopted by the World Bank, UNICEF, UNDP and UNESCO in March 1990, it was reaffirmed that at present almost 100 million children and youngsters in Third World countries have no opportunity, at all, to attend a primary school. Even among those who do have a chance to complete the 6 to 9 years of basic school education now compulsory in many countries, only a minority does really obtain the qualification for further education and (vocational) training. Who does not fail to meet the formal enrolment requirements for secondary or technical schools, will at the latest in the lessons have difficulties to keep up, because what is officially taught in the primary school curricula, often has not really be learnt and understood.

At primary school – especially in rural areas and in the urban squatter areas – the children learn very little, be it because of
– irregular school attendance or premature drop-out, due to the (in)direct costs involved for the families, a distance too great between home and school, a lack of interest in school education on part of the parents and/or children, or the necessity to help in the household or in the field, or to earn money through some odd-jobs elsewhere;
– inadequate qualification of the primary school teachers in terms of professional competence and/or pedagogical skills, or their lack of motivation to teach children from the informal sector or to work in rural areas or in/near urban squatter areas, at all – largely due to poor pay and the low social status associated with these jobs.

The specific reasons and situations vary from case to case and from region to region. It can be generally stated, however, that primary education leaves a great deal to be desired in almost all developing countries, with the quality of the education as well as the chance for attending school generally decreasing with the distance to urban areas, and the more the children come from poor and socially marginalized families.

This reduces later opportunities and options as regards employment and vocational training for children from the informal sector already from very early childhood on, which basically applies to boys and girls alike. Girls, however, are much more often denied school attendance, let alone the completion of primary school, purely for gender reasons.

Without an improved primary school education in content and standard fairly comparable with the urban middle-class standard of primary education, children in the rural areas and from socially marginalized urban families, will continue to be denied access to the formal vocational training system – if not formally, then de facto. Even a non-formal occupation-oriented training can then hardly be more than patchwork, and will – neither among the people from the informal sector themselves nor among potential employers – ever get rid of the stigma of a second-class "vocational training for the poor";

or it must – which is often impossible – combine basic education and vocational training.

The lack of a proper basic education and learning experience will later make it difficult for most people to adequately deal with information, technical innovations and social change. Many feel themselves as being unintelligent or inferior, and they fully realize that they are often cheated by traders.

As there are many – also young – adults among the one billion of completely illiterate people and the unknown large number of so-called secondary illiterates, the need for basic education not only relates to children and youngsters of school age, but with functional (back-up) literacy programmes also to older generations.

To improve the living and working conditions of people in both the urban and the rural informal sector, there is, therefore, a tremendous need for

– improving the quality of primary school education with respect to both content and teaching methods, which also should include some practical skill training suitable to be applied in subsistence work and to create a basic understanding of technics, however without turning primary school education into a "non-formal education for children", in which the general education is neglected;

– a corresponding training (and remuneration) of primary school teachers, including a specific preparation and motivation for work with target groups from the informal sector;

– primary school curricula which do not make accompanying out-of-school tuition absolutely necessary, since most children in the informal sector have no time after school and their parents normally do not see the need for this;

– additional primary schools with an environment-adapted endowment in both rural areas and urban squatter areas, to avoid that school attendance is rejected already because the next school is too far away, in view of the travel time and costs involved and the social reservations of parents;

– in many countries also for pre-school education, especially for children in rural areas and from socially disadvantaged families, since they will otherwise hardly be able to keep pace at primary school where curricula are often based on the assumption that some basic knowledge – such as reading the alphabet or recognizing numbers – has been acquired already in a pre-school;

– occupation-oriented literacy programmes in adult education, in which the necessary reading, writing and mathematical skills are

taught in the context, e.g. of health care and nutritional education or agricultural extension training;
- finally – as a key aspect – awareness creation among parents, children and teachers for both the importance of basic (school) education and its occupation-relevant potentials, and – especially in rural areas – the advantage of some practical occupation-oriented education related to the respective environment-determined options, in addition to general education.

However, especially regarding this last aspect, the opinions and the subjectively perceived needs of the rural population, in particular, are definitely ambivalent and controversial. Quite a few parents and youngsters reject school curricula with practical skill training components as inferior with the argument that they do not provide the qualification required for secondary school education and, thus, imply a disadvantage. Chances of vocational training and employment in the modern sector are often over-estimated because of a lack of proper information, or because of the hope and observation that secondary school education seems to be a guarantee for later employment there[31]. Especially in rural areas relatively close to the urban centres, many parents do not see why just their children should not be able to obtain one of the much sought-after positions in the civil service, even though their performance at school cannot match such ambitions[32].

Many teachers also have problems when it comes to teaching practical subject-matter. After all, they did not take up this profession to then work "with their hands", but because they have, in some way, internalized a western-oriented urban educational ideal. Most of them belong to the urban middle class, anyhow, and have had little prior contact with social groups from the informal sector. Those who do come from rural areas or have a lower-class background, mostly view the teacher profession as a chance of rising up the social ladder, in other words moving away from manual labour. In addition, the teacher training usually provides neither the technical nor pedagogical preparation to meet the demands of teaching

---

31 This discussion takes place almost everywhere in rural areas with parents who are basically "education-conscious". Insofar as they (finally) tolerate practical subjects at school which are oriented to realistic occupation opportunities and options, this often seems rather to result from a resigned acceptance of a "second-best" solution than from a feeling of being convinced about the benefits.
32 According to information from the GTZ, a study – which was unfortunately not available – conducted in Swaziland revealed that in well over half of the cases the parents of children who had given up school at both primary and secondary level are *still* convinced that their children stand a chance of further school education.

practical skills, not to mention adequate motivation in this respect. As regards an understanding of the importance of a qualitatively good basic education for later employment opportunities, for the development of self-help potentials, for the access to further occupation-oriented or formal vocational training, and, above all, for the ability to comprehend and apply imparted knowledge and skills, still a considerable awareness creation is required, both among the people from the informal sector themselves – especially in rural areas – and among teachers and teacher trainers as well as among educational experts and development planners.

5.2.4 *Awareness Creation and Education on Health Care and Nutrition*

Especially in the rural areas, but also in the slums of large urban areas – with their growing drug addiction problem – the health, hygiene and nutrition situation is so serious that it often has direct and irreversibly adverse effects on the quality of life and the ability of people, especially children, to work and learn. From early childhood, illness and malnutrition damage the physical and mental ability to learn. People who are hungry or ill, not only find it more difficult to learn, but also to find a job. Observations and talks in any village or urban slum in Africa, Asia or Latin America make it clear that priority assistance needs are in this field.

Especially local NGOs working directly with people from the informal sector to improve their living and working conditions, realize the twofold importance of education in health care, hygiene and nutrition[33]

– to improve the health and nutrition situation as well as the learning environment of the children as a goal in itself;

– to develop the learning capacity, and to maintain or restore the strength to work, and to thereby indirectly contribute to improve the occupation opportunities of people who are already socially and economically disadvantaged.

The consequences of inadequate education and information on health care, hygiene and nutrition in rural areas could hardly be expressed more clearly and comprehensively than in the rationale of a project proposal of an NGO in India for setting up of a basic health education service in a number of remote villages:

33 The "World Charter on Education for All" also points this out in Article VII (Draft B) under the heading "Enhancing the Learning Environment".

111

- The lack of basic medical knowledge, health workers and midwives and health care centres with obstetric facilities leads to increased (risks of) illness for pregnant women with congenital defects for their children, and serious infant illnesses which could, in principle, be prevented;
- Inadequate sanitary facilities, uncovered water containers and insufficient information on the importance and possibilities of hygiene and health care create an objectively desolate hygiene situation resulting in numerous typical "diseases of the poor", which for the subjective feeling of inevitability leads to an apathy among adults, which again is passed on to the children, also determining their hygienic behaviour and health;
- The serious health disorders of women resulting from malnutrition accompanied by strenuous physical work, poor housing conditions and the traditional cooking with firewood often lead to – in some cases irreversible – prenatal damage to children;
- Because of lack of information on (the importance of) vaccination for children, these are often not carried out, even if they are available nearby and free of charge;
- Whereas the significance of traditional medicine is declining in many regions, superstition and quackery are still widespread, and the high illiteracy rate prevents other education through written information[34].

This description relates to a rural area. But it is on the whole just as applicable to the situation in most slums in urban areas, where the complete inadequacy of sanitary facilities, water supply and sewage systems, and the difficulties – often coinciding with a lack of interest on the part of the municipality and/or the residents – of proper refuse disposal give raise to catastrophic hygiene and health conditions.

In view of this situation, there are urgent qualification needs in two respects, namely for

- awareness creation and education especially for women in the informal sector on the importance of personal hygiene, preventive health care and child care and a reasonably balanced nutrition as well as on simple techniques for safe water storage and drinking water treatment, for healthy food preparation and preservation, and for waste disposal in residential areas;
- correspondingly, the training of social/health workers and midwives from within or close to the people from the informal sector,

---

34 Summarized from a project proposal of the "Centre for Rural Education and Development Action" (CREDA) in Mirzapur of September 1990; on the training and education work of CREDA in general cf. Section 6.3, point (1).

preferably of elder and/or married women as they normally enjoy high social respect in their communities.

Whereas the latter are directly occupation-oriented qualification needs, the education and advisory needs mentioned first have – apart from their immediate relevance for an improvement of the living conditions of people from the informal sector – more indirect and long-term occupation-relevant effects by helping to improve their physical and mental learning potentials and their general working strength.

5.2.5 *Social Education for the (Re)Integration of Rural and Socially Marginalized Target Groups*

A fact which is as banal as it is underestimated in its significance is that employment opportunities, business success and social as well as professional recognition are determined not only by technical skills and qualifications, but also by factors such as individual social behaviour, the personal impression made on (potential) employers, clients or creditors, and the ability to adjust to an unfamiliar social environment which requires a certain understanding of the "rules" applying there.

Accordingly, the need for and the importance of social education is primarily to help people from the informal sector

– to understand – also in rural areas – the norms and behaviour patterns of urban-industrial culture and life and acquire them to the extent required for (re)integration into a rapidly modernizing society;

– to develop greater self-confidence, a sense of self-esteem and social assertion, and overcome the feeling of psychological and social isolation, especially among youngsters and women in urban slums, which also means

– to strengthen their ability to meaningfully select and assess information and their capacity to absorb (technical) innovations and social change;

– to develop a positive identification with a permanent life and/or occupation – including subsistence work – in the informal sector through respective awareness creation and value teaching.

In a normal socialization in the urban-style middle class, this kind of social learning process is normally understood as integral part of education at school and in the family environment. For most people from the informal sector, however, the situation is fundamentally different.

The already described general conditions of survival in the villages and in the slums of the big cities socialize people in a different way, in an urban environment again different than in a rural area. Because of the feeling of being "second-class citizens", the exclusion from (supposed) development opportunities in urban areas, the permanent (self-)exploitation and desperate prospects, many people in the villages tend to develop – despite the inner dignity they mostly retain – lethargy, resignation, a sense of uncertainty and a lack of self-confidence. In urban slums, on the other hand, the destroyed self-esteem turns more and more often, especially among the youth, into psycho-social isolation, aggressiveness and a susceptibility to drug abuse. Under the pressure of economic poverty and social marginalization individuality, traditional values, social structures and often families crumble.

(1) Rural target groups, above all children and youngsters,
need, therefore, also social education and value teaching aimed at helping them to develop a perspective for life and occupation within the rural environment and/or the subsistence economy. This is the more important as – when confronted with "modern" urban-style civilization or hearing about it from neighbours returning from urban areas and/or in the media – a large number especially of young rural people view their way of life as an anachronism and not (any more) as just another, but as valuable way of life – not only because of the poverty, but also because of its non-urban character. To them "village" is a synonym for poverty, backwardness, exploitation and hopelessness, whereas "town" stands for opportunity and progress[35]. In this situation it is necessary
 – to strengthen the ability of the rural people, especially youngsters and women[36], to interact as equals with "the town", through

---

35 This does not necessarily contradict the above described indicators of a change in attitude towards a growing preference for a life in a rural area, provided there are some development prospects. Often, both views and/or feelings exist side by side, and even represent at the individual level a typical conflict of decision.

36 Social education, especially for women, is regarded as necessary not only because they are generally most disadvantaged – especially as regards training and education – but also because normally the women again are the main social educators in the families. Furthermore, women are often more receptive to innovations, with a strong sense of whether they are of benefit to them or not. Finally, they often – especially women in the villages – have an inner strength, a purposefulness in their action, a sense of responsibility and stamina to gradually improve the situation of their family, which distinguishes them in a perceptible way from many men. When moving from rural to urban areas, women and girls also apparently are not so easily "distracted" as (young) men. This is certainly not to generalize, but nevertheless significant to observe.

education for a self-confident communication with urban(ized) people and a constructive attitude towards modern ways of life and developments, based on their identification with rural life, its culture and its norms.

Of course, such an orientation in social education has a basis only if there actually are prospects of an improvement of the rural living and working conditions. In this context, the introduction of applicable, manageable and affordable "appropriate" technologies is just as important as a rural primary school education which, at the same time, provides a general education reasonably comparable to urban school standards and some basic vocational education corresponding to the given rural occupation opportunities.

Furthermore, past experience has shown on many occasions that any kind of one-sided technical vocational training for rural youth, or a merely technical agricultural training for small farmers is more often than not inadequate in view of the difficulties which they have afterwards in recognizing the scope of possible application or, at least, in the independent application of what they have learnt. In addition, without an awareness creation towards rural perspectives, many young people in the villages will continue to view vocational training and education as a stepping stone to urban areas – with the undesirable result of further migration to the conurbations and the individual frustration of still not finding any (reasonably paid) employment there.

(2) Street children and (young) prostitutes
are two extraordinary difficult social groups in the informal sector, which are hardly – and without accompanying social (re)integration measures normally not at all – accessible for directly occupation-oriented training and education measures. In view of their (often very) young age and their steadily growing number, this cannot mean to simply ignore them as target groups for education and vocational training even though there is a tendency to overlook them as economically seemingly irrelevant "marginal groups". But, they are only marginal insofar as they find themselves on the fringe of society, a position they are normally unable to leave (again) without help. In terms of numbers, they are since long much more than a marginal phenomenon in most large urban areas in the Third World, and they are the most sad manifestation of what fate and living conditions may happen to people from the informal sector.

Many of the street children and prostitutes belong to the second and third generations of urban squatters, but probably as many come from rural areas, and their "entry age" is becoming lower and lower. Their possible perspectives and future options, and thus their assistance needs, cannot be recognized and comprehended in an only superficial look at their situation. But it must be really understood where most of them come from and why[37].

Education and training alone certainly cannot prevent the fate as a street child or prostitute, but without basic education and some kind of occupation-oriented qualification many young people are doomed to it to secure their own survival or to support their families. Therefore, especially for these target groups – as for the children in urban slums who often grow up under similar circumstances, and the children in rural areas working sometimes in bonded labour in agriculture or in carpet manufactures – occupation-oriented training and education is an extremely important chance

37 As less is generally known about street children than about any other target group in the informal sector. A brief "statistical portrait" of the street children of Madras and Salem in India is given with reference to the already cited studies by the Bosco Institute of Social Work. The majority are boys (88.3 %). Almost two thirds are not older than 14, roughly 5 % younger than 8. About 40 % live with their parents to whom they also have close emotional ties. Their level of education is extremely low, with 46 % illiterates and a further 41.5 % with only five years of primary school education which is virtually worthless. Most of them (82.7 %) work, over half of them as "rag-pickers", at least 5–8 hours a day; 42.5 % work 9–12 hours and 5.8 % work over 13 hours a day. They earn 25–100 rupees a week – roughly the same as their fathers, in cases where they still have one. Only about one third contribute what they earn to the family income, the others work to support themselves. For almost 90 % going to the cinema, preferably (77.1 %) to see violent and battle films, is the only spare-time activity. The majority (57.5 %) live on the streets because of poverty and/or unemployment of the parents, roughly a quarter because their parents abandoned or mistreated them. About 8 % state to be orphans. Their first priority is obviously to obtain food, which they somehow manage to do. However, 56.7 % have nowhere to stay, and two thirds – among the girls even 83.1 % – have to depend on the use of public toilets and washing areas. Over 70 % have only the clothes they wear. Consequently, they are unable (and suffer from it) to look "decent", which is why they are despised by society and often persecuted by the police. The result is "psycho-social deprivation ... (and a) very poor self-image" (p. 26). Nevertheless, many of them still have "dreams" of education or vocational training, which over half would like to do, and of a permanent job (33.1 %) or a "business" of their own (18.9 %); 16.6 % would like a "complete" education. Almost a third, however, especially long-term street children have already given up hopes for a better future.

The situation for boys and girls is basically similar, but in all respects somewhat worse for the girls. Almost two thirds (62.7 %) have no work, none of them has more than 6 years primary school education (42.2 % none at all), and only very few girls have training possibilities (5.1 %). "If it is said that the boy street children ... have a very bleak future, then it can be said that the girls have no future at all." (p. 32) Nevertheless, the majority (89.8 %) still have – in view of their actual situation fairly irrational – hopes of employment and education. The conclusion: "The street is a comfortless classroom where the harsh realities of life are learned at a tremendous cost in human abasement." (p. 28)

All figures and quotes are taken from *BOSCO INSTITUTE* (1990).

– to make it unnecessary for children, in the first place, to lead a life as a street child, a prostitute or in other forms of bonded labour;
– to help to socially (re)integrate those who are already struggling through life as street children and (child) prostitutes;
– under certain conditions also to motivate and train young prostitutes still in contact with their families in rural areas and also supporting them financially, as "animators" to promote development in their home villages[38].

However, for any occupation-oriented training and education addressing street children or young prostitutes, it is important, even more than for other target groups from the informal sector, that
– beside a basic (back-up) general education
– special importance should be attached to social education and recreation pedagogics, especially initially, in order to psychologically and socially stabilize these children and youngsters;
– to this end, prior to the actual training and education, personal and stable social relationships to social workers must be established, to reduce mistrust and inhibitions and to motivate and encourage them to participate in a training, at all;
– these children and youngsters must be actively convinced and recruited for such measures, since simple "advertising" of occupational training courses on posters or in the mass media – except perhaps for cinema spots – normally is not enough to arouse their interest;
– in case that the parents are still alive and contacts exists, they also should be included, if possible, within integrated programmes, since family ties apparently are often fairly close and it is basically the poverty of their parents which forces children onto the streets or into prostitution.

Not to respond to the need for social education and value teaching, which exists to some extent in all social groups in the informal sector – the younger the people, the more – would mean to exclude a large number of them right from the very beginning

---

38 Positive experience has been made with such a – private – initiative among young prostitutes in Bangkok, who have been reasonably successful in their business. Together with them, an attempt was made to identify reaonable investment opportunities or needs in their families in rural areas. The prostitutes themselves then made their transfer payments, at least partly, dependent on its investive use, e.g., in animal husbandry or for the purchase of agricultural implements. Furthermore, they facilitated for the advisers of their initiative the social access to the villages, which helped to create a basis of confidence between them and the villagers within a short period of time.

from any (successful) occupation-oriented training and education. And it would also negatively affect the sustainability of such measures.

5.2.6 *Training and Education Measures Designed with Regard to Target Group-specific Learning Opportunities and Potentials*

Often, the need to design (occupation-oriented) training and education measures in a way that their actual development options and occupation opportunities as well as their learning opportunities and potentials are reflected adequately and realistically is articulated more strongly and more precisely by the people from the informal sector than their qualification needs as such. Whereas most of them normally have only relatively vague ideas of the desired training contents, the majority definitely realize what – regardless of the relevance of the contents – makes it impossible for them to participate in training and education measures or to make use of advisory services, and what impairs their learning success, if they do participate[39].

(1) Those who are already occupied
as small or micro-entrepreneurs, as wage workers, or in any kind of self-employment or subsistence work, will normally only be attracted by a training course or an advice service, if
– it can be attended with a prospect of success also outside of working hours, or if attendance does not have adverse effects on their occupational activities;
– the direct and indirect costs involved, the daily amount of time required including travelling to the training location, and the total duration of the training all seem acceptable;
– the training can be resumed, possibly during the next cycle, if it needs to be interrupted because of additional workload, e.g. during the harvest season or to meet a business contract;
– the training or advisory service offered is considered useful to them personally or to their business, i.e. the content seems relevant to their problems and applicable within their given opportunities and options;
– they assume the training to be carried out in a way that they are

---

39 Cf. also on this aspect, Section 4.2.1.

able to understand what is taught and to incorporate it into their present know-how and experience;
− information on the training − and sometimes necesssarily also some encouragement − comes in due time in advance.

(2) Women and girls
especially if they are in all their activities more or less strictly confined to their homes due to social reasons and/or household commitments, will − apart from the a.m. aspects − normally only then be able to consider participating in training and education, if such measures
− are offered nearby − for women farmers in their villages − and, if necessary, also provide child care facilities for the duration of training hours,
− are organized with a schedule which is flexible enough with regard to their other workload which usually varies seasonally;
− especially in Islamic countries and communities with very traditional ideas, are exclusively targeted on women and girls;
− do not involve high costs, since most women have little or no money at their own disposal, and paying for their training and education often is rejected by their families as a waste of money;
− do not set formal enrolment requirements as regards previous school education, and take into account in both curricula and didactics women's mostly low level of basic education;
− mainly impart knowledge and skills which can be applied within their range of options (including technologies affordable and socially accessible for them), for example, to improve the housing environment and/or the family nutrition situation, to create an income source based on home production, or to reduce their workload;
− will, at least, be tolerated also by the men in their social community.

(3) Smallholder and subsistence farming families, but also unemployed rural youth
should be offered not only agricultural extension services, but any training as much as possible in their own or at most a neighbouring village, since
− "idle time" in rural working life, although it can account over a longer period for a good half of a person's time, does normally not occur as longer phases, but rather for a few hours a day or sometimes one or two days a week, which makes a longer absence basically unacceptable for almost everybody occupied in farming, or

presupposes a real turning-point with a clear decision in favour of training instead of work;
- parents are often unwilling to allow their children, even older ones, to attend a training which requires overnight stays outside for "safety" and/or cost reasons, the former being a particular restriction for girls;
- the financial means which can be set aside for training and education, are already extremely limited in rural families so that (additional) costs for transportation or even accommodation often are an argument against an education and training which would be appreciated, in principle.

Especially smallholder and subsistence farming families will normally respond to advisory services or training offers only, if they
- clearly correspond to their needs and given options, and also take into account their restrictions as regards learning possibilities and especially their learning capacity influenced by the rural environment, and thus promises a practical applicability – with calculable risks – of what has been learnt;
- are designed with a long-term perspective and on a continuous – not necessarily permanent – basis, for example, with a periodical "back-up" advice or a nearby information and advisory service which can be consulted any time;
- allow all family members who (are able to) work in the business to be included;
- are essentially based on principles of practical and active learning, using teaching methods which stimulate people's learning capacity and build on their already existing knowledge and skills.

As a principle, preferably members from within or familiar with the village community and socially accepted by the target groups, should be trained as social multipliers, trainers and advisers, in particular, for the implementation of longer-term occupation-oriented training and education measures. This could be – depending on the specific culture – older men and/or women, (retired) village school-teachers and/or persons with a religious or traditional authority.

The advantage of such locally rooted trainers or development workers is that they are already integrated into village life as social multipliers, and will
- not normally, after participation in a training of trainers, migrate at the next best opportunity to town in search of a better income;
- require only a minimum of cash income from their training activity, since they either already have a certain basis of livelihood

in the village and/or can at least partly be paid in kind by the village community for their services;
– see – as some kind of motivation – their training work as contribution to improve their own village, and as a source of social recognition;
– finally, not encounter language problems and – if they are carefully selected – no social barriers to communication within the village.

Following the considerations for a multi-dimensional identification of possible target groups for occupation-oriented training and education measures, relatively broad scope was also given to the description of their major qualification needs. This was to make clear again from just another aspect how heterogeneous and complex the informal sector is, not only in its (target group) structure, but also as regards the occupation-oriented qualification needs of the people living there.
It also might have emphasized again how important it is, therefore, before intervening with measures for occupation-oriented training and education to obtain a fairly clear picture of the target groups to be addressed, their specific living and working conditions, their maximum possible occupation-relevant opportunities and options, and their learning opportunities and potentials. Only then specific qualification needs and development options can be understood and, correspondingly, be considered in the formulation of realistic targets for training and education measures and their target group-specific design.

5.3 Conclusions as to the Overall Objectives of Occupation-oriented Training and Education for Target Groups from the Informal Sector

Although the design of measures for occupation-oriented training and education of different target groups from the informal sector will ultimately vary from case to case depending on the frame conditions, people's development options, learning and occupation opportunities and specific qualification needs, the basic scope of their assistance and qualification needs as just described, nevertheless, leads to the conclusion that such measures should be oriented towards certain overall objectives.
Directly and indirectly occupation-oriented training and education measures of varied kinds should be combined with regard to the

respective specific target groups, regional and cultural aspects in such a way that, as a whole, they will contribute towards

(1) Transfer of occupation-relevant knowledge, skills and abilities applicable within the given scope of opportunities and options which can enable the people from the informal sector to sustainably improve their living and working conditions and make them more humane, be it through small business (creation), self-employment, or reasonably paid wage-employment in the modern or in the informal sector, or through subsistence work and self-organization to sufficiently meet their various basic needs;

(2) More equal opportunities for people from the informal sector by combining technical training also with social education to strengthen their social competence, since this, after all, is decisive for their social (re)integration and their participation in the economic and social development of modernizing societies, with a special emphasis to be put also on particularly disadvantaged groups such as women, street children or rural youth;

(3) Strengthening their "information processing capacities" and communication skills
to ensure that people from the informal sector will become better able
– to recognize and pursue their own information needs and possibilities, independently acquire, assess and creatively apply (new) information relevant to them, and hence also get more and sustained benefit from any training or advisory services;
– to express and emphasize their own interests in a self-confident communication with traders or (potential) clients also from the modern sector, with administrative officials or development advisors and the like;
– to deal – also in the rural areas – with the economic and technological changes and social transformation in areas relevant to their life and work, and to understand and master, as much as necessary and beneficial for them, the "rules" of a society with an increasingly urban-industrial character, in order to gradually overcome their economic and social marginalization.

(4) Strengthening the self-help potentials in the villages and in the urban squatter areas
especially in view of the situation that a large number of people will definitely be unable to settle in the modern sector, and hence will need

to find a perspective for improving their living and working situation also in the subsistence economy in order to gradually develop a positive attitude towards a possible permanent life in the informal sector.

In the following chapter, different approaches of various (counterpart) institutions will be assessed with reference to these overall objectives regarded as meaningful and desirable for occupation-oriented training and education measures addressed to people from the informal sector, and by taking into consideration their above described scope of qualification needs. It is asked to which extent they are, in principle, suitable to reach such target groups in view of their own objectives orientation and their institution-specific instruments and scope of action, and whether these approaches (can) at all respond to these people's occupation-oriented qualification needs. Special attention will also be paid to the question as to what extent they have already been adopted by Government-run vocational training institutions and in (bilateral) vocational training assistance, or at least, in principle, could and should be so.

6. Approaches for the Occupation-oriented Training and Education of Target Groups from the Informal Sector

Vocational training and education which is to have real relevance and sustainable benefits for people from the informal sector, must aim at stabilizing or extending the scope of development options and occupation opportunities actually accessible to them. An integration of such measures into the existing or planned formal education and vocational training system of a country in a way that they will be really accessible and useful to target groups from the informal sector, however, will hardly be possible to realize – and definitely not with reference to *one* particular concept – in view of the differences in development options, social and educational background, learning opportunities and potentials and, accordingly, qualification needs and possibilities between people from the informal and the modern sector, and even within the informal sector, as outlined before.

Instead, depending on the number and type of identified target groups, their qualification needs and their development options, quite different approaches will be found suitable in different situations, often even a combination of measures so far viewed as clearly distinguished alternative options only. They might also have to be embedded in a broader integrated development approach in order to realize the ultimate development objective of improving the living and working conditions of people from the informal sector.

Therefore, the elaboration of any one particular "standard concept" for occupation-oriented training and education for these target groups makes little sense. Even if it were complex to the utmost possible extent – and hence almost unmanageable, anyhow – it could still only inadequately comply with the conditions and needs relevant to the different target groups. Instead, an attempt was made to identify various approaches as basically suitable "conceptual modules" to be taken into consideration in the planning and design of programmes or measures for occupation-oriented training and education of target groups from the informal sector. Their actual suitability must then be examined and their design adapted, depending on the frame conditions and target group needs in each specific case.

The typologically partly extremely different approaches presented below[40] refer to
– broader occupation- as well as specifically vocation-oriented qualification through formal, non-formal or informal training and/or education, aimed at either improving the chances of employment in the modern or in the informal sector, and/or increasing the possibilities and quality of subsistence work;
– the business advice and training for (potential) small and micro-entrepreneurs and self-employed persons, aimed at strengthening existing or helping to create new small businesses and (self-)employment opportunities;
– directly or indirectly occupation-oriented training and social education especially of rural target groups within more integrated development strategies;
– some considerations on primary school education as part of or preparation for occupation-oriented training and education.
They will be assessed as to whether their development and training objectives, their instruments and the scope of action of the (counterpart) institution concerned are basically suitable to reach target groups from the informal sector in view of their specific qualification needs and learning opportunities and potentials. Furthermore, it is asked to which extent they (could) have a positive impact on the employment and income situation of people from the informal sector, or on an improvement of their living and working conditions in general.
Furthermore, it was chosen to discuss also general aspects, where applicable, in the context of a specific project experience. The initially converse attempt to summarize them in a kind of cross-sectional presentation was dropped, since in the then necessary generalization of statements too many key aspects essentially important to explain the success, difficulties or only limited applicability of a specific approach, would have disappeared.
This is the more relevant, since – as the examples presented will show

40 The description of the various approaches mainly refers to secondary information. Wherever they are based on direct information from the project visits in Thailand and India, this is mentioned accordingly. The selection of just these project examples does not mean that they were the only or very special projects of the respective type. From the host of project descriptions screened, in cases of similarity, normally the more recent ones were chosen, especially if additional information could be obtained in discussions. The information gathered during the reconnaissance mission – especially on training and education approaches of local NGOs and church-related organizations – were, of course, particularly taken into account, since they are based on extensive on-site information and discussion, and personal observation.

– not so much the programmatic general objectives or the target groups themselves make the essential differences between various approaches and their success or difficulties in reaching the target group(s) and achieving sustainable learning results and positive employment impacts, but rather details of the actual design of measures and the way of programme/project planning. It will also become clear that many of the occupation-oriented training and education approaches are not necessarily bound to one specific type of (counterpart) institution. The final considerations in this chapter will, therefore, refer to the question as to what extent the approaches described below could and should be applied within bilateral vocational training assistance, too, in order to better reach target groups from the informal sector.

6.1 Individual Qualification for a (Labour) Market-oriented Occupation and/or for Subsistence Work

Individual occupation-oriented training and education can – as regards both the objectives orientation of intended measures and the interests of the target groups addressed – seek to provide a qualification primarily to improve income-earning and employment opportunities on the (labour) market of the modern and/or informal sector, or primarily for subsistence work including home production to (partially) compensate the lack of cash income, to reduce the burden of subsistence work or to improve housing conditions.

Formal, non-formal and informal training and education assume different roles and also are accessible and attractive for the various target groups to a different extent.

The following examples of
– "classic" vocational training oriented to clear (industrial) vocational profiles in (partly) Government-run training centres;
– approaches to dual vocational training in cooperation with private enterprises and (small) workshops;
– informal training through apprenticeship in small and micro-enterprises or in private commercial training institutes;
– broader occupation-oriented training and education with reference to environment-determined (potential) occupational options, also in the subsistence economy;
– vocational training and education with a socio-pedagogical approach in various Don Bosco institutions

show, however, that with regard to target groups from the informal sector, the suitability of an approach is neither necessarily determined along the formal – non-formal – informal line of distinction which is difficult to mark anyway, nor generally and clearly depending on a particular nature of the (counterpart) institutions.

6.1.1 *"Classic" Vocational Training and Education in (Partly) Government-run Training Centres*

The experience with the formal and non-formal vocational training of young people in the training centres of the (largely) Government-run vocational training institutions in Latin America[41] and in a "Non-Formal Education Centre" in Thailand exemplify the basic difficulties and limits generally faced in a vocational training which is both strictly oriented to classical industrial vocational profiles and centre-based. They are effective not only, but particularly to target groups from the rural as well as from the urban informal sector.

(1) Vocational training and education to qualify for employment in particular in the modern sector
is the main task of the Government-run vocational training institutions in Latin America[42]. Their training centres have always

41 In African and Asian countries, the system of *formal* vocational training does not differ substantially from the vocational training institutions in Latin America as regards its basic structure and the formal and de facto enrolment requirements. Here too, training in Government-run training centres is almost exclusively geared to meet manpower demand in the modern sector, in particular in African countries "mainly for jobs which do not exist", as *FLUITMAN* (1989), p. 214, claims. Its relevance is even less in view of the fact that, according to an *ILO* study (1988), not even 1 % of the relevant age-group are actually in a formal vocational training (p. 18). Where a demand for skilled workers does exist, as in Thailand, Indonesia or the Philippines, employers complain – like in Latin America – about the insufficient quality and excessive theory bias of vocational training in the Government-run training centres, as the Regional Adviser on Vocational Training in the ILO Regional Office in Bangkok said in an interview.
Non-formal training and education in government training centres also exists in most Asian and some African countries, according to the *ILO* (1988) in Niger, Zambia, Malawi, Nigeria and the Ivory Coast (pp. 11, 26, 28, 32 and 35), for the same informal sector target groups as in Latin America. They reveal similar conceptual and structural weaknesses, with the same result that their efficiency is just as low as their acceptance and reputation among the target groups addressed, if they are, at all, aware of such training possibilities.
42 All of the (semi-)governmental vocational training institutions in Latin America, set up between 1942 and the end of the 1970s, have more or less the same vocational training and education curricula and are to supply the modern industrial sector with skilled labourers. As regards training and education offers specifically for target groups from the informal sector, the SENA in Colombia, the INA in Costa Rica, the SENAI and SENAR in Brazil and the INTECAP in Guatemala deserve a special mention.

offered formal vocational training courses lasting up to three years, in the classical industrial skills, addressing primarily urban youngsters aged between 14 and 20. The enrolment requirement is secondary school education, although not always with graduation. Even this does not appear to be a very restrictive formal barrier in view of the high percentage of secondary school graduates among the young people in the urban squatter areas in Latin America, normally only those youngsters can attend such a long-term vocational training, who
– do not, at least during the period of the (full-time) training, need to earn their own living or contribute towards the family income, since there is – different from the situation in some production schools – no possibility to earn income within or beside the training;
– live near the training centre or can afford the costs of transportation and, if need be, accommodation at the training location;
– live in a social environment in which information on vocational training is available, at all, and such training is considered as relevant or, at least, an opportunity which should be used;
As they fail to meet at least one of these preconditions, the majority of youngsters from the *urban* informal sector – girls almost completely – are if not formally then *de facto* excluded from participation in formal vocational training. More than a few who begin nevertheless, are soon forced to give it up because they have to earn money (again). In the *rural* areas, the number of secondary school graduates is so small that for rural youth vocational training is normally out of reach already for *formal* reasons. At the latest, the cost involved and social obstacles generally turn the participation in a formal vocational training lasting several years into a complete illusion.

Apart from this, also a growing number of those who finally graduate from a vocational training institute, end up – often as unemployed – in the informal sector, because they cannot find employment in a modern industrial enterprise. This has led to mounting criticism of the centre-based and only *industrial* occupation-oriented vocational training. Indeed, it appears to be a particular problem of Government-run vocational training centres that the training very often fails to meet the skill requirements in both the modern and the informal sector. Their facilities, equipment and curricula normally are
– inadequate to fulfil the requirements for the qualification of skilled labourers in the modern industrial sector in terms of the technological standards prevailing there;
– at the same time, so out of touch with the working conditions and the actual technical possibilities in small and micro-enterprises that

the graduates are not trained to use simple technologies and to cope with material supply problems, irregular electricity or water supply and other everyday problems of small and micro-businesses and overcome them as much as possible through technical and organizational improvization, let alone as business owner.

In view of this situation which is worsened by the steadily increasing number of young people in urban areas seeking training and employment, some vocational training institutions[43] in the mid-1970s extended their – still priority – focus on the formal qualification of skilled workers to be employed in modern industrial enterprises by offering also *non-formal* training courses to improve employment opportunities also for target groups from the informal sector.

They were and are intended to train unemployed and underemployed persons in urban squatter areas and in rural areas with a low-level of education, who have no access to the formal vocational training system, for jobs with low qualification requirements in the modern, but also in the informal sector.

The non-formal character is that there are neither formal enrolment requirements nor graduation certificates. Extremely brief training periods of 2–3 weeks only are aimed at enabling course attendance also for those who can be absent as "income-earners" just for a short time. More than simple and selected technical skills from industrial vocations, however, cannot be taught in these short courses[44].

Despite the different objectives and target group orientation, there was no change in the training curricula which remained completely oriented to the classical vocational profiles[45]. The same teaching

---

43 This was probably done most extensively and professionally by the SENA in Colombia with its PMU, PPPU and PPPR programmes, cf. e.g. *CINTERFOR/ OIT* (1982) and *CINTEFOR* (1987), pp. 40 ff.; approaches in other countries are described in *ARNOLD* (1987), pp. 95–107 (INTECAP Guatemala), pp. 114–123 (INAFORP Honduras), pp. 152–166 (INFOTEP Dominican Republic), pp. 167–170 (INSAFORP El Salvador); in *CORVALAN* (1985), pp. 83 ff. (MOBRAL Brazil); and pp. 88 ff. (SECAP Ecuador); in *GOODALE* (1989), p. 58, (INACAP Chile), and in *MÖLLER* (1986) who in particular, describes the reasons for the failure of the INCE programme in Venezuela, cf. esp. pp. 130–155.
44 This relates especially to the SENA programme. The INTECAP in Guatemala carries out a ten-month non-formal technical training for youngsters in rural areas, during which also accommodation is provided and a small grant. This training in the basics of industrial skills is mainly aimed at improving the employment opportunities for semi-skilled and odd-job workers in the modern sector, and, in *this* respect, is similar to the orientation of the Southern Institute for Skill Development (SISD) in Thailand described in Section 6.1.2, Point (2); cf. *CINTERFOR/OIT* (1982), pp. 146 ff.
45 One non-formal training approach more oriented towards the actual occupation opportunities of informal sector target groups in Costa Rica, is described in Section 6.1.4, Point (1).

methods and materials as in the formal training courses were used without adaptation, and the same instructors were assigned to carry out the non-formal training, without any specific preparation[46]. In order to reach the target groups in rural areas and in the urban periphery, the SENA initially sent mobile training units to "give technical instruction to the people"[47], without prior classification of the target group-specific learning opportunities and potentials, training needs and realistic occupation opportunities. Later on, permanent regional centres were established instead. In order to increase the employment impacts of the measures, in the meantime also local (labour) market analyses are carried out in both the modern and the informal sector, and the training courses offered are selected accordingly.

These non-formal training programmes were started at a time when there were still hopes to fight the growing unemployment through training measures providing semi-skilled qualifications, assuming that the modern sector could also, and in particular, absorb less qualified workers in larger numbers. From the disappointing experience in this regard, in the meantime most Government-run vocational training institutions have drawn the consequence to limit themselves again to their original and primary task of training qualified skilled labourers to promote modern economic development in their countries.

They are *not* prepared to adapt the curricula and organization of their vocational training programmes to the specific learning opportunities, qualification needs and occupation opportunities of target groups from the informal sector so as to actively engage in building up – by means of vocational training – their weak or submerged "economic potentials". *Instead* they are deliberately concentrate on those target groups which, as a result of their education, socialization, and – as regards the short-term training courses – previous job experience, already show some "economic development potential" for small or micro-entrepreneurship or a qualified wage employment in the modern or also in the informal sector, and who, thus, can really benefit from a classical – but short-term – vocational training.

This orientation responds to the advanced training needs of skilled labourers and also small and micro-entrepreneurs with a broad spectrum of trade-specific evening classes, also to channel

---

46 Cf. *CINTERFOR/OIT* (1982), pp. 145 f. and *CINTERFOR* (1987), p. 39.
47 *CINTERFOR* (1987), p. 39.

technological innovation into smaller enterprises. Enrolment requirements are primary school graduation and sound technical skills. This makes these courses, in principle, also accessible for small and micro-entrepreneurs from the informal sector with little school education, but work experience and interest in upgrading their technical skills[48].

Conclusion

(i) For young people from the informal sector in general, *formal* vocational training is almost inaccessible either de facto due to its structure, or – especially for most of the rural youth – already formally since they are unable to meet the enrolment requirements.

(iii) The attempt by Government-run vocational training centres to bring *non-formal* vocational training also to more remote and socially disadvantaged target groups, and thereby inform them – often for the first time – about the availability of vocational training accessible to them, is commendable. However, the lesson to be learnt – especially in view of the self-critical assessment of success by the institutions themselves[49] – is that such institutions should not be overloaded with a range of economic, educational and social policy tasks which altogether are too heterogeneous, since this

– is confronted, on the one hand, by budgetary limits, with the result that in particular programmes for economically "marginal" groups (can) only receive marginal financial allocations.

– leads, on the other hand, to friction in the "corporate identity" of these institutions, resulting in misallocations of personnel and motivation problems of staff who find it difficult in their daily work to reconcile the extreme variety – indeed often polarity – of institutional objectives[50].

Also the people from the informal sector, who require really target group-specific measures and particularly qualified instructors and advisers, are hardly helped by an objectives and target group orientation in their favour, which then is not applicable *in practice*.

(iii) The major objective of the Latin American vocational training institutions orientation to train skilled or semi-skilled labourers above all for wage employment in the modern sector is undoubtedly hampered by the prevailing overall economic situation, but as much

---

48 This assessment is shared by the World Bank; cf. *IBRD* (1989a), p. 196.
49 Cf. *CINTERFOR/OIT* (1982), pp. 146 ff.
50 This problem is also seen by *LOW MURTRA* (1987), pp. 113 f., who describes the existence of "two SENAs" in Colombia.

by their orientation towards only classical industrial vocation profiles, and the inadequate design of the formal and non-formal training courses. The curricula mostly neither meet the qualification requirements for skilled workers in the modern sector nor for a qualified employment in the informal sector. Especially with regard to the only restricted employment opportunities available to young people from urban slums or rural areas, they fail to take into account their particular qualification needs, not to mention their specific learning opportunities and potentials.

(iv) Nevertheless, the availability of skilled labourers in sufficient number and with good technical qualifications is crucial for a country's economic and technological development. Government-run vocational training institutions of the "Latin American type" should, therefore, concentrate on this task and the correspondingly suitable target groups, and they should adjust their formal vocational training programmes to include more innovatory subjects in response to the demand of the modern sector.

Focusing these considerations to a certain extent also on the improvement of non-formal training for people from the informal sector, may make sense wherever existing or potential regional employment opportunities fairly correspond with the maximum level of qualification which may be achieved in such a training[51].

(v) Partner organizations in bilateral vocational training assistance – as far as Germany is concerned, especially the Industrial Occupations Promotion Centre (ZGB) or the GTZ – should promote such adaptions in the programmes of the Government-run vocational training institutions, for example, through assistance in the elaboration of curricula and teaching materials to meet the qualification needs of young people with regard to the actual skill demand in the modern industrial – and service – sector. Training needs analyses including studies on (labour) market potentials could provide useful information in this context, as could tracer studies among former graduates *and* drop-outs on their social background, current employment and income-earning situation and – in case of the drop-outs – reasons for prematurely quitting the training.

(vi) On the whole, however, the possibilities for (better) reaching especially target groups from the informal sector in cooperation with vocational training institutions of the "Latin American type" are

---

51 The experience of the already mentioned Government-run non-formal training centre SISD in southern Thailand shows that this is possible, under certain conditions; cf. Section 6.1.2, Point (2).

viewed as rather limited. This also applies to the necessary pedagogical-training and motivation of instructors to be assigned to train people from the informal sector – the more as an institution such as the ZGB probably itself has learning and experience deficits here.

However, the conclusion should not be drawn – as other examples will show – that it is basically impossible to provide in cooperation with (partly) Government-run institutions occupation-oriented training and education which would really correspond to the qualification needs and given occupation opportunities of people from the informal sector. This will only prove particularly different wherever these institutions have developed a structure with a clearly different orientation – which may well be justified – with respect to their institutional objectives and to the qualification, work experience and interests of their staff.

(2) A qualified non-formal training of rural youth
was the objective of the "Metal Work Training Project" which has been carried out in northern Thailand with the Northern Region Non-formal Education Center (NRNFEC) in Lampang as the project executing institution, with personnel assistance from the German Volunteer Service (GVS; German: DED)[52]. During the pilot phase between 1985 and 1988, an attempt was made to introduce the concept of a training in three phases lasting altogether 7–8 months – with a "Workshop Management Training" during the last 2–3 months – in the metal work training programme at the Non-formal Education Centers in initially four provincial capitals[53]. The idea was to train rural youngsters from the villages of the respective provinces so that they were afterwards able to set up small workshops of their own in their villages. The participants should have at least six years primary school education – which in the meantime is quite normal in Thailand – and a few years job experience, resulting in an age of around 18. Girls could not feel addressed by these courses, since traditionally in Thailand they do not work in metal work trades.

52 The project was visited as part of the reconnaissance mission to Thailand in June 1990. A – slightly too positive – brief description of the pilot phase can be found in *MELLER* (1989). The project design is described in greater detail in *PETCHARUGSA/MELLER* (1988).
53 Since the end of the pilot phase, the project's training activities have mainly been concentrated at the Provincial Non-formal Education Centre (PNFEC) in Chiang Mai. At the same time, the efforts to establish courses in the PNFECs of the three other provincial cities were said to be continued with assistance of a GVS development worker. The catchment areas of these PNFECs are to encompass – as in Chiang Mai – four provinces each.

In its implementation the project has been confronted by various problems which appear to be symptomatic for non-formal training programmes, especially in Government-run institutions:
– The reputation of non-formal education as a "second-class education" which hardly improves prospects of a reasonably paid employment, is equally shared by the training institution, their instructors, the target groups and – because of the normally low quality standard – potential employers;
– The target group which is mainly intended to be addressed – older youngsters from the villages – is hardly reached at all;
– The learning success of the training participants in terms of the training objective normally falls short of expectations;
– The high degree of fluctuation among the instructors makes a systematic training difficult and the training of non-formal trainers – who do mostly not have particular pedagogical qualifications – a never-ending task, if it takes place at all.

The difficulties in inducing young people from rural areas to attend the courses[54] are mainly attributed to the fact that
– most villagers already regard training centers in the provincial capital as too distant, not only in terms of travel distance[55], especially since little is really known about the type of courses offered;
– apart from this, the training courses from their design and organization are often not acceptable to the target group because of the training location, the costs involved the schedule and/or duration or the basic education and skill background required as precondition, including the ability to learn in a school-like manner.

The course planners seemed not to be bothered by these problems, whereas the instructors frankly expressed their critical views, when it came to the question of reaching the target group and taking into account their learning opportunities and potentials. They
– above all see the difficulties which result for most young people when moving from their villages to town to take part in a training course from the associated confrontation with all kinds of innovations;

---

54 Most training participants at the PNFEC in Chiang Mai, northern Thailand's booming economic centre, come from the city or nearby villages. They are at most between 14 and 15 years old, which is reason enough why hardly any of them subsequently sets up his own business. The project staff assumes that between 4 and 7 of the by then altogether roughly 200 course participants at the four PNFECs may have tried to set up a workshop. Only three of the roughly 60 participants in the pilot project courses did so.
55 This was again confirmed in the target group interviews in two villages in the NRNFEC catchment area.

– regard the specific village education and experience which shape the way of thinking and learning behaviour different as compared to urban youth, as a major reason for the often persistent problems young villagers have to comprehend and practically apply even simple technical facts[56];
– against this background, consider the period of five months of technical training as sufficient enough to impart to the young people basic skills on metal work and repair useful in the village environment, but not enough to train them for a qualified job, and certainly not for setting up their own metal workshop[57];
– on the other hand, are convinced that, for cost reasons alone[58], this is the maximum training duration acceptable for rural families, especially if the village is so far away that accommodation has to be rented in town.

The technical qualification of the instructors working in the project was said to be not bad. For the other courses at the PNFECs, however, it is generally viewed as poor. Qualified instructors either regard this (often only sideline) activity as a temporary solution. Or they have a sense of social commitment, but can afford to carry out the job of non-formal instructor only as long as they are still unmarried.

---

56 Most of the eight training participants interviewed also shared this view with regard to themselves, and some of them said that they had only begun the course because they had been "dragged along" to it by a friend while they had nothing better to do. They feel particular learning problems in theory lessons as well as in technical work. None of the boys interviewed has any thoughts yet of setting up a business afterwards.

57 A tracer study carried out by the PNFEC in Chiang Mai in May/June 1990 revealed that almost all participants in the metal work training courses there initially look for a kind of "apprentice-job" to further consolidate their skills, which most of them also find thanks to the comparatively high standard of the training and the shortage of skilled labour, especially in the region of Chiang Mai and Lamphun. Another few go for further vocational training at a technical college. Only about 10 % of them go back to work in their villages – which are near the city anyway. As regards the three other PNFECs included in the project, at most 50 % of the course participants find a job afterwards, at all, though often not in nearby areas but also in Chiang Mai or in other towns, and not necessarily in the metal trade. The others return to their villages without (self-)employment.

58 The course participants pay one Baht per training hour, which amounts to roughly 600 Baht for a five-month course, plus living expenses in town. For comparison: in an economically rather well developed village in this region, well over half of the families (= households) have an annual income of between 5,000 and 15,000 Baht, but roughly 15 % less than 5,000 Baht. These figures from 1987 will not have changed dramatically since then. In a less developed neighbouring village – which is more typical for the general situation in northern Thailand – none of the families has an annual income exceeding 15,000 Baht. Over a quarter of the families have to manage on less than 5,000 Baht. This has to feed on average a family of four or five and, among other things, pay for the agricultural inputs for the coming year; cf. *LOHMAR-KUHNLE* (1987), pp. 9–17 and 26–32.

For the implementation and monitoring of the planned two- to three-month "workshop simulation" as third phase of the training, in which the participants "(should) practise how to run their own workshop and learn what it means to be the boss"[59], none of the instructors are qualified without further training, neither as regards the required know-how in business administration and organization nor as regards the different didactic skills required to impart entrepreneurial instead of technical skills[60]. For the same reason, there is still a lack of qualified personnel, even after a five-year project period, hampering the realization of the planned back-up advisory assistance for participants who want to set up their own workshop.

A training of instructors for that purpose proves fairly impossible mainly because of the already mentioned rather high fluctuation and/or their low level of commitment. Both result from their below-average pay on a lesson-by-lesson (hourly) basis, payment only for the course training itself, but not for preparation time, for the maintenance of the machines used or for additional tuition of course participants outside of course time[61]. On top comes the poor reputation of non-formal training for which most instructors feel they are over-qualified, anyhow. Finally, the location of the training centres in rather small rural towns is generally considered as unappealing[62].

For the reasons described, it must be assumed that the very few course participants who have in fact set up their own small workshop, would have done so anyway. As regards their categorization as "village craftsmen", it sets thinking that a former course participant presented as particularly successful, may have established a workshop in his home village not far from town. According to his own statements[63], his market, however, is hardly at all this village, but within a radius of about 100 km the entire economically booming

---

59 *MELLER* (1989), p. 20, although the impression given there that this third phase is already an established component of the Metal Work Training Project was not confirmed.
60 This was stated as one reason for the difficulties to realize the phase of "management training" as preparation for self-employment as rural craftsman – the component for which the project was originally selected for a visit.
61 In this respect the GVS tried with some success to improve the situation by persistently demanding that instructors working in the project should also be paid for the six lessons (hours) they actually give a day, instead of the statutory maximum for non-formal training of three hours per day only.
62 Especially because of the appeal of the urban location, the problems of finding instructors are the least extreme in Chiang Mai, also since there it is comparatively easy to increase the total income through a second job.
63 Khun Kasem was interviewed during the visit to the project.

region where there is a substantial middle-class purchasing power. He claimed that he can only earn a just about adequate income because the quality of his metal work – as a result of the training course – has become known to clients from this wide area. The generally good road infrastructure and a pick-up hired from an uncle for a fee, allow him sufficient mobility. He is convinced that as a simple village craftsman he could not survive.

Conclusion

(i) In order to actually reach their target groups, non-formal training institutions generally must recognize that, precisely because of the reduction or elimination of formal enrolment requirements, they address target groups with more restrictive learning opportunities and potentials and different qualification needs than those assumed for formal vocational training courses. This must be taken into consideration when deciding on schedules, location, curricula contents and didactics of non-formal occupation-oriented training and education. Especially in rural areas, the lower level of information and the tendency of rural people to mainly assimilate only information relating to their closer vicinity, must be taken into account. Active information on the availability of non-formal training must be provided at village level as well as encouragement of the villagers to think about a participation in view of the possible impacts on their employment opportunities.
(ii) The instructors in non-formal training must be prepared for work with these target groups – which are hardly familiar with systematic learning and how to deal with new technology – through advanced training in pedagogical skills.
(iii) Under certain circumstances, the concept of non-formal vocational training as qualification for setting up a village workshop – and hence a contribution to rural (self-)employment creation – can be meaningful. It is confronted, however, with the fundamental dilemma that in the more remote villages market saturation is reached quickly due to the limited demand for the kind of products village workshops can produce and the low purchasing power of the villages. The closer the villages are to urban areas, on the other hand, the more purchasing power is there, but the village workshops are also much more exposed to the competition from a wide range of supply in modern goods and services in the market.

Therefore, a non-formal training programme – especially when relatively strongly oriented to a particular vocational profile – which is aimed at promoting the establishment of rural workshops through young villagers, should not be "simply set up", without a concept and (enough) skilled staff for advisory assistance to the potential rural entrepreneurs. During the planning phase also a fairly precise market analysis should be carried out, not only on the rural demand in principle, but also on the quantitative absorptive capacity of the local and regional markets for the type of products and services which (additional) rural workshops can provide[64].

(iv) In view of the objective difficulties to reach a significant number of people in the villages – women hardly at all – even with the already relatively decentralized occupation-oriented training offers of rural training *centres*, existing institutions of this kind should shift more to a training for intermediary target groups with a social multiplier function. They could probably better qualify village school teachers, local social workers or village craftsmen to extend occupation-oriented skills and advisory services to rural target groups directly at village level. If such a concept is supported within a programme of (bilateral) vocational training assistance, e.g. for the elaboration of adequate curricula and advisory assistance in the organization of such training of local trainers, this approach would most likely significantly contribute to improve the training and subsequently occupation opportunities in the villages, in particular for women.

6.1.2 *Forms of Dual Vocational Training in Cooperation with Private (Small) Enterprises*

Individual qualification of young people in some sort of so-called dual vocational training – in the sense that the practical training takes place in – also small – workshops of private enterprises, while the corresponding vocational theory training is done in a normal, not necessarily Government-run training centre – is actually found more often than could initially be presumed from the respective literature which mainly describes Latin American experiences.

64 The case of the Rural Trade School in Salima/Malawi shows that vocational training for rural business creation can, in fact, be successful under certain conditions; cf. on this aspect Section 6.2.2., Point (3).

Following, forms of dual vocational training are described as they exist
- in some Latin American countries[65] as – often difficult to establish – cooperation between the Government-run vocational training institutions and private enterprises primarily from the manufacturing industry of the modern sector for the qualification of skilled workers;
- also, for example, at a Government-run non-formal vocational training centre in Thailand, with an interesting model for the qualification not of skilled but of semi-skilled workers for employment in relatively labour-intensive rural industrial enterprises;
- in initial stages in some West African states, especially in Nigeria[66], as a supplementation or extension of the informal apprenticeship training in small and micro-enterprises through Government-organized centre-based theory lessons and efforts by the Government to introduce certain standards for (also informal) vocational training in the private enterprises;
- finally, as private initiatives like, for example, in a workshop centre in the Ivory Coast.

(1) Dual vocational training as introduced in Latin American countries

is a formal vocational training of youngsters lasting at most three years. As regards its primary objective of training skilled workers for the demand of modern industrial enterprises, its orientation to classical industrial vocational profiles and consequently the target groups addressed, it hardly differs from the above described exclusively centre-based formal vocational training of the "Latin American type". At the end of a dual vocational training, too, a recognized certificate attests that the apprentice now is a qualified skilled worker in his trade.

The idea underlying the promotion of dual vocational training is to shift the responsibility for vocational training as far as possible from

---

65 According to a study by *CINTERFOR/OIT* (1989), "dual vocational training" programmes orientated to the skilled labour demands of private *enterprises* in the modern industrial sector, in order to increase employment opportunities there, are currently being introduced by the Government-run vocational training institutions in Peru (SENATI), Guatemala (INTECAP), the Dominican Republic (INFOTEP) – in cooperation with the Regensburg Chamber of Crafts – and in Paraguay (SNNP).

66 Also in the Ivory Coast, Togo and Algeria, according to *BAS* (1989), p. 491, and in Sudan and Malawi, according to *IRBD* (1989), p. 83; as regards Ghana cf. *HAKAM* (1983), pp. 64 f.

Government-run vocational training institutes to the private sector. The intention behind is,
- through the expected reduction of the share of Government costs for vocational training in one place, to realize a better countrywide coverage, and
- through the stronger emphasis on practical vocational training in "real" workshops of private industrial enterprises, to achieve a qualification of graduates which is more compatible to the needs of modern industry.

Both these effects are hoped to ultimately increase the total number of apprenticeship places as well as the subsequent employment opportunities of the apprentices.

For the majority of boys and girls from the urban slums and even more for those from the rural areas, however, this type of dual vocational training is no better chance for an occupation-oriented qualification than the described exclusively centre-based formal vocational training, since it confronts them with just the same formal and de facto enrolment restrictions. Therefore, no need is seen here for any further discussion – extending beyond the following remarks – on the advantages and weaknesses of this concept of dual vocational training for developing countries in general[67].

Conclusion

(i)   The assumption that a shift of the larger part of vocational training into private enterprises would significantly increase the number of apprenticeship places and subsequent employment opportunities for the graduates, may prove to be correct in individual cases. On the whole, however, the number of jobs – especially in the modern sector – will only increase to a noticeable extent, if the overall economic development creates a corresponding labour demand. Otherwise, private enterprises will hardly train more apprentices than up to their own immediate need, let alone employ them after training.

(ii)   Many enterprises – generally medium-sized and smaller ones –

---

[67] For more information on this question cf. the references in part II.1 of the bibliography. According to information from discussions with GTZ staff, the number of young people involved in formal dual vocational training in Latin American countries is low, anyway, roughly 3,000 in courses carried out by the SENATI in Peru and "a couple of hundred each in Paraguay, Guatemala and Ecuador".

will have difficulties anyhow, at least initially, to cope with the requirements related to workshop-based vocational training, not only for internal organizational and financial reasons, but also because of the inadequate number and pedagogical qualification of skilled workers who could be assigned the task as instructors[68]. They are unlikely to be keen on making their situation even more difficult by taking on young people from the informal sector as apprentices, who often have a sub-standard of school education and also must be expected to be particularly "difficult" in their social behaviour.

(iii) There will certainly be cases where the payment of an apprenticeship grant during the workshop based vocational training will enable secondary-school graduates to take up a formal vocational training, who would otherwise simply for financial reasons have no such opportunity. On the whole, however, especially for young people from the informal sector, this form of dual vocational training will be as well- or little-suited and accessible as the exclusively centre-based formal vocational training, even though just secondary school attendance but not necessarily the graduation[69] is an enrolment requirement.

(2) "Cooperative Training Courses" for the non-formal qualification of semi-skilled workers

were introduced at the Southern Institute for Skill Development (SISD) in Songkhla (Southern Thailand) under a GTZ project[70]. At the SISD, one of the 11 regional centres for non-formal education of rural youth under the Department of Labour, six- to twelve-month normally exclusively centre-based courses are offered in 14 different technical fields. For the first time in 1989, a form of dual – here called "cooperative" – non-formal vocational training was introduced, initially for the "electrical engineering" and "mechanics" courses, and one year later also for the "air conditioning" course.

The clearly job-oriented objective of the SISD's "Cooperative

---

68 This is often pointed out, for example, in *ZIEBART* (1989), pp. 157 ff., who also refers to the problem that external "mentors" are normally poorly accepted on part of the enterprises to train their workshop staff as instructors in dual vocational training programmes.

69 According the experience of the SENATI in Peru, the importance of secondary school education should not be over-estimated, anyway. Even apprentices who graduated, are normally unable to solve even basic problems such as unit conversion or the interpretation of simple technical drawings, because they lack basic knowledge in mathematics or physics. Hence, introductory courses in these subjects are inevitable, anyway; cf. *FAJARDO* (1988), p. 46.

70 All the information presented here has been taken from the final report on the project carried out by the GTZ between 1979 and 1990.

Training Courses" is to give a sound basic technical qualification – focusing on work quality and a relatively wide scope of applicability of the imparted skills – to disadvantaged rural target groups such as school drop-outs and unemployed youth. Probably due to the trades selected, however, apparently no women or girls are included. These qualified semi-skilled workers earn less than skilled workers, but more than untrained odd-job or casual workers.

With a wage level and qualification which both correspond to the demands of the comparatively labour-intensive small and medium industries in the rural areas, they have significantly better employment opportunities. While the employment rates among participants in the ordinary – only centre-based – non-formal training courses thanks to the quality of the training, already reached roughly 70 %, it increased to 84 % in the "Cooperative Training Courses".

Furthermore, by involving the region's industrial enterprises for the practical training to be (partly) carried out in their workshops, the number of participants in the "Cooperative Training Courses" could initially be doubled, in the "mechanics" course in the second year even be trebled.

From the beginning, for these courses a deliberate selection of participants was made in favour of those applicants who obviously want the training for immediate subsequent application of the imparted skills in an income earning activity (again). They are assumed to not be keen on further training in a formal vocational training institute towards a "white-collar" career. This is also tried to be prevented by that the successful completion of the SISD "Cooperative Training Courses" do *not* lead to a higher *formal* qualification.

Mainly three indicators suggest that the orientation towards a non-formal but sound enterprise demand-related qualification of semi-skilled workers – instead of a formal vocational training of then too expensive and often over-qualified skilled workers – responds to both the labour requirements of rural industries and the qualification needs and learning opportunities of rural target groups with little prior education and job experience:

– The interest in the "Cooperative Training Courses" among the target groups is so great that enrolment quotas had to be fixed for each province in its catchment area[71];

71 The extraordinary positive response among youngsters to the "Cooperative Training Courses", in particular, was confirmed in a discussion with two participants from villages located relatively close to the provincial town of Songkhla.

- It was apparently possible to overcome both the reservations on part of the instructors to approach industrial enterprises and the latter's reserved response – already described as typical in Latin America – as regards the provision of apprenticeship places for the "Cooperative Training Courses", supported by the positive frame condition that the demand of rural industries for semi-skilled workers is by no means satisfied yet in the region[72];
- The Department of Labour has begun, in its own initiative, to introduce "Cooperative Training Courses" in other regional non-formal training centres, too.

Conclusion

(i) The experience of the SISD shows that – especially in newly industrializing countries with a policy aimed at a decentralization of industries into rural areas – a sound non-formal vocational training not of skilled but of semi-skilled workers, which is clearly oriented to the local labour demand, can be a way of promoting rural economic development and, at the same time, creating employment opportunities for rural target groups which have no access to the formal vocational training system.

(ii) With a deliberately selective choice of course participants according to the a.m. criteria and the reputation as a training institution whose courses do indeed increase the employment opportunities for the participants, it proves possible also for a Government-run *and* non-formal vocational training institution to actually reach target groups such as unemployed and young rural people and to motivate them to attend non-formal training courses.

(iii) In principle, the same concept of sound non-formal qualification as semi-skilled workers is also conceivable for young women, in trades fairly common and accessible to them, even though there will probably be greater difficulties in implementation: On the one hand, for reasons explained earlier, mostly only women who live close to the training centre will consider taking up the offer. On the other hand, it will normally be more difficult to persuade private enterprises to provide apprenticeship places for women, since women may be a common phenomenon in most countries as unskilled cheap labour, but not as trained odd-job, let alone skilled workers.

---

72 It is not known, however, whether and to what extent the enterprises incur (part of the) costs for this apprenticeship training.

As it is a well-known experience that the readiness for social innovation in this respect is not particularly great, especially not in rural areas, probably specific women's development programmes will be needed here, possibly in cooperation with local women's organizations or other NGOs.

(3) An approach to dual vocational training including existing forms of informal apprenticeship training

is what the National Directorate of Employment (NDE) has been trying to introduce in Nigeria since 1987 on a countrywide scale with its "National Open Apprenticeship Scheme" (NOAS)[73]. In view of the problems of acceptance at enterprise level confronting the concept of dual vocational training in Latin America, and the fact that there target groups from the informal sector are largely excluded also from this form of vocational training, the NOAS approach which incorporates the tradition of informal apprenticeship training in (West) Africa, deserves a closer look to be taken, even though a period of only three years of implementation is too short to really assess the employment impacts of such a large-scale programme.

The NOAS approach is presented as a concept for vocational training which is low-cost, potentially covering a relatively large area and oriented to realistic occupation opportunities and practical skills, and hence could be able to meet the labour qualification requirements of enterprises with quite different technological levels as well as reach a large number of young people from the urban and rural informal sector, including girls.

The core elements of the NOAS "Youth Employment Program" can be summarized as follows:

— Places are found for unemployed primary and secondary school-leavers in (semi-)public and private enterprises of all sizes as well as with master craftsmen in small and micro-enterprises in the informal sector for a practical vocational training in one of 81 occupational fields or trades in which employment opportunities exist. Depending on the occupational field the course duration is from a few weeks, e.g.

---

73 Cf. *ILO* (1988), p. 32; and *BÖHM* (1990), pp. 9–13; special reference to the NOAS is also made in *IBRD* (1989), p. 83. The NOAS is apparently carrying out altogether three programmes to improve the youth employment situation – apart from the "Youth Employment Program" described here, the introduction of "Mobile Schools" and a programme for new business creation through small and micro-entrepreneurs. There is no further information available on the latter programs.

on "bakery", up to three years, e.g. on electrical engineering, metal work or motor mechanics;
– There are deliberately no standardized curricula in view of the sometimes very different skill requirements and production technologies in the "training enterprises". However, the quality of the workshop training which in the small and micro-enterprises, by and large, has the character of informal apprenticeship training, is to be regularly inspected by NDE staff, so-called Monitoring Officers, based on the "reporting books" of the apprentices[74];
– As an incentive to provide apprenticeship places, the NOAS pays the enterprises a subsidy of 150 Naira per apprentice and year as compensation for the loss of the traditional apprenticeship fee, whereas the apprentices themselves receive a modest grant of 50 Naira/month;
– Apart from the workshop training five days a week, the apprentices also have to attend "saturday classes" in vocational theory, arithmetics and English. The vocational theory training is carried out by master craftsmen or technical teachers against payment, normally in existing school or other communal facilities;
– Although the NOAS-supported training is not completed with a certificate, the apprentices may afterwards on their own, i.e. without an apprenticeship subsidy, enrol for a further apprenticeship year at one of the country's four Trade Test Centres with the aim of passing this test for a formal certificate.

During the first three years, reportedly 200,000 young people have started a vocational training under the NOAS. Thanks to the monthly grant, this apprenticeship scheme is open also to a larger circle of young people from the informal sector. With the NDE's placement support, also girls apparently obtain an apprenticeship more often than usual. Only about 20,000 of the roughly 50,000 graduates so far, however, have afterwards found employment in an enterprise or set-up their own business. A parallel "Resettlement Program" with incentives for young rural-urban migrants to return to (the vicinity of) their home villages during or after the NOAS-supported apprenticeship, which could help to increase the (self-)employment rate, is still in its early stages.

---

74 According to information obtained in discussions, there is only one "Principal Monitoring Officer" with five staff for this task at each of the 22 "State Offices". The consequence is that the same enterprises are inspected at most once every three months, and "good enterprises" not at all, due to lack of time. In Lagos, each "Monitoring Officer" reportedly is responsible for about 400 apprentices at a time.

Conclusion

(i) The positive conceptual and – in principle – exemplary aspects of this approach to dual vocational training incorporating elements of informal apprenticeship training, are
– an obviously only limited need for regulatory intervention through Government institutions;
– the potentially broad impact at comparatively low cost for the Government, by making use of the existing system of informal apprenticeship training and existing school or other communal facilities for the vocational theory training in the "saturday classes";
– the additional "saturday classes" through which – different from normal informal apprenticeship – at least some basic vocational theory and general education can be imparted. That this will inevitably remain inadequate in view of the limited number of lessons, should not be overrated as a major disadvantage in view of the subsequent (self-) employment opportunities realistically given for the majority of young people either in a (rural) small or micro-enterprise, or in the subsistence sector as often intended anyhow[75];
– the openness or flexibility of the curricula for the workshop training, which allows to include "training enterprises" with very different levels of economic and technological development, thus providing – especially through the small and micro-enterprises in the informal sector – apprenticeship opportunities also for young people with rather poor school education and little chance for apprenticeship in a modern sector enterprise;
– the broad range of vocational training offers in occupational fields in which (self-)employment-opportunities actually exist, giving a chance for useful training also to those who want or have to (further) apply their acquired knowledge and skills, in the first instance, in an occupation in the subsistence sector, although it is not clear to what extent the instructors employed under the NOAS are qualified for the corresponding kind of training;
– the intention of gradually introducing through monitoring inspections in the "training enterprises" a certain standard to what essentially still remains informal apprenticeship training;
– the basically dynamic concept of vocational training, which

---

75 Nothing is known, however, about whether and in what way the inevitably very different learning opportunities and potentials of the apprentices many of whom are from the urban informal sector and as many have only recently migrated into town from a rural area, are taken into account accordingly.

integrates elements of non-formal, informal and, in the final stage, formal occupation-oriented training through the option of undergoing formal Trade Tests after an additional year of training, though this has to be financed – which seems wise – by the apprentices themselves.

(ii) Some major critical remarks on the NOAS approach are that the – undoubtedly necessary – payment of a fixed subsidy for each apprenticeship place might well be an incentive, especially for economically weak small and micro-enterprises, to take on apprentices beyond the local or regional labour demand in their trade[76], the more so as the (self-)regulatory "guild-like" limitation as in traditional apprenticeship training is not (intended to be) effective under the NOAS;

– the question remains unanswered just how far such an approach can really be introduced with reasonable success – in particular as regards the rural areas – without corresponding training for master craftsmen in small and micro-enterprises and for local teachers in the "saturday classes". No special attention seems to be turned to an adequate (advanced) technical and/or pedagogical skill training of the trainers, nor to a differentiation in the programme design to reflect the varying learning opportunities and potentials among young people from the informal sector;

– many of the (semi)public "training enterprises" are clearly large enterprises, such as the Railway Authority with alone 400 apprentices, which puts the number of 200,000 young people accepted as apprentices in a different light – not necessarily indicating a pronounced integration of small and micro-enterprises as "training enterprises".

(iii) Regardless of the unclear calculation method leading to this figure, the fact that only about 40 % of the apprentices who have so far completed a NOAS-supported vocational training subsequently found some income-generating (self-)employment, shows that the employment impacts of this vocational training approach – like any other – does not only depend on the quality of the concept, but very much on the overall economic situation as reflected in the labour market and the general economic potential.

(iv) Nevertheless, a dual vocational training concept such as the NOAS, which is essentially based on the use of the existing structure of informal apprenticeship training and also provides training opportunities oriented to subsistence occupation, appears,

[76] This reportedly is also an increasing tendency in the ordinary informal apprenticeship training; cf. on this aspect Section 6.1.3, Point (1) and (2).

in principle, worth to be (further) promoted also within (bilateral) programmes of vocational training assistance. They should, however, have the features mentioned in (i).

As regards the apparent pedagogical as well as (advanced) technical training of the teachers and master craftsmen engaged as instructors in the "saturday classes", a long-term assistance to strengthen a suitable Government institution to be responsible for the policy guidelines and standards of vocational training, by improving the professional competence required for this task, in particular their capacity to undertake labour market analysis and vocational training planning, would be necessary, as well as to establish nationwide functioning local administrative units and facilities for vocational theory training like the "saturday classes".

It would also be conceivable and meaningful to integrate into a dual vocational training programme also advisory services for the enterprises to disseminate innovative or improved appropriate technologies in various occupational fields.

(4) A workshop centre for informal dual apprenticeship training has developed in purely private initiative during the past eight years in a district of Abidjan in the Ivory Coast[77]. In the currently five training workshops of the "Port Bouet Pilot Centre" each year roughly 190 young people from the informal sector are trained, regardless of their previous school education, in various crafts where there is a confirmed local demand, namely in repair of motor vehicles, refrigerators and air conditioning systems, and in furniture making and tailoring. Because of the kind of business, girls have apparently not – at least not yet – been addressed.

The set-up of this small workshop centre dates back to the initiative of a clergyman who started it in 1983 together with a group of unemployed young people and with a certain support from the local municipality in the city district of Port Bouet.

The workshop centre is characterized by the following elements:

– The instructors are skilled craftsmen from the informal sector, who were allowed to move with their former "street workshop" permanently into the workshop centre, if they, in return, would take on between one and three young people as apprentices in their trade;

– Depending on the trade, this apprenticeship lasts up to three

[77] The history and apparent success of this model are described in brief in *FLUITMAN/SANGARE* (1989), pp. 114 f. The information presented there was confirmed and complemented in certain respects in a discussion with a visitor from the Ivory Coast, who said to be familiar with the centre in Abidjan.

years, with each apprentice in his second year taking on the technical fields and some key qualifications useful for small business organization;
– Upon admission the youngsters have to pay a one-off training fee. Apart from that, there are no other enrolment requirements;
– The observation of a minimum standard in the workshop training is regularly checked by the management of the workshop centre, in which also the local municipality is represented.

Conclusion

(i)   With this form of dual informal apprenticeship training in small workshop centres where micro-enterprises doing the workshop training and off-workshop vocational theory lessons are combined in one location, young people from the informal sector have – also without previous school education – the opportunity to participate in an occupation-oriented technical training in a type of workshop which in structure and work routine resembles their own subsequent employment opportunities, while at the same time some general education and vocational theory is imparted.
By settling the "training micro-enterprises" at the workshop centre, apart from a quality control of the training also a certain social protection and social education can be provided for the apprentices.
(ii)   Even if they are unwilling or unable to set up their own business immediately after finishing training, the extended period during which they grow up, so to say, in the atmosphere of a micro-enterprise can – similar as in the normal informal apprenticeship – contribute more towards qualifying the youngsters as potential small and micro-entrepreneurs or for self-employment than any special training course aiming at that purpose, the more so as young people with a socialization in the informal sector are likely to acquire also business skills and some kind of market feeling easiest by "watching" and "doing".
(iii)   The recruitment of local craftsmen as instructors from among those who have good skills but not (yet) an established workshop, for whom the offer of establishing their own workshop at the centre hence is both incentive and chance to take on their own apprentices, is undoubtedly an approach suitable not only in Abidjan to create apprenticeship places especially for young people with very low school education and, at the same time, give micro-entrepreneurs

or self-employed craftsmen a chance to build up a more stable business.

(iv) In its function as an information and advisory centre, the workshop centre can familiarize both the apprentices and the master craftsmen with innovative techniques and products which can be applied and produced, respectively, at the technological level of small and micro-enterprises[78].

(v) Altogether, the approach to set up, in collaboration with local NGOs and/or responsible Government institutions, decentralized small workshop centres for informal or non-formal vocational training, which by and large support and organize themselves, appears worth to be promoted also within the framework of (bilateral) vocational training assistance, e.g. by GTZ and/or NGO donors. Thereby, the training, occupation and income-earning opportunities for some relevant target groups from the informal sector, namely unemployed youth and weak micro-entrepreneurs and self-employed craftsmen – especially in urban areas – can be increased. This approach is particularly attractive in those countries or big cities where there are numerous skilled workers and self-employed craftsmen without a secure and sufficient income basis and nowhere near enough jobs to be created in the modern industrial and tertiary sector even in the long run.

The "small size" of such workshop centres should not be taken as a quantitative counter-argument, since a greater employment impact may possibly be brought about by several small centres of this kind rather than by one single large and expensive project. Such small units are more flexible and closer to the market and the relevant target groups.

6.1.3 *Informal Occupation-oriented Training*

For the majority of people from the informal sector, work and training are not separate affairs. Since also children and youngsters – often from early childhood on – have to contribute to the family income with their own work, they can usually only consider an apprenticeship, if they find a workshop where they can also earn

---

[78] A similar approach has been adopted by the BGZ/GTZ-supported "Foundation for the Promotion of Vocational Training and Small Industries" (MEKSA Foundation) in its vocational training schemes in Turkey.

some money in a kind of odd-job apprenticeship. Even this is becoming increasingly difficult in urban areas, too, due to the growing number of young people looking for jobs and training. In many cases, it is only possible through the connections of friends and relatives. Young people from rural areas – insofar as they do not (have to) stay in subsistence farming anyway – have even less opportunities for such an informal training, in the rural areas themselves because of the small number of off-farm enterprises there, as newcomers to urban areas looking for an odd-job apprenticeship because of the lack of social contacts and problems of adjusting to urban life.

On the whole, informal apprenticeship training is most common in the form of some sort of "odd-job apprenticeship", the appearance of which is, by and large, similar in all developing countries. A peculiarity is the almost guide-like traditional apprenticeship in some West African countries. A modern and apparently increasingly significant form of informal vocational training are the commercial training offers of private training institutes and master craftsmen.

(1) Informal odd-job apprenticeship
still is the most customary form of vocational training for young people from the informal sector. Theoretically, this possibility is open to everyone, but in reality mainly to boys, since most artisanal trades are male domains. Regardless of the statutory minimum age of 16 years for any kind of apprenticeship and employment, as in most countries, there are many children found in private workshops as helpers or odd-job apprentices. Quite a few are only 8–9 years old, some even younger.

Those who do not have the opportunity of skill acquisition by watching, helping out and learning from their fathers in the family's own workshop, have to try to be accepted in any workshop as "helper apprentice".[79] The workshop owner does normally pay him a small amount for his work and perhaps provides accommodation – often only the latter, sometimes just a place to sleep in the workshop – and one or two meals a day. Although this is not to contribute to the

---

79 There are quite a few descriptions of the training and working conditions in odd-job apprenticeship in Africa, e.g. *HOPPERS* (1985), pp. 99–139, *KING* (1975), *FAPOHUNDA* (1990), pp. 77–79, or *McLAUGHLIN* (1979); for Asia cf., e.g. *KAZI* (1989), pp. 149–152, with Pakistan as an example for the rather similar situation throughout Southeast Asia; for Latin America cf., e.g. *PALMA* (1987), pp. 45–47.

family income, the boy's family is at least not financially burdened by the training.

The odd-job apprenticeship can last for only a short while or longer (up to seven years), but without special training periods and objectives. Odd-job apprentices, instead, often just assume for long the role of helpers in all kinds of work, and are only gradually entrusted with more qualified tasks. It also is no exception that odd-job apprenticeships are extended beyond training necessity, since many workshop owners do not primarily consider themselves as masters of an apprentice, but are interested in exploiting them as cheap – because unskilled – labour as long as possible[80].

Learning in odd-job apprenticeship is hardly systematic, with no particularly specified training content or schedule, and mainly through observation and imitation[81]. Its type and quality depends on the work to be done, the skills of the master, and his willingness to impart (some of) his own skills to his odd-job apprentices. Specific entrepreneurial skills enabling for setting up a business later, such as business organization, calculation of prices or negotiation techniques can hardly be acquired, although a little more – simply through observation – than in a merely centre-based vocational training. Normally, activities of this kind are not carried out in the presence of apprentices, and exclusively by the owner of the enterprise, who – as already pointed out – often would need himself some training in these skills.

Since also on part of the youngsters themselves the apprenticeship generally is not regarded as a "real" apprenticeship in which certain demands could be made regarding the extent, type and duration of the training, but rather as an income-earning activity with the additional chance of skill acquisition, it does not have a particularly binding character. Depending on their own interests or emergencies, each side, therefore, feels fairly free to terminate the relationship, if necessary also at very short notice.

---

80 The importance of odd-job apprentices as cheap labour is also reflected in the fact that in many small and micro-enterprises they often account for over half of the workers. This is reported by *ZDUNNEK* (1988) for Nigeria and *HOPPERS* (1985) for Lusaka. In many Thai small and micro-enterprises the situation is similar. In all too many cases, the availability of cheap odd-job apprentices is vital for the economic survival of small and micro-enterprises, not only in the informal sector.

81 This type of skill acquisition probably explains the phenomenon that especially informally trained craftsmen and workers often have – especially in Asia – an astonishing talent for copying "prototypes", whereas their innovative skills are less developed.

With a growing number of secondary school graduates, especially in urban areas – also from the informal sector – there is a tendency in informal vocational training, too, for better educated youngsters pushing those with less or no school education out of the latter's former "domain" of vocational training possibilities. As a consequence, the majority of young people from the informal sector, who already have almost no access to formal vocational training, have increasingly less chances also of informal apprenticeship training. This, by the way, clearly confirms the need for improved and generally accessible primary school education for the children from urban slums and in the rural areas.

The inadequacies and weaknesses of this form of informal occupation-oriented training should not be overlooked. They refer mainly to

– the limitation of technical skill acquisition to the knowledge, skills and experience of the owner of the enterprise and/or his workers and their willingness to impart it to the odd-job apprentices, and the largely missing chance to also acquire some entrepreneurial skills with regard to own business creation;

– the (almost) total lack of vocational theory training, let alone some required (additional) general education, as well as to the fact that learning is almost exclusively based on imitation – which does little to stimulate creativity and innovative skills[82];

– the often patriarchal and arbitrary behaviour of the workshop owner towards his odd-job apprentices who run the risk of being immediately dismissed in case of disobedience;

– the fact that especially small and micro-enterprises are often somehow forced to exploit the labour of the cheap, yet gradually better trained odd-job apprentices in order to sustain their own

---

82 Experience shows that (traditional) small and micro-enterprises hardly act innovatively at their own initiative. The ability and willingness to acquire new technological information is all the more limited, the less such information is easily related to the perceived business environment of the enterprise and previous work experience, and the more own initiative is required to obtain it. The adaptation of possible innovations also takes place extremely hesitantly, if at all, without external impetus. However, especially the repair and maintenance of machines, electrical appliances or motor vehicles and the production of goods or the provision of services, which are influenced – more or less directly – by the technological or fashionable changes occurring in the modern sector, require a flexible adjustment to resp. adaptation of new technologies, materials or designs, and the acquisition of correspondingly required new technical know-how and skills.

existence, with the result that the training is often neglected even where the workshop owner has good intentions.

Conclusion

(i)   Despite these weaknesses, the informal training in form of such odd-job apprenticeships must be acknowledged as the often only possibility for the majority of young people from the informal sector to realize some kind of occupation-oriented training beside the need to earn money or at least not to be a financial burden for the family. Also with respect to the fact that it has always existed – and apparently not without achievements – its capacity and significance as a low-cost and widely available vocational training option for socially disadvantaged young people with little school education, should be recognized and promoted. It should not be overlooked, however, that informal apprenticeship training is only possible where small and medium-sized enterprises with an artisanal structure and production exist.
As this is the case in rural areas only to a very limited extent, for the majority of young rural people even this form of vocational training is a rare option unless they migrate to urban areas.
(ii)   Within the framework of (bilateral) vocational training assistance, some careful promotion and regulatory measures sensitively adapted to the prevailing conditions, are conceivable in order to, at least partly, offset the negative aspects of informal training, for example, through
– direct subsidies for enterprises providing odd-job apprenticeship places, possibly with an additional bonus payment for each apprentice who finds adequate (self-)employment after the training, in conjunction with
– protective regulations for the youngsters, especially as regards some certainty that the odd-job apprenticeship will be continued until a level of qualification agreed on in advance has been reached, and a commitment by the "training enterprises" to observe a certain minimum training standard, both in return for the subsidy payments;
– financial grants for the apprentices, enough to also cover the indirect costs of the training;
– offers of short-term vocational training for *all* persons working in the enterprise, and, in addition, a compulsory off-workshop vocational theory training and related general education for the

apprentices in order to at least partially compensate for the immanent tendency of small and micro-enterprises – and thus informal apprenticeship training – to be technologically stagnant and adverse to creative learning[83];

– apart from the training, advisory services for the "training enterprises", wherever desired, so as to give the owners an incentive to accept some intervention in the odd-job apprenticeship training and, at the same time, assistance to improve their business situation in such a way that they will not have to rely anymore on the maximum exploitation of the labour of the cheap apprentices;

– an arrangement with the owner of the enterprise to the effect that also an odd-job apprentice – as was customery in traditional informal apprenticeship – is given the opportunity to gradually familiarize themselves with business organization tasks and the network of business and social relations, which would enable him to later use these informal channels of obtaining information, materials and loans, in case he sets up his own businesses;

– a special cooperation with skilled workers who had worked in the modern sector before setting up their own small or micro-enterprises where they often also train apprentices[84], with regard to the aspect that these skilled workers often acquired in their previous jobs modern technical knowledge and skills, and hence are generally more able and willing to apply innovative technologies. Furthermore, they may contribute during the apprenticeship training to "socialize" the apprentices for their easier occupational and/or social integration into "modern" society.

(iii) Altogether, however, any intervention in the structure of informal apprenticeship training must set out to maintain its character as informal vocational training system especially for young people from the informal sector, since it would prove difficult to otherwise provide a similarly accessible option for vocational

---

83 For this reason, the National Vocational Training Institute (NVTI) in Ghana tried in cooperation with the Accra Technology Centre to familiarize masters and apprentices with innovative technical equipment and techniques through advice and demonstration training directly in small and micro-enterprises. Especially for the apprentices, additional supportive short training courses were offered at the NVTI. In practice, however, this measure is rather unpopular with many masters who fear to lose their already semi-skilled apprentices after that additional training. The apprentices themselves often can hardly keep up with the theoretical lessons because of their low level of general education. Finally, the intended transfer of innovative technological know-how from the apprentice to the master hardly takes place in reality, since the traditional hierarchical relationship between master and apprentice rarely allows either of them a reversal of their roles; cf. *HAKAM* (1983), pp. 64 f.

84 Cf. *FAPOHUNDA* (1990), p. 78.

training to them. This rules out any kind of assistance which would be accompanied by massive, but selective financial allocations and excessive Government intervention.

(2) The guild-like informal apprenticeship
has a special tradition especially in some West African countries[85] For many artisanal trades in which skills have been handed down from one generation to the next, it is still today the prevailing form of vocational training, although more recent studies[86] indicate that the permanent economic crisis does gradually also undermine the socio-cultural basis of the traditional apprenticeship. It is moving closer to the above described odd-job apprenticeship training which has long since been common in the more modern artisanal trades anyway, also in West Africa.

The traditional apprenticeship is occasionally presented as an exemplary or even alternative model for the vocational training of young people from the informal sector, since it is seen as to be open to youngsters between the ages of about 15 and 25 without any school-leaving certificate[87]. The main differences to the odd-job apprenticeship training are that
– one essential condition usually is that the apprentice belongs to the ethnic group, kinship or relatives of the master, and the commitment by the apprentice's family to pay him an apprenticeship fee. In return, the master takes a rather complex obligation to care for the apprentice, which consists of giving him accommodation and food, and imparting to the best of this abilities all his knowledge and skills to his apprentice to enable him to later work as skilled craftsman in his own business;
– at the end of training the apprentice often receives from his master some tools, sometimes even a machine on borrow, and initial social support to set up his own business, which includes the formal admission as journeyman in the respective artisanal trade, this

[85] Especially for Ghana, cf. *HAKAM* (1983); for Nigeria, cf. *OYENEYE* (1980), pp. 373–384; and for Zambia, cf. *HOPPERS* (1985).
[86] Cf. e.g. *HOPPERS* (1985), p. 104; a vivid account of this change is given in an interview with an originally traditional master tailor from Sierra Leone, who explains why he himself had no choice but to depart from the system of guild-like apprenticeship training; cf. *UNIVERSITY OF SIERRA LEONE* (1987), pp. 19–31.
[87] This impression is more implicit rather than explicit from the relevant literature. Own observations in a number of African countries indicate more that, especially in urban areas, these guild-like and generally old-established artisanal enterprises – at least in the meantime – well attach importance to the school education of their apprentices.

opening up to him a network of social and economic relations supportive to his business development;
- a kind of "guild regulation" guarantees – or at least did so in the past – that the masters of a "guild" only trains as many apprentices as have a secured chance for subsequent (self-)employment.

In the informal apprenticeship, too, the apprentice can learn "only" as much as the master's knowledge and experience can teach, although the master usually takes great pride in training competent journeymen. Although learning also takes place on the basis of observation and imitation, there is continuous guidance by the master or an experienced worker. The apprentice is increasingly integrated into the work process, until he has acquired all the skills and knowledge required to independently make the products of that trade. The duration of a traditional apprenticeship is left to the discretion of the master. It depends on the trade, age, level of education and learning ability of the apprentice, and varies between a few months and five years.

A formal, i.e. recognized apprenticeship certificate cannot be acquired this way. Nevertheless, this guild-like apprenticeship has a recognized high (market) value. Correspondingly, depending on individual and family ambitions and the market situation, the youngster can after training work as a journeyman in his master's enterprise or in any other with a similar production and organizational structure, or look for – and normally find – skilled labour employment in the modern industrial sector. Many apprentices in traditional artisanal trades also choose to initially work as self-employed itinerant "service craftsmen" and to set up their own workshop later with greater experience and a certain amount of savings[88].

What has contributed to erode the traditional system of guild-like informal apprenticeship is the fact that for mere economic survival many small and micro-enterprises even in the traditional crafts have started – because of the apprenticeship fees – to accept more apprentices than they themselves or other enterprises can possibly take on afterwards, or the local or regional market can absorb in the medium term as self-employed craftsmen[89]. This has led – due to the

---

[88] At least up until the beginning of the 1970s apparently all three possibilities were actually open to these apprentices, whether because of the good quality of their training or the better employment opportunities at that time; cf. *HAKAM* (1983), p. 63.
[89] *HAKAM* (1983), pp. 59, 68 f., points out that many traditional craft enterprises nowadays rely on the apprenticeship fees for their survival.

large number of apprentices – to a deterioration of the quality of the training, the more so as there are masters who no longer maintain their traditional profession ethics. Since many of these apprentices cannot find adequate employment, which means that their families paid the apprenticeship fee in vain.

Conclusion

(i) As regards accessibility of the guild-like informal apprenticeship for target groups from the informal sector, it must be understood that these apprentices normally come from a relatively small circle of traditional yet "established" urban society. The really traditional crafts are as a profession by no means open to "everyone".
In view of the desolate economic conditions in African countries, most young people from the informal sector there are, anyway, less likely than ever able to consider an apprenticeship for which they have to pay instead of earning a little money. To girls the traditional apprenticeship is hardly accessible, at all, for reasons of socio-cultural tradition.
(ii) As regards *quantitative* employment impacts, the traditional apprenticeship, therefore, can hardly be considered as generally more efficient as compared, for example, formal vocational training in Government-run training institutions, especially since the departure from the guild-like regulations for the admission of new apprentices makes their subsequent income-earning and employment opportunities in the meantime also fully dependent on the overall economic situation and the competition on the labour market.
One difference, however, is that the knowledge and skills acquired in informal apprenticeship are easier applicable also in the subsistence sector than those from formal training in a vocational training centre.
(iii) On the whole, the guild-like informal apprenticeship as prevailing in West Africa appears to be an evolved and self-contained system rooted in the socio-cultural and economic context of its evolution. It is fair, therefore, to be sceptical about its applicability to other regions, which does not mean that it is not worth retaining it in countries where it still exists. Regulatory or even directive intervention, however, would be inconsistent with its very character.

(3) Commercial private occupation-oriented training offers have existed in bigger cities in Africa since the 1970s, for example, the "garage schools"[90]. They developed when master craftsmen realized that income from apprenticeship fees – especially in fields of modern service crafts, such as repair work – can be more lucrative than their own productive work. The "garage schools" were purely commercial training places, often also providing accommodation, in which a master craftsman took on between 10 and 20 apprentices at the same time, as opposed to one or two in the normal informal apprenticeship. Among the growing number of rural-urban migrants they were apparently in very popular demand – not the least for the possibility of accommodation – despite the high apprenticeship fees charged.

Following their recognition by the Government as technical colleges, the training became oriented to formal certification, which led to an increase in training costs. The former "garage schools" then ceased to be an opportunity for occupation-oriented training for poorer young people from the informal sector.

A more recent form of informal occupation-oriented training are the commercial private training institutes which are opening in growing numbers especially in the big cities in Asia and Latin America in response to the qualitatively and quantitatively insufficient vocational training in existing Government-run vocational training institutions.

In cities such as Bangkok or Lima their training courses provide a qualification mainly for jobs in the modern commercial service sector. While these training institutes themselves do not necessarily belong to the informal sector, they are attended in particular by secondary-school graduates from the urban informal sector with the aspiration of acquiring sufficient knowledge for a simple office job[91]. The fact that the (also female) course participants – just as in traditional apprenticeship – are willing to pay an often substantial fee for the training should not lead to the conclusion that they all come from better-off families. On the contrary, many youngsters, but also dismissed employees from enterprises in the modern sector view these courses as their only hope of (again) finding employment. They often borrow the money for the course fees with the idea of paying it

---

90 This is described particularly for Kenya in *KING* (1977), pp. 50 f.
91 Similar approaches can apparently also be found in Nigeria where typing offices have been established to train secretaries. The course participants pay a fee, and while being trained also carry out contract work for the typing office; cf. *ZDUNNEK* (1988), p. 42.

back from the income of a subsequent job. Women are met at these training institutes in above-average numbers.

Conclusion

(i) The primary advantage of the training offers by commercial private training institutes is their comparatively easy accessibility for, in principle, everyone from the informal sector with primary education and a certain mobility, especially also for women. However, this is an option more in urban than in rural areas. As regards the employment generating effects, the repeatedly mentioned limitations resulting from the overall economic and labour market situation also apply here, of course.

(ii) The commercial private training institutes should not, because of their profit orientation, be ruled out right away as an alternative for a labour market-oriented occupational qualification of various target groups especially from the urban informal sector. Instead, a cross-country study should be carried out to obtain more detailed information on the way they operate, the kind and quality of the training offered, and the qualification of the trainers employed[92]. This would allow a more sound assessment of their possible contribution to occupation-oriented training and education for target groups from the informal sector, and maybe even their suitability as counterparts in bi- or multilateral vocational training assistance.

(iii) A promotion of commercial private training institutes as regards type and quality of the training offered as well as an increase in the number of such institutes could well be considered within the framework of (bilateral) vocational training assistance. Conceivable could be

– organizational and management assistance for new or existing institutes, or financial support for their adequate endowment, especially for institutes in (the vicinity of) urban squatter areas or in small rural towns, and/or to introduce (more) training courses especially suitable for women;

– the provision and/or joint development of curricula and teaching aids, especially also for training courses oriented to the occupation

[92] This is similarly also suggested by World Bank staff; cf. *MIDDLETON* et al. (1990), p. 35, and pp. 19 ff. with comments on the promotion of "private training". The significance of private "backstreet colleges" as a possibility of training and educating informal sector target groups is also pointed out by *KING* (1989), pp. 29 f.

opportunities particularly of target groups with little previous school education;
– the advanced professional and pedagogical training for the teaching staff of these training institutes, to be provided at Government-run vocational training institutions and/or by local NGOs;
– agreements on minimum standards regarding the training quality and the content of the curricula, the observation of which could be "rewarded" with fee subsidies to the course participants, which would positively influence the appeal of the training institutes concerned and hence their market share among potential training clients.

6.1.4 *Training and Education Related to the Environment-determined Occupational Options*

In view of the fact that in future, more than ever, not all job-seekers and not even all graduates will be able to find employment in the modern sector, approaches of non-formal occupation-oriented training and education will become increasingly relevant which turn greater attention to the environment-determined opportunities and options realistically given to the majority of people from the informal sector, including work in the subsistence sector.
The experience with the "Talleres Públicos" in Costa Rica and the "Village Polytechnics" in Kenya show – in different aspects – the discrepancy between wishful thinking and real opportunities in which occupation-oriented training and employment prospects of target groups from the informal sector have to be realized. The "Community Polytechnic" visited in India, on the other hand, is an example that an environment-adapted, also subsistence-oriented approach to vocational training can well have very positive results, if there is a thorough on-site planning and a flexible implementation which takes into consideration the actual learning and occupation opportunities of the target groups concerned.
As a completely different approach, yet one also responding to the environment-determined needs and options of people from the informal sector, finally also training measures within the framework of Government or municipal infrastructure programmes are worth

mentioning, although the imparted skills are rather limited and purpose-oriented.

(1) The "Talleres Públicos"
which the INA set up as "public workshops"[93] in peripheral urban areas and small rural towns in Costa Rica, are combined production and training facilities in which men and women of all ages (beginning at the age of 12) also without any school education, and no other enrolment requirements, have the possibility
– to use the available tools and equipment to produce goods for their own consumption or for sale, provided that they have sufficient technical skills;
– to participate in a technical training which is purpose-oriented with regard to their realistic occupation opportunities, also in the subsistence sector, and adapted to their learning opportunities and potentials, and for which they merely have to make a – timewise flexible – commitment to attend a minimum number of hours per month.

The skill training offered and the type of equipment provided are decided for each "public workshop" with respect to the local qualification needs and labour demand as identified beforehand by the INA. The objective of the technical training is to qualify the participants to an extent that they afterwards will be able
– to meet their own basic needs to a greater or qualitatively better extent than before through subsistence work and thus to perhaps also reduce their family's need for cash income;
– if intended, establish a small – maybe cooperative – business, or to work in self-employment, and especially for women to start or improve their own commercial home production;
– if possible, to take part in more industrial vocation-oriented training courses qualifying for a wage-earning employment in the modern or in the informal sector.

The training by (local) INA trainers – in the level depending on the actual local level in technology – takes place either as individual advice on request, or in group work. It is based largely on modular learning units similar to the "Modules of Employable Skills"

---

[93] Cf. *CHANG* (1985); also *LENHART* (1989), pp. 197 f.; it should be noted, however, that this is not a major change in the INA's vocational training programme, but rather a kind of pilot programme. The "Talleres Públicos" of the INA to a certain extent also served as a model for a similar programme of the INFOTEP in the Dominican Republic; cf. *ARNOLD* (1987), pp. 152–166.

(MES)[94] developed by the ILO. As an advantage, the MES training approach allows to choose individual learning programmes suited to the specific qualification needs, starting level of technical skills and time constraints of each participant. On the other hand, it may be over-optimistic to expect the meaningful application of modular learning units – which have been developed also for self-training purposes – to be mastered with little guidance by people from the informal sector with their particular learning disadvantages as described above.

As the MES concept, in particular, is repeatedly presented – not necessarily in connection with the "Talleres Públicos" – as a suitable instrument for (autodidactic) training especially of target groups from the informal sector for reason of its low costs and time-flexible adjustment, a few critical remarks may be in place here:

– The use of MES learning materials not only requires sound skills in reading, writing and mathematics, but also – especially for self-training – the ability to learn unguidedly and systematically on the basis of logically structured didactic material. This is expecting too much not only of illiterates and people with little school education. Even skilled craftsmen who can read, write and even do calculations reasonably well, have – as experience shows – difficulties to think in abstract terms and to understand and apply technical drawings without any guidance;

– Since the MES have been developed on the basis of industrial technologies, both the training – and learning – of many MES qualifications and their application at work requires tools and equipment, often a workshop, which, at best, will be found in modern industrial enterprises, but normally not in a small or micro-enterprise, let alone with a village craftsman in the informal sector;

– A consequence of the segmentation in partial qualifications is

---

94 The MES are based on vocational profiles prevailing in industrialized countries, the overall qualifications for which are respectively segmented into partial qualifications which can be applied separately. In theory, it is possible – over any length of time – to obtain the overall qualification in such an occupation by successively acquiring all partial qualifications. Another possibility is to acquire only partial qualifications from one evocational profile, or – through any combination of partial qualifications from different vocational profiles – a kind of cross-vocational qualification which often tends to meet best the qualification needs of the target groups in question. From the conceptual idea of the MES, qualification should be possible in training courses as well as in private studies. The ILO elaborated training manuals for students and additional training material for MES instructors. For a detailed description and critical appraisal of the MES concept cf. *MASLANKOWSKI* (1987), pp. 135–145; *LUSZCYK* (1987), pp. 147–172; and *HANSEN* (1987), pp. 163–176.

that technical interdependencies are not easily realized and understood, especially since vocational theory is normally not taught. As regards this lack of vocational theory, the MES concept, by the way, has the same weakness as the merely practical training in informal apprenticeship.

In the "Talleres Públicos", these shortcomings can be partly offset, in principle, by technically and didactically adequately trained instructors. Although there are among them reportedly also local craftsmen or advanced training participants, they can, in practice, often not really cope with the requirements. As a result, there is a tendency for people with little previous training and education not to start a training at all, for fear of uselessness, or to drop out after a short while, the more as nobody is obliged to carry on.

For this reason, many of the "Talleres Públicos" often operate less as training centres, but indeed more as "public *workshops*" where people with sufficient technical skills but no suitable tools at their own disposal go to use the equipment available at the workshops free-of-charge. In this function, the "Talleres Públicos" are extremely useful, and the fact that they are highly frequented for this purpose proves the respective demand.

Conclusion

(i) The MES and similar modular vocational concepts were probably put to most meaningful use in a field in which they have hardly been applied so far: in the advanced training of technical instructors who could in this way – perhaps even in private studies – indeed acquire additional partial qualifications to improve their technical know-how. In conjunction with some (advanced) pedagogical training, the MES could be used to qualify technical trainers and advisers to small and micro-entrepreneurs – also in rural areas – trade-specifically and with special focus on the given (self-)employment opportunities, technical possibilities and skill level, and the specific learning opportunities and potentials of these target groups. Such "training of trainer" courses could, for example, be held at existing vocational training centres.

(ii) Where modular training concepts are applied for first-time technical training, as also partly in the "Talleres Públicos", the chances and success of learning, especially for fairly unskilled participants, will depend decisively on the availability of qualified and committed instructors. In view of the discrepancy between the required and existing learning opportunities and potentials, as normally observed in reality, the MES cannot be regarded as a particularly suitable instrument for the occupation-oriented qualification of young people or even adults from the informal sector, and certainly not for autodidactic purposes.

(iii) As regards the "Talleres Públicos" themselves, they are apparently very popular and undoubtedly meaningful in their function as publicly accessible workshops, especially in areas with only few artisanal workshops.

As an approach to non-formal vocational training for young people with little prior (vocational) education, however, they can say to be suitable in their present form only with reservation – at least according to available information – in view of the inadequate number and reportedly also inadequate qualification of the instructors, a problem which will be hardly solved without external assistance.

(2) Vocational training of rural youth with regard to their environment-determined (self-)employment opportunities

was intended with the "Village Polytechnics" (VP) set up in Kenya following independence[95]. They were originally established by churches with the idea to qualify primary-school leavers[96] through a rural-based non-formal vocational training for self-employment in or near their villages, in an effort to reduce rural-urban migration and to induce an endogenous rural development.

The original VP concept can be summarized as follows:

– The training content and curricula, laid down with participation from the village communities, were adapted to the development and employment options determined by the rural environment, and to the target group-specific learning opportunities and potentials;

– The material, financial and human resources were mainly to be provided through the village communities' own contributions in the

---

95 A detailed description of the "Village Polytechnics" and the process of their gradual formalization which finally in 1979 ended in extensive Government regulation and ultimately a take-over by the responsible ministry, is given by STURMANN (1990). Since 1985, they have been called "Youth Polytechnics" in order to dispel the colonial associations of the term "village"; *ibid.*, p. 96.

96 It was hoped that the non-admittance of youngsters without primary school graduation, combined with a minimum age of 16, would ensure that the VP graduates would be able – both age- and educationwise – to afterwards go into self-employment. The decision to exclude secondary-school graduates and not to issue formal certificates of graduation was to prevent the enrolment of young villagers whose training aspirations were obviously oriented to subsequent employment in the urban modern sector.

form of training fees, cash donations, transfer of land and hut to the VP, and the commitment of local craftsmen as voluntary instructors as well as through contract work by the VP workshops for the village communities;
– Most of the practical training were to take place directly in the villages in the workshops of local craftsmen and within home production;
– Apart from the technical qualification, the youngsters were also taught some entrepreneurial skills required to run a rural workshop, the setting up of which would be facilitated by back-up tuition, initial support from the instructors in the acquisition of orders and the provision of a first set of tools and material.

The VP concept, thus, contained quite a few elements for which it still – or perhaps again – appears not at all unsuitable for rural target groups, especially in more remote areas, and not just for primary school leavers. It is, therefore, worth examining which factors led to its failure in Kenya at that time.

Since they were established, the core problem for the VPs – which finally led to their formalization and the abandonment of the approach to orientate the training to the rural environment-determined (self-)employment options – apparently was the non-formal character of the training itself. This did in no way corresponded to the real aspirations of the youngsters and their parents for a subsequent employment in town.

Furthermore, the assumption that the VPs could be financially sustained primarily by the village communities themselves was unrealistic, since also at that time the majority of the villages were subsistence farmers who – for the reason just mentioned – were unwilling and normally also unable to bear the financial burden or to set aside working time to make contributions in labour or kind instead. The VPs, thus, remained dependent on external financial assistance, which was problematic insofar as their training and development concept did not correspond with the development ideas of national educational policy planners.

Finally, most of the VP instructors themselves were graduates from a formal vocational training institution, and hence not well-prepared for the various tasks facing a non-formal instructor, even more at village level. Due to their lack of personal contact with the village community and the rural living and working conditions, they were often neither motivated nor able to identify the actual qualification needs of young villagers and their rural employment opportunities. Instead, they offered the standardized vocational training courses for carpenters, bricklayers or tailors, familiar to them from their own vocational training. A practical training in the village workshops or in the home production was just as seldom as a back-up tuition for graduates who really wanted to set up their own workshop.

Altogether, the youngsters ultimately were qualified neither for an employment in town – which most of them basically wanted – nor for a successful start into self-employment in the rural areas. Under all aspects, therefore, the VP training made no sense to them and was increasingly rejected. The result was a rapid formalization of the training courses following the take-over – and finally renaming – of the VPs by the Government. Secondary school graduates who have to struggle with all the known problems stemming from the shortage of jobs in the modern sector, since then have been the target group almost exclusively.

Conclusion

(i) The failure to meet the original objectives of the VPs certainly cannot be explained only be referring to the fact that a non-formal qualification for self-employment in the rural areas did not correspond to the aspirations of the target group, which were oriented towards training for wage employment in the urban modern sector, because of the expected higher income and social prestige[97].

With the growing disillusion among the rural population as regards their employment opportunities in town and especially in the modern sector, a concept like the VPs will probably, anyway, have a more positive appeal – particularly in Africa – nowadays than in the development euphoria during the first 10 to 15 years following independence, especially in more remote villages[98].

(ii) Therefore, the basic elements of the original VP content should still be regarded, in principle, as a suitable approach for occupation-oriented training and education of rural youth – girls and boys – of

---

[97] This view is taken by *STURMANN* (1990), esp. pp. 83, 116 ff. Other reports already in the 1970s, however, stated that even at that time also in Kenya young people were looking for apprenticeship in the informal sector, due to lack of other employment or vocational training opportunities; cf. *KING* (1977), pp. 59 and 170.

[98] The National Vocational Training Institute in Ghana would also appear to take this view. In cooperation with the GVS, it has set up since 1977 until now six rural Vocational Training Centres where "rural builders" are trained in the sense of a polyvalent qualification oriented to their environment-determined (self-)employment opportunities. A critical yet positive short report is given by *GRÅN* (1989).

all ages, since it takes into realistic consideration their environment-determined (self-)employment opportunities. Especially in rural areas (still) fairly detached from industrial development and related (labour) markets, and also from modern "urban" influences, the VP concept may well be a viable approach.

Some modifications, however, should be made, if it is to be promoted in the context of (bilateral) vocational training assistance:

— The training itself and related employment aspirations of the rural target groups should be consciously oriented — also by means of social education — towards subsistence occupations, too, and a qualitative strengthening of their self-help potentials, with accordingly adapted curricula;

— Qualifications needed for social and communal services as well as the introduction of innovative environment-adapted technologies should be made part of the training objectives and the training contents;

— In particular, the more immobile poor rural target groups which, for some reason, are tied to the villages with hardly any occupation-oriented training and (outside) employment opportunities — like most married women, subsistence farmers and their children, school drop-outs or (semi-)illiterates — should be addressed with high priority;

— The instructors must be better prepared as regards both their technical and socio-pedagogical skills and their motivation for work in a rural environment, and be recruited, as far as possible, among local master craftsmen and journeymen, and — for "women trades"

— also among apt older women particularly respected in their communities.

(iii) To what extent Government institutions may be able to undertake the planning and implementation of such an approach, will largely depend on the country's policy orientation in the fields of rural development, basic and vocational education, and employment creation programmes for economically and socially disadvantaged groups in society.

In many cases, local NGOs or church(-related) institutions will be more likely found suitable, and may also show greater interest. Wherever possible, cooperation models between Government institutions and local NGOs or other self-help organizations ("linking") should be considered to set up as effective as possible institutional (counterpart) structures. Within the framework of (bilateral) vocational training assistance, such linking models should actively be promoted through institutional strengthening measures for Government institutions *and* NGO.

(3) Non-formal training for rural youth oriented to their environment-determined, largely subsistence-based (self-) employment opportunities

is offered at the Community Polytechnic in Yellareddy (CPY)[99]. The CPY was set up by the Council for Technical and Vocational Training (CTVT) of the Church of South India[100], with financial assistance from the EZE, in a distantly rural area in Andhra Andhra Pradesh (Central India) for the non-formal occupation-oriented training of young rural people with no (much) primary school education.

Within a preparatory pilot phase between 1985 and 1987, a comprehensive socio-economic study was conducted in the 31 villages of the CPY's catchment area as part of the planning process. This was to find out the level of school education, the locally available resources and the level of technological development in the villages as well as to identify the priority training needs of the rural people with regard to subsistence work and potential (self-)employment opportunities for (additional) rural craftsmen.

Among other things, the study revealed that there were hardly any primary and secondary schools in this region. Only 9.2 % of the children attend primary school up to five years or more, i.e. over 90 % also of young people are illiterate. For the overwhelming majority of rural youth, therefore, the question is not whether and with what kind of training they could seek employment in town, let alone in the modern sector. But they will have no other option than to further organize their survival basically in the rural subsistence economy – if not sheer poverty will ultimately drive them to a big city where they end up at the lower levels of the urban informal sector.

This was the understanding of the initiators of the CPY. Hence they saw –right from the beginning – that the objective of an occupation-oriented qualification of school drop-outs and young illiterates from the villages must also be very much subsistence-oriented.

99 The CPY was visited during the reconnaissance mission to India in June 1990; for a brief description cf. *LANZET* (1989)
100 The CTVT has a wide range of activities, with conceptual and practical work in the fields of education, occupation-oriented training, community development, and programmes for "awareness creation" and "leadership training". It also regards itself as documentation and information centre especially for appropriate and rural technologies. In the latter field, in particular, the CTVT is interested in more support and exchange of ideas, according to its director.

Consequently, the CPY intends to impart to the young people such know-how and skills which
– are definitely in local demand, because they are essential for providing goods and services for basic needs, so that the youngsters will later have the chance of at least occasionally obtaining some cash income – or equivalent revenue – as self-employed rural craftsmen;
– they can, at the same time, usefully apply in subsistence work to improve their own housing and living environment, although in reality there will mostly be a combination of both gainful and subsistence self-employment;
– will – in the long run – help to raise the technological level in the villages, and contribute to stimulate the rural market economy with a needs-oriented and affordable supply of local products and services.
Especially with regard to the last-mentioned objective, the CPY hopes to gradually develop into a kind of "information and service centre on appropriate technology" for the surrounding villages. It is convinced that rural demand which in turn is the basis for income generation from non-agricultural work, can only be generated in a simultaneous process of appropriate technical skill training for rural people on the one hand, and awareness creation and information in the villages about suitable technologies available and affordable for them to improve their living and working conditions by their own efforts, on the other hand.
As conclusion from the findings of the above mentioned preparatory study, in the first stage the CPY's training programme was decided to be implemented as follows:
– During an initial phase, priority is given to a training of know-how and skills required to better meet the basic needs in housing, later also in water supply, and then for the improvement of local transportation;
– In view of the extremely low level of school education, formal enrolment requirements of any kind made little sense. But for the same reason, the technical vocational training must be accompanied by some general and also social education, without which the intended training in basic accounting and other necessary skills for small business administration would be impossible;
– A certain vocational theory training is considered important, yet limited to the minimum required to develop good practical vocational skills. Emphasis, thus, is on practical training. Learning how to do technical improvization and how to make optimum use of locally available materials is also part of the training;

- Both the equipment of the CPY workshops and the training content are adjusted to the technological level, available resources and assumed development potentials in the region. The training content in detail is to be flexibly adapted to changing market and employment opportunities in the area;
- The technical standard of the training courses is kept at a level to which skilled local craftsmen still can be trained to become technical instructors at the CPY.

With a technical skill training which is compatible to the technological development level prevailing in the region, it is hoped to demonstrate to young rural people that (self-)employment in the rural areas and an improvement of the rural living conditions are in fact possible – and often more sustainable – without a great deal of external "modern" technology. The other purpose is to counter the aspiration among the young people that the training at the CPY would also qualify for employment in town.

At present, there are four one- resp. two-year training courses for carpenters, bricklayers, electricians and welders, which implies that only boys can be trained[101]. The duration of the training can be individually extended, if the instructors and the student feel this is necessary. All of the youngsters between the ages of 13 and 25 come from very poor lower-caste families from villages within a radius from the CPY of roughly 15 km. The applicants whose number is far above the current capacity of the CPY, are mainly selected with respect to their technical skill and aptitude[102].

---

[101] An expansion is planned for the near future with training courses in sheet-metal work, blacksmithing and spray lacker coating. In the next phase, training opportunities are intended to be created for girls and women, too, through mobile training units directly in the villages, taking into account their immobility rooted on social tradition and household obligations.
In cooperation with the Medak Diocese of the Church of South India, the CTVT has also set up a "Self-employment Training Centre for Girls" (SETCG) near the rural market centre of Wadiarum. Here, women and girls from the surrounding villages have the opportunity to attend functional primary education and/or occupation-oriented non-formal training courses which with a flexible course timetable particularly take into account the agricultural cycle. The courses are oriented to the qualification needs of the women with regard to the "profit potential" of the occupational fields and activities compulsory or accessible to them. Training at the SETCG is always accompanied by basic education as well as awareness creation and training in the fields of nutrition, health care and hygiene. Particularly interested and apt participants of the typing course are given the possibility to afterwards attend a (further) non-formal secretarial training course at a polytechnic in Hyderabad, in which they also learn how to operate PCs. The graduates of this course stand a good chance of finding a job, since there is a considerable, still largely unsatisfied demand in private enterprises and public administration for employees with this qualification.

The practical training is five days a week. A great deal of the building skills are acquired by gradually constructing the workshops and accommodation facilities of the CPY under the guidance and supervision of the instructors. A further weekday is reserved for lessons in vocational theory and general education, social education, and – for the advanced students – basic training in business administration.

All the instructors are skilled craftsmen from the area, who have a reasonably well-paid employment at the CPY and, thus, are motivated to stay.

Conclusion

(i) Altogether, the CPY approach of a non-formal vocational training oriented to the realistic (self-)employment opportunities as determined by the rural environment and economy – and hence also subsistence-oriented – can be viewed as an extremely suitable and exemplary approach to occupation-oriented training *and* education of young people in rural areas. This is said with regard to the planning process as well as the objectives orientation and the implementation design. There is no reason seen why such an approach should not be applicable in its core elements also in other rural areas, and also within the framework of (bilateral) vocational training assistance.

(ii) It would certainly do injustice to the CPY approach to consider as conceptual weakness the fact that special training offers for girls have not yet passed the planning stage, or that there was a relatively high number of drop-outs. Instead, both should be understood as indication – or confirmation of what is well-known, in principle – that

– setting up a vocational training institution for target groups from the rural informal sector, in particular, which really takes into account the local environment-determined conditions – including socio-cultural factors – and occupation opportunities, can only take place step-by-step, since the necessary learning process to understand the relevant social and economic context is generally slow;

---

102 According to the CPY Director, a total of 129 youngsters have started a training since the courses began in 1988 until June 1990, 28 of whom quit – mainly because of marriage. Of the 101 graduates, half now work as self-employed rural craftsmen, whereas 35 have returned to the CPY for further technical training. The remaining 16 do also work, but in fields other than the ones in which they received training.

– consequently, the objectives pursued by such a rural vocational training institution can only be achieved over a longer period of time;
– negative statistical data often reflect socio-cultural factors which are beyond the influence of any such project, and which may even have to be accepted as part of normal life for the target group concerned.

(iii) It cannot be overlooked that the success of the CPY – as regards both the training measures and the construction progress – is owed decisively to the technical qualification and management skills of its Director, an engineer with many years of professional experience in the construction trade. Without him, it would hardly be possible to master the complex task of the CPY construction planning and supervision, curriculum development, training of the instructors, social work, and CPY management at the same time, and all this with a very limited number of personnel. Furthermore, both he and his wife who has taken on the task of primary and social education of the youngsters, appear to have an outstanding sense of social commitment and extraordinary pedagogical skill

This fundamental problem of any approach which involves working directly with and for poor people, to depend on the *long-term* availability of advisers, managers, instructors and social workers who have technical competence and pedagogical skill as much as human qualities and social dedication, will be taken up in greater detail at a later stage.

(iv) Another essential aspect of an approach such as the CPY's is the cooperation of Government agencies and/or foreign (NGO) donors with local NGOs, at least if it is taken up in the framework of (bilateral) vocational training assistance. As much as many of the instructors and especially the managers of NGO projects often have above-average technical, organizational and socio-pedagogical skills – especially in relation to the local context – as much are they still part of the (local) project structure. This makes them sometimes personally too involved and self-identified with their work, and hence occasionally routine-blinded. Therefore, they need exchange of know-how and experience with external advisors and stimuli from outside – a need which they themselves often appear to realize much more clearly than their external partners.

For information, advice or even just an exchange of ideas, however, local NGOs require and expect "real" partners in discussions, not project "scrutinizers" who merely pop in to superficially assess the status-quo achievements and problems of a project under the aspect of possible (further) financial assistance. They need and rightly expect from their donors to send persons who can "get involved" with the local people and situation, who can listen – especially before giving advice – and who do not simply present their "universal" know-how and preconceived project ideas, but are also prepared to be persuaded by evidence or better arguments from a local partner[103].

(4) Non-formal training within the framework of infrastructure programmes

in the fields of housing, irrigation or road construction are a completely different way of imparting technical skills directly applicable within the environmental context of urban squatter areas or rural areas. Within the framework of Government programmes for low-cost housing, the SENA in Colombia[104], for example, involves the local population in squatter areas for the purpose of skill training in the (re)construction of their own houses, provided that some sort of self-organization does already exist among them. During the various construction stages they are concurrently trained on site in the different construction skills required for the work. In addition, they receive organizational support from qualified staff, and, if needed, also a building loan.

Such practical vocational skill training oriented to the environment-determined needs and employment opportunities in combination with low-cost housing construction in squatter areas is to impart to (semi-)skilled odd-job craftsmen, unskilled casual labourers, unemployed youngsters or women construction skills which will enable them to further improve their own housing environment

---

[103] Without some rethinking in this respect among development planners and advisers, it is going to be difficult to realize long-term cooperations with local NGOs, for example, in the sense of the "linking concept". Yet this would be particularly necessary and desirable for occupation-oriented training and education measures addressed to people from the informal sector, who are much more accessible and familiar to local NGOs. Disappointing experience, resignation when facing the "arrogance of experts", fear of being steamrollered, and also self-respect often make especially the grassroot-type of NGOs reluctant towards such cooperation. "A kind of survey and base-line study on the ... NGOs and their activities" (*GTZ* (1988), p. 78, translated), would – with the attitude expressed in this approach – be taken by many NGOs included in such a survey as a reassurance of their reservations rather than an invitation for cooperation. They do not want to just be "examined" as regards their suitability as information source on socio-cultural features or as facilitator for better reaching poor target groups, yet with no real vote when it comes to the project design. What local NGOs claim more and more, is simply to be taken serious as competent and equal partners with a contribution to make to a dialogue.

[104] Cf. *CINTERFOR/OIT* (1982), pp. 150 ff.

through individual or community subsistence work also beyond what is provided under the Government housing construction scheme, or to easier find – at least occasionally – paid employment in the construction trade.

The (self-help) groups are also trained in basic accounting as far as required to self-administer the loans which they receive under the Government construction programme. Furthermore, they are supported by social workers to strengthen their self-help potential. This supportive measure is intended to increase their capability for self-organization and social action to such an extent that they will be (better) able to plan, initiate and implement measures to improve their living conditions in their own initiative and responsibility.

Conclusion

(i) The possibility and feasibility of such integrated construction-cum-training measures is decisively determined by external factors, in particular whether a suitable mode of financing their own share in the building costs can be offered to the target group, and whether the families have formal title-deeds. Furthermore, some members of the families must have enough time to take part in the training and to do the construction work. Finally, the target population must already be organized in such a way that the building contractor and the training institution can cooperate with a fairly stable self-help organization with a reasonable capability for out-of-the-group communication and business-like negotiations.

Such infrastructure programmes with a related purpose-oriented skill training component hence require a careful preparatory planning, perhaps a preliminary phase to initiate a self-organization process within the target group, as well as an altogether integrated approach in which training is a key but not independent component.

(ii) The employment and income-generating effects of such purpose-oriented and limited training measures will largely depend on
– the given general level of education and technical skills among the target group and their ability to afterwards apply the imparted new skills and knowledge also without guidance, especially since the size and heterogeneity of the target group will normal allow no real training, but rather how-to-do demonstrations;
– the availability of building material for own building purposes at prices which people can afford, and the general employment opportunities in the construction trade of the modern or the informal sector.

At least, however, can the acquired skills be applied in the maintenance and repair of people's own housing, and hence contribute to save money. This effect should not be underrated in view of the increasingly deteriorating income situation of many families in the informal sector.

6.1.5 Vocational Training and Education with a Socio-pedagogical Approach in the Don Bosco Institutions

The educational institutions of the Salesians of Don Bosco are in high esteem in many countries[105]. This is particularly true for the technical schools, because the quality of the vocational training which is consciously oriented to the existing labour demand results in relatively good chances for the graduates to afterwards find a job, even in the modern sector. This reputation often induces also middle-class families to try and obtain a training place for their children, even in technical schools which were set up for poor children from the slums. Nevertheless, many of these vocational training institutions do (almost) exclusively take on children and young people from very poor families.

The origin of the Don Bosco (technical) schools and most of their experience is in big cities where most of them are established in the immediate vicinity of their target groups – children and young people without education and without a chance in society – in or near the slum areas. In all schools, training and education is based on the concept of "preventive education"[106], which for the technical schools results in a concept of vocational training with a socio-pedagogical approach.

---

105 The Don Bosco institutions of the Salesians are named after the founder of the first of this kind of schools for orphans in Turin in 1841. St John Bosco was a charismatic and socially committed Catholic priest. He devoted his life to the education and vocational training of deprived children and youngsters with the aim of (re-)integrating them into society. The congregation of the Salesians of Don Bosco – thus named after Saint Francis de Sales on whom Don Bosco modelled his work – concentrates its activities mainly on boys and their families, whereas the sisterhood of The Daughters of Mary, Help of Christians – also called the Salesian Sisters – takes special care of girls and young women.

106 This philosophy of "preventive education" as opposed to "repressive education" is described in *ANDERSON S.D.B* (year of publication unknown), pp. 340–359, as "making the ... regulations of an institute known and then watching carefully so that the pupils may, at all times, be under the vigilant eye of the rector and (guiding) assistants who, like loving fathers, can converse heart-to-heart with them; ... giving advice, and ... correction, in a charitable ... spirit. ... it tries to do without even the slightest chastisement. ... Never, ... are the pupils left alone. Certainly this system implies some difficulty for the educator, but zeal will help to overcome this obstacle" (p. 350).

The fundamental objectives orientation is "to build up self-confidence and self-esteem in people who are marginalized in society, by accepting them as human beings with a dignity, and by giving them the opportunity to learn for a better life. And even those who are too old for a regular education, may learn a trade or anything, not necessarily for later employment exactly in this field, but for the experience that they may achieve things in life by means of their own efforts"[107]. In this wholistic perception, a person has to be trained and given educational guidance to develop all his abilities, and not just looked at and trained as a unit or manpower. With their conviction that *initially* the social background does not say anything about a person's abilities, but that the aptitudes and talent of children who grow up in poverty are threatened to be submerged at an early stage, the Salesians put great emphasis on beginning education – also via family counselling – already in childhood.

In an attempt to compensate as far as possible for the social handicaps of children and young people from the informal sector as regards their employment opportunities, a high-quality vocational training is provided, though largely confined to typical vocational profiles, in the "classic" artisanal trades, but in conjunction with a social education towards "normal" social behaviour, self-esteem and a certain "work ethic". Furthermore, their background is taken into account insofar as for children from poor families not only the education and vocational training itself is free, but, wherever possible, they are taken on as boarders, or at least given one – for many the only – meal a day.

In the socio-pedagogical approach which aims at building up trust and self-confidence, own understanding of necessities and personal values among the children and youngsters, also recreational activities and group experience through games, sports and "holiday camps" are seen as important aids for personality development, especially among children who have been socialized in the poverty of the urban slums or on the streets. They often show a tendency towards inner withdrawal, and leisure time as an – also psychologically – necessary regeneration phase is, of course, absolutely unknown to them.

The Salesian approach of establishing and maintaining an extensive as possible network of contacts to Government and private employers is not only to ensure the right and up-to-date identification of their qualification demands for skilled workers, but

---

[107] Father Tarcisius Rathnaswamy, head of the institutions of the Don Bosco Beatitudes in Madras.

also to facilitate the job placement of graduates who cannot find employment on their own. Furthermore, it is tried thereby to finance at least part of the operating costs of the technical schools through Government and private customer contracts.

Because of their acknowledged success especially in the field of formal and partly also non-formal vocational training – in terms of employment impacts and the ability to actually reach the people from the informal sector – various Don Bosco institutions addressing different target groups and working under different frame conditions, were visited during the reconnaissance mission, namely

– two "classic" Don Bosco Technical Schools – which in some respects resemble production schools – for formal and non-formal vocational training in Bangkok and Madras;

– two rural vocational training institutions in Katpadi and Poplur, which are partly similar, but partly extremely different in their frame conditions and problems;

– the three Anbu Illam ("House of Love") for street children in Madras,

– a centre for training and social education of young people, rural families and social multipliers in Ennore[108].

The aim was not to just have a look at the facilities of these institutions, but to take the opportunity of own impressions and onsite discussions with headmasters, instructors, social workers and students to really understand the key elements of the Salesian approach to vocational training, and hence be able to distinguish the elements possibly applicable also by other institutions from those tied to a congregational organization like the Salesians.

(1) Formal and non-formal vocational training for youngsters from the urban informal sector

is carried out by the *Don Bosco Technical Institute St Joseph's* (DBTI), one of the typical technical schools of the Salesians with

---

108 More detailed descriptions of all the institutions visited during the reconnaissance mission to India were submitted to the BMZ in an additional volume (in English). This also includes a description of the Don Bosco Beatitudes in Madras, who have created with their school education, vocational training and social welfare institutions impressive facilities and a care network covering all ages and needs of the poorest sections of the population, for roughly 5,000 families and 230 lepers. This very comprehensive approach to work with and for people from the informal sector definitely could serve as a model, and is perhaps not necessarily bound to church-related institutions. As regards the occupation-oriented training and education, however, the Beatitudes institutions do not basically differ from the vocational training and youth centre at St. Joseph's. Therefore, a more detailed description was confined to the additional volume.

production school character[109]. In three-year formal training courses 200–250 youngsters from the nearby slums are trained in metal work and welding[110]. Because of the experience of the Salesians that at least a basis knowledge in reading, writing and arithmetics is essential for the learning success, applicants must have eight years of primary school education. The same applies to the two-year non-formal training as mechanic or electro-mechanic, and to the three-month courses for semi-skilled electricians.

For the non-formal training with altogether about 200–220 students, the proven ability to read and calculate is considered sufficient. Hence, the completion of primary school education is no enrolment requirement for the one-year training course as motor mechanic, and also not for the training courses for girls in typewriting and "oecotrophology".

As a rule, the DBTI which is located in the middle of a slum area, admits only youngsters from families with a "poverty certificate" (entitling to rice subsidies) issued by the Government. This is to ensure as much as possible that only young people from the intended target group are actually admitted.

At the DBTI Youth Recreation Centre recreational facilities and organized events are open to the students, and – in turns – also to

---

109 The term "production school", as reintroduced to the discussion on development and vocational training assistance by *GREINERT*, can be applied to the Don Bosco technical schools only to a limited extent, even though some of these institutions finance up to 40 % – occasionally more – of their operating costs through external contract work carried out in their training workshops. Although there are efforts to realize, increase or maintain this self-financing share in as many technical schools as possible, this nevertheless has subordinate priority for the Salesians. Top priority is given to a comprehensive theoretical and practical vocational training in conjunction with social education. The Salesians themselves when they occasionally call their technical schools "production schools", see the emphasis on the "school" as opposed to mere workshop training, as they attach such great importance to the inclusion of vocational theory, general education and social education in their vocational training. The concept of production schools as presented by *GREINERT*, on the other hand, rather emphasizes dovetailing, almost equal relevance of contract work for financing the operating costs and technical training in the training workshops. Some of his suggestions on how to organize production schools in developing countries, cf. *GREINERT* (1990), esp. pp. 18 ff., however, are realized in most of the Don Bosco technical schools, such as, for example, the autonomy of the institutions vis-à-vis the formal education system, the endeavour for a top quality vocational training in accordance with the technological level prevailing in the region, or the practical job orientation of their training and education approach.
110 Vocational training in good work, in the meantime, is only carried out in advanced training courses for graduates from the Technical School in Katpadi (see Point (2)), who are taken in as boarders. Urban youngsters reject woodwork because of its low social (caste) image and the increasingly poor employment prospects for this trade in urban areas.

about 500 children from the adjacent slum area in an attempt to arouse their interest in education and/or vocational training and, at the same time, to take socio-pedagogical care of them. In addition, evening tutorials at primary school level are given to about 400 boys and 120 girls, in order to help them keep up at school.

A DBTI-run Social Service Centre located directly in the slum cares for about 2,000 families, with a focus on health care. For that purpose, about 60 young women from these families have been trained by Salesian sisters as social workers in the fields of nutrition, preventive health and child care.

The fact that normally all graduates from the formal vocational training courses and also a fairly large number from the non-formal courses subsequently find employment, is mainly owed to

– the orientation of the training content to the labour qualification requirements of potential employers;

– the quality of the training, which is ensured by qualified teachers most of whom are DBTI graduates with an additional – DBTI-financed – training at a Teachers College;

– the normally positive attitude of the graduates towards work, their reliability and awareness for work quality, resulting from the social education;

– the DBTI's support in finding jobs with private and Government employers.

Difficulties in finding employment are experienced especially by the participants of the short courses. For them the training period of 3–12 months is actually not enough to achieve good and sustainable learning results, especially since they are often older and thus more difficult to train and educate. Girls in general have – also due to the social pressure from their families – the greatest problems to find after the training employment outside of their homes.

According to the school principal, the DBTI – like the Don Bosco Technical Schools in Bangkok and in Katpadi – is able to recover between 30 and 40 % of its operating costs – especially costs for personnel, workshop maintenance, boarding and a daily meal for the day students – through work orders from external customers. This contract work is usually carried out by students in their final year of training. In terms of the demand which is pretty high due to the good quality of the products, this recovery rate could still be increased at least temporarily. More contract work, however, is rejected for the reason that the students, due to their only limited work experience, still work relatively slowly – and should do so, since product and work quality and sustained learning effects are given priority over a higher recovery rate of operating costs through self-financing. Furthermore, the youngsters should not for that purpose run the risk of having their energy efforts and labour unduly exploited.

(2) Formal and non-formal vocational training for rural youth is carried out by the Don Bosco Technical School St Joesph's Home in Katpadi, a rural city with roughly 1 million inhabitants, and by the non-formal training institution Don Bosco Agro Tech in Polur, which is located in a completely rural area. Both institutions are about 450 km from Madras. Despite their different frame conditions and working environment, they do have some similar problems which result from their orientation to a rural target group and their location in a rural area.

(a) In *St Joseph's Home*, the biggest vocational training institution in the area far and wide, 120–150 rural youngsters with 8–10 years of primary school education – not necessarily graduation – receive a formal vocational training in good work (3 years) and welding (1 year). The two-year non-formal training for motorbike and rickshaw repair, and car-spraying, respectively, and an 18-month training course for band musicians address, in particular, school drop-outs and young illiterates. The girls in a non-formal tailoring course account for 10 % of the total number of students.

The emphasis at St Joseph's Home is clearly on formal vocational training. The graduates from these courses generally find a job, thanks to the extended network of contacts to private and Government employers and the reputation for good-quality training, which both extends beyond Katpadi. Both also helps to recover part of the operating costs, especially through customer contracts in wood works. About 500, the annual number of applicants from Katpadi and the surrounding rural area exceeds by far the capacities – for which there also is a statutory limit as far as the formal training courses are concerned – of altogether only 100 new students per year. This should, however, not hide the fact that, especially for the participants in the non-formal courses, employment opportunities are very limited, even though there are quite a few industrial small and medium-sized enterprises in Katpadi. But the non-formal training courses offered at St. Joseph's Home do – apart from the welding course – not meet their labour qualification requirements, as the Director himself admits. So far, however, this has not been considered as an indication for any change required, the more so as the non-formal training courses appear to be regarded rather as a kind of social service for young people with little other chances.

Also in establishing their own workshops, most non-formal students are hardly successful, "partly because of lack of capital and local purchasing power, but mostly because of the mentality of the rural boys", say their instructors. They give them all the technical help and personal advice they may require, but do not – and probably cannot due to their own lack of corresponding qualification – prepare them within the training for the setting up of their own business.

The example of the band musician course which was initiated by a retired leader of a police music corps – who was himself educated by the Salesians in Katpadi – shows that sometimes just unconventional fields of activity provide chances for non-formal training with subsequent employment opportunities. All the 35 participants of each course so far found employment thanks to the placement help of their instructor.

This course is also an indication of the basic willingness of the Salesians to provide training also in "non-classic" fields, if only this improves or creates employment opportunities for young people with little school education. They, however, thereby recur almost exclusively to experiences within their order and to opportunities arising from their own connections. Little is known by them about innovations and approaches outside of this frame of experience and contacts, even though, for example, in the field of appropriate technologies – particularly in India – there is a great deal which would be worth to be incorporated especially in the non-formal training courses, with regard to the rural environment-determined occupation opportunities and options of their target groups. Those school directors and teachers who would like to learn more in this respect have few sources of information and points of contact, just because they are (still) very unfamiliar with appropriate technology approaches and the related information networks. This, however, must be understood as a result of life in a relatively "secluded" and self-contained world rather than a sign of arrogance.

(b)   At the *Don Bosco Agro Tech* in Polur, a so far purely non-formal vocational training centre which is still in its initial phase, this restriction has even more serious effects than in St Joseph's Home in Katpadi. For the 100–120 boys coming from villages in the area the school director and the teachers can hardly see any income-generating employment opportunities after their training in one of the three courses for electro-technical repair, wood work, and maintenance and repair of lorries and agricultural machinery, respectively.

Major reasons are the low level of rural school education – most of the youngsters did not finish primary school and many are almost illiterate – and the adverse learning opportunities and potentials on which the rural environment has a restrictive influence. The process of learning hence is slow in all three technical fields, and the work quality can only very gradually be raised to a not more than moderate standard. Job placement for these young people in larger enterprises, therefore, is virtually impossible. The problem is compounded by the desolate economic situation in the villages of the – very extensive – catchment area of Agro Tech, where there are also hardly any gainful employment opportunities.

Agro Tech, thus, is confronted with considerable structural problems stemming from its rural environment and target groups, and, at the same time, it is urgently needed just therefore. As regards its occupational relevance and employment impacts, the problem is aggravated by the fact that – like in Katpadi – the school director and the teachers in their idea of crafts and technical skills to be imparted to rural youngsters, quite rigidly follow the – in urban areas successful – Salesian concept of a vocational training which tries to qualify disadvantaged young people as much as possible for wage- or self-employment in one of the common artisanal trades.

Their clear perception that almost all their students will – also after training – have to further live and work in the subsistence sector, has not (yet) induced a reflexion on possibilities to extend or reorientate the training to include more appropriate technologies and skill training in agriculture-related, also subsistence-oriented occupations. A broad vocational training deliberately oriented to the skill demands in modern *rural* industries also would certainly improve the chances for young rural people to find employment.

Up to now, Agro Tech has – beside the vocational training – "merely" tried within its extremely limited scope of possibilities to help to improve, in the medium term, the level of basic education in the area by carrying out supplementary primary school tutorials for boys and girls from nearby villages.

(3)   (Re-)Integration of street children through social education and some non-formal vocational training
has been attempted by the Salesians in India for a number of years now in several big cities by setting up so-called "Anbu Illam" ("House of Love"). The main target group are street children with no parents, both boys and girls, but in separate institutions. Furthermore, they have started to conduct systematic sociological studies

among street children in order to learn more about their living conditions, needs and perspectives [111].

Under the "Rag-Pickers Reach-Out Programme", by now three Anbu Illam have been set up in Madras for the social education, occupation-oriented training, and, wherever possible, family reintegration of boys whose home are the streets of Madras, where they earn a living as "rag-pickers", load carriers, porters at the station ("station boys") or through some other kind of odd-jobs.

The *Mannady Anbu Illam/Broadway* was the first of these houses, set up five years ago in a densely populated district right in the city centre, and deliberately located in a plain-looking building. Street children can come (back) there any time, even after running away. In the meantime, about 80 street children up to the age of 16 live in this home and non-formal training institution under the care of a Salesian who for the children is father, teacher and social worker all rolled into one. The experience of the first years shows that youngsters above the age of about 16, generally spoken, are much more difficult to educate – sometimes requiring different education and training methods – and can often still be helped only by directly occupation-oriented measures, or even simply by providing a place to stay. Therefore, the *Park Town Anbu Illam* was set up in addition as an open home, information and contact centre especially for older street children, most of them "station boys" from the nearby railway station. Here, they live more independently than the children in the Mannady Anbu Illam, but are still included in education and non-formal training measures, if they want to be. The *Anna Park Anbu Illam* was under construction at the time of the reconnaissance mission, as a home, training and work centre for young "rag-pickers" whose activities are planned to be better and more profitably organized there by setting up a kind of cooperative for the sale and recycling of the waste products collected by them.

Accompanying the "father of the street children" on his regular evening tour to the various information and contact points, waste collection points and "paper shops" of former street boys, to the three Anbu Illam and the street families in "his" district which he also looks after, gives an idea of how it may be possible to approach street children, to socially (re)integrate them in a slow process of building up trust and confidence, general and social education and occupation-oriented training, to create employment opportunities for them,

---

111 The studies already mentioned earlier are carried out by the Bosco Institute of Social Work in Tirupattur; cf. *BOSCO INSTITUTE* (year of publication unknown) for Madras and *ibid.* (1990) for Salem.

and to reconcile some of them with their families, which is always the aim but by no means always achieved.

It also makes clear what, in principle, is obvious: To work with and for street children does not only require social-pedagogical skills and – if the social work approach is to be employment-oriented – some vocational know-how, but also a kind of dedicated commitment which is very hard to find.

Approaching street children in Madras takes place in various stages and in various ways:

– At night, when they can only be distinguished from other poor children, the "father of the street children" roams through his district and talks to them, often many times, before they come along to the Anbu Illam – always of their own free will – for the first time;

– Once they are there, they are given socio-psychological support and pedagogical guidance, receive primary school and social education and take part in basic non-formal training courses, e.g. tailoring;

– At various places of the district where former street children – sometimes with their families – live and which the father visits every evening, points of information and contact have been set up for street children of all ages who want to make contact but who do not dare to go to one of the Anbu Illam straight away;

– The "paper shops" set up as commercial micro-enterprises by some former street children, with the help of the Anbu Illam, also serve as points of contact and, what is more, are a visible sign of the possible successful "career" of street children. The commercial purpose of the "paper shops" is to be a delivery point for the waste products collected by the "rag-pickers", from where the waste paper is sold to dealers who resell it for their part to recycling factories[112].

The Salesian approach of occupation-oriented training and social integration of street children is dynamic. Following a period of observation, it is decided for each of the children and youngsters whether they should, after some preparatory education, be integrated into the formal Salesian school system for an education up to secondary level, or better attend one of the formal or non-formal vocational training courses, or remain (for the time being) "rag-pickers" as the best possible solution.

In the latter case, the aim then is to give them a positive attitude to this job by making them aware that this not only helps them earn a living

---

112 For the cooperative of the "rag-pickers", the purchase of an own vehicle is considered so that the waste products can be sold to the factories directly. During the visit it was also suggested that the Anna Park Anbu Illam should gradually build up its own waste recycling production for further income generation.

in an honest way, but that they – instead of the municipality – also fulfil the important task of refuse disposal for the community. With the planned cooperative in the Anna Park Anbu Illam it is hoped to give them a perspective for creating a "proper" business, not only under financial aspects.

For older street children and those who have been on the streets for many years, it is tried – apart from social education – to find a simple yet relatively stable wage-employment. Or they are helped to create a business for self-employment, as owner of a bicycle rickshaw and later perhaps a motorized rickshaw, or initially as a night-time load carrier. Wherever possible, however, this is not considered as the "end of the road" but as a stage in their occupational "career".

For work with street children, too, the guiding principle of Salesian education and vocational training is to help each individual to get as far as possible – in occupation and in social life – in accordance with his/her abilities to be developed over a longer period. But never the second step must be taken before the first by immediately and suddenly dragging the youngsters out of their social milieu, which would for most street children mean a second social uprooting in their young life.

(4) Social education, awareness creation and social leadership training

for target groups in the role of social multipliers – such as teachers, youth and social workers, "school liders", men and women with social authority in their (village) communities, social animators and leadership trainers – is the task of the Don Bosco Youth Animation Centre (DBYAC) in Ennore, roughly 25 km from Madras. The two Salesian fathers who run the DBYAC, are highly qualified professional social workers. Their work is guided by the understanding that all development in quality and sustainability ultimately depends on people's social and mental development. Development work hence requires – even for occupation-oriented training to improve employment opportunities – pedagogically qualified instructors, social animators and leadership personalities ("liders") who are motivated in their work through a high sense of social commitment. They are needed in the schools as much as in the urban squatter areas and in the villages. The DBYAC addresses both men and women. But a particular emphasis is on women whose special role and influence in the process of children's (social) education is clearly perceived.

Apart from the training courses for these target groups of social multipliers, weekend seminars and two-week holiday camps on "achievement motivation" are organized at the DBYAC for both urban slum and street children and for youngsters from poor rural families. For many of them, this is their first experience ever of leisure time. The intention is to create for the young people an atmosphere in which they may reflect about themselves, their ideas and further options. Often it is only then that an interest in education or training comes up, for which they are then sent to a suitable Don Bosco school or vocational training institution.

As a measure for self-help promotion among the rural population and for awareness creation on their own development potential, regular family counselling is carried out by the DBYAC staff directly in a fairly large number of villages.

Like the Anbu Illam for street children, the work of the DBYAC is entirely dependent on external financing – mainly from the Salesian Congregational Province of Madras – since in both cases the "non-profit" social education component is the priority aspect as compared to occupation-oriented training.

Conclusion

(i)   As regards its ability to actually reach target groups from the informal sector and its positive employment impacts, the remarkable success of the Salesian vocational training cum social education approach must probably largely be attributed to

– the above-average – yet technologically not "over-dimensioned" – quality of the vocational training, which helps to give socially disadvantaged youngsters a "competitive edge" on the labour market. The training quality is secured by a qualified vocational *and* subsequent (socio-)pedagogical training for the teachers at the DB institutions;

– the incorporation of social education and value teaching as part of the vocational training. This does not only positively influence the process of personality building for children and youngsters socialized in poverty[113], but also improves their employment opportunities,

---

113 Meeting children and youngsters in projects – not just those of the Salesians but also of local NGOs – in which occupation-oriented training and social education are regarded as two equally important elements of a comprehensive educational concept oriented to personality development, is impressive. Most of them appear to be more "alert", learn more actively, are more open in approaching strangers, and generally show more self-confidence as compared to their peers who come from a similar social background with comparable learning opportunities and

since they are guided to develop a normal social behaviour, self-esteem and a sense of good workmanship and reliability;
- the fact that the social background of the target groups, i.e. also the economic poverty of the families, is taken into account insofar as for children from poor families the training is (almost) free-of-charge, and day students receive a free meal a day, wherever possible. Hence, "social welfare" is recognized as a – to a certain extent – necessary component of any vocational training assistance addressing poor target groups. This approach makes access possible for a much larger number of young people from the informal sector as compared to Government training institutions.

The problem of fluctuation among the teachers as a result of inadequate pay, however, the Don Bosco Technical Schools have to face in almost the same way as other vocational training institutions. Although they have the advantage of being able to recruit new qualified teachers among their own graduates, their additional pedagogical training at a Teacher College again and again is an investment of relatively short-term benefit for the Don Bosco institutions.

(ii) Some elements of the Salesian vocational training cum social education concept are largely confined to the specific conditions and possibilities of a congregational structure. This is particularly true as regards
- the individually "life-long" and institutionally "endless" time perspective in the work, which allows to get to know people and establish a "natural authority" and acceptance within the target groups in a completely different manner as it is possible for a project manager with a limited contract period, who is "guided" by project objectives to be realized within a comparatively short period of time – although the question is whether this needs necessarily to remain the norm;
- the selfless and benevolent commitment – yet with no illusions – to help to improve the living conditions of the economically and socially disadvantaged, which can be expected only in the rarest cases from professional development advisers, especially since it also requires the ability to endure the psychological strain of permanent encounter with all forms of poverty and patience with people whose

113 (...continued)
potentials and who participate in a mere technical training in a non-formal vocational training institution. Among the street children in Madras, even an outsider can, from a difference in social behavior, differentiate between newcomers in the Anbu Illam and those who have been educated and trained there already for some time.

socialization makes it difficult to initially establish learning discipline and motivation;

– the network of contacts to private enterprises and Government institutions, which the Salesians in many countries have developed over decades to facilitate the job placement for graduates as well as the acquisition of contract work for the training workshops to partially finance operating costs;

– finally – at least in India – the autonomous Salesian education system comprising all levels, which enables them to fully pursue their own ideas on a child's (further) education also at a level to which children not meeting formal requirements would never have access in the public education system – not even with preparatory education and supplementary tuition. Especially for the educational and occupational options of street children, this means that assistance measures will not automatically lead to an early dead end – which is a high risk in a detached development project.

That a socio-pedagogical approach in occupation-oriented training and education for target groups from the informal sector, however, needs not necessarily be bound to a church(-related) training institution, is proven by the work of quite a few local NGOs[114]. Also the long-term character of training and education measures is conceivable in other than congregational institutions, too. However, it requires development workers who are willing and able to take on long-term contracts for a continuous work in one place.

(iii) A certain weakness the vocational training concept of the Salesians reveals in its relatively one-sided bias to the "classic" vocational profiles. As their own experience shows, this does not significantly contribute – not even with the backing from the Salesians' extensive network of contacts – to improve the occupational prospects of rural youngsters and young people, in general, who have access only to non-formal training due to their poor school education.

In this respect the Don Bosco institutions should do more, to not only take into account – as is done in an exemplary way – the learning opportunities and potentials of the poorest groups in the informal sector addressed (and actually reached) by them, but to better respond to their actually given opportunities, too. This could – beside the emphasis on excellent training quality – be realized by introducing skill training in various fields of appropriate technologies, which for rural youth, in particular, should

---

114 Cf. the two examples described in Section 6.3.

also be subsistence-oriented, and possibly extend to their families in the villages.

(iv) Under this aspect, the Don Bosco vocational training institutions should be suggested to undertake advanced training for their school directors and teachers – if desired with advisory assistance within a bilateral measure for institutional strengthening of vocational training institutions – in order to

– extend their knowledge and competence in the *technological* field with regard to the possible introduction, production and/or application of innovative and appropriate technologies not only but especially in non-formal vocational training courses, and make them familiar with available respective information sources;

– increase their understanding of *economic* interrelationships and, consequently, their willingness to also include elements of a subsistence-oriented occupational qualification for self-employment, subsistence work and community self-help activities in their concept of vocational training for young people from the informal sector.

(v) Altogether, the vocational training with a socio-pedagogical approach in the Don Bosco institutions is a concept for occupation-oriented training and education for target groups from the informal sector, which is definitely worth to be promoted. Many of its elements could well be applied also by other institutions within the framework of (bilateral) vocational training assistance, provided that they can find not only professionally competent but also in terms of human qualities suitable staff.

The Don Bosco vocational training institutions themselves are – due to their acknowledged competence and social commitment – generally strong and, in a positive sense, self-confident local institutions. (Bilateral) vocational training assistance projects would be well-advised, if they seek cooperation with them, wherever possible. Especially in the planning stage of assistance measures for occupation-oriented training for target groups from the informal sector, they can be expected in most cases to be a valuable source of information and ideas.

6.2 *Business Advice and Training for Small Enterprise Development and Self-employment Promotion*

In view of the absolutely inadequate number of jobs available in the private enterprises of the modern sector, even in the long term, and the decreasing role of Government institutions and public enterprises as "compensating employers", quite a lot of hope in development policy is pinned on the creation and stabilization of gainful employment opportunities through the promotion of small and micro-enterprises and self-employment.

It should not be overlooked, however, that at both the micro- and macro-level the possibilities of earning a living through business creation and self-employment are just as limited by a region's overall economic situation as are the employment impacts of vocational training for wage employment. To sell the products and services offered, there must be a demand sufficient in quantity and with a substantial enough purchasing power among the (potential) clients. Also, required (raw) materials and working equipment must be available and affordable, and possible sales markets must not only be there but also accessible for small and micro-entrepreneurs. In reality, the limitations from these factors normally exceed by far what has been assumed in theory, and they increase significantly with the distance from industrial-urban centres and the rate of inflation in the country.

Nevertheless, the promotion of (potential) small and micro-enterprises and self-employment through specific training offers and advisory services is an important means of improving the economic situation of people from the informal sector. The success of such measures, however, will create its own limits through the increased competition of a growing number of businesses. The development potential attributed to this approach, therefore, should not be overrated.

Furthermore, a great deal of knowledge about markets and mentality is required to design training and advisory measures which do expect neither too much nor too little from the target groups as regards their given experience, skills and abilities. Their general learning capacity is often just as overrated as their understanding of the relevance of some kind of systematic business management and production planning. Particularly, the latter normally is hardly increased through only abstract teaching and advice, since many (potential) small and micro-entrepreneurs – especially in rural areas – and even more the (often only temporarily) self-employed persons are (almost) illiterate, and, what is more, their view of their economic activities nowhere near resembles the business-science way of thinking.

They are generally underrated, however, as regards their practical experience, their resourcefulness and their talent for technical and organizational improvization. Instead, there is a risk that these strengths will be under-appreciated or even damaged in the over-emphasis of all kinds of planning, which can be observed in advisory assistance and training courses. When a small and micro-entrepreneur cannot intellectually and/or in the business reality combine the two elements – improvization and planning – he will finally opt for the "tried and tested" approach of muddling through, which, of course, will not result in a great learning success.

With the following approaches to small and micro-enterprise stabilization and new business creation by means of training and advisory assistance, concepts are introduced first which are based on the assumption that for the realization of any significant employment impacts it can only be meaningful to assist small or micro-entrepreneurs and self-employed persons "with development potential". This view then is challenged by the experience of two programmes which show that it is very well possible to promote business creation and self-employment also for people from the informal sector, who at first glance seem to have hardly any economic development potential, provided that there is an adequate planning and implementation strategy.

6.2.1 *Training for Small and Micro-Entrepreneurs "with Development Potential"*

In Latin America, both Government-run vocational training institutions and private organizations try through specific training and advisory programmes to promote those small and micro-entrepreneurs who evidently have an economic development potential for employment creation and income generation. As this kind of small and micro-enterprise promotion – as already critically stated above – often tends to be equated with "informal sector promotion", it has been assessed as to which extent it actually may create occupation-oriented training opportunities suitable and accessible for target groups from the informal sector.

(1) A Government programme for countrywide business training and advisory services for small and micro-entrepreneurs,
which in the meantime has been adopted by several Government (-run) and private institutions also in other Latin American

countries, was originally developed by the SENA for Colombia[115].
As target group addressed is the "small or micro-entrepreneur with development potential"[116], who is defined as someone
– whose business has enough economic potential to assert itself on the market and, thus, secure the job and a fairly sufficient income for the entrepreneur himself and his workers resp. employees;
– who shows the main features of informal business, i.e. a very limited internal division of labour and low productivity, (almost) no access to credit on market terms, little influence on purchasing and selling prices, and a considerable dependence on the developments in the modern sector[117].

The training and advisory measures for this type of small and micro-entrepreneurs "with development potential", who are mainly engaged in manufacturing, small-scale trade business and other services, primarily aim at improving their entrepreneurial skills and know-how[118]. Sound technical skills are just as much presupposed as several years of work experience as a small or micro-entrepreneur and sound abilities in reading, writing and arithmetic.

Accordingly, small and micro-entrepreneurs who attend these training courses normally have a sound general education, many even formal vocational training. They often set up their own business only after many years of job experience, because they considered self-employment more appealing and lucrative than wage-employment[119].

The topics of the trade-specific evening and weekend courses in the training centres – for which normally fees are charged – generally include accounting and cost calculation, investment planning, business and work organization, personnel management, product design and marketing, and occasionally technical drawing. The training content is decided on the basis of a prior market analysis and assessment of the potential business opportunities of the enterprises in the trade concerned.

The theoretical training is to be supplemented by advisory services for the enterprises, to support the practical application of the

---

115 Other programmes for the promotion of cooperatives or joint ventures between several small or micro-enterprises are – also in the opinion of the SENA – definitely not suitable for the typical informal sector enterprises, because of the high demands made on the existing business and workshop structure and the entrepreneurial qualification of the owners; cf. *CINTERFOR/OIT* (1982), pp. 149 f.
116 Cf. *CINTERFOR/OIT* (1982), pp. 162 f.
117 The description is mainly based on *CINTERFOR/OIT* (1982), pp. 147 ff.
118 Cf. *ibid.*, p. 114.
119 Cf. *GRAF* (1989), pp. 132 f.

imparted knowledge, and to elaborate business-specific investment plans adapted to the development potential of individual enterprises. However, this does not involve credit offers.

Conclusion

(i)   Due to the considerable demands this programme makes on its participants as regards job experience, professional qualification and level of general education, it can only marginally reach the type of small and micro-entrepreneur and self-employed persons predominantly found in the informal sector. At most, these "modern" small and micro-enterprises will feel addressed which can hardly be distinguished from a small enterprise in the modern sector, anyhow, or the character of entrepreneur who by nature is innovative and risk-prepared. Due to the trades selected, women are de facto largely excluded

(ii)   Programmes of this type generally expect instructors and advisers to know a great deal about the business reality of small and micro-enterprises and the respective local market conditions. It remains to be asked to what extent the staff at Government-run vocational training institutions (can) fulfil such requirements.

Furthermore, working with typical small and micro-entrepreneurs and self-employed persons in the informal sector, requires pedagogical skills and an understanding of their mentality, their learning opportunities and potentials and their environment-determined (business) options, which the overwhelming majority of instructors in Government-run vocational training institutions are unlikely to have.

(iii)   For these reasons, it cannot realistically be assumed that by means of such programmes especially small and micro-entrepreneurs from the informal sector will actually be reached, or, if so, adequately trained and advised.

(2)   Training and advice to improve the entrepreneurial skills of small and micro-entrepreneurs

is the aim of the "Desarrollo de Pequeñas y Micro-Empresas" (DESAP) programme carried out by the Foundation Carvajal[120] in

120 The Foundation Carvajal was established in Cali in 1977 in the private initiative of a private enterprise group of the same name, to implement the DESAP. In the meantime, the concept serves as a model and has been introduced – by other organizations – in about 80 towns in Colombia and, with advisory assistance

Cali/Colombia. Different from the just described programme of Government-run vocational training institutions, in which business advice and training for small and micro-entrepreneurs is regarded as a general means of sector promotion, and hence not intended to respond to the needs of individual enterprises and persons, the DESAP is based on an entrepreneurship philosophy which regards entrepreneurial creativity and the willingness to take business risks – associated with a sound knowledge of market-oriented business management – as the key to a country's economic and social development. Accordingly, the programme is shaped to meet the business assistance needs of individual persons and small and micro-enterprises.

The activities of the DESAP itself are deliberately restricted to the target groups of small and micro-entrepreneurs and the self-employed in Cali where the Foundation Carvajal is located. This is to ensure intensive training and advice on the basis of a precise knowledge of the local market and business situation, which is oriented in each case to the individual and business-specific potentials and qualification needs of the course participants[121].

Anyone who wants to participate in a DESAP training course, must – beside a general ability and willingness to expand the business – already have several years of entrepreneurial experience and sound technical know-how in his occupation as well as enough school education to be able to follow the courses in the spoken and the written word. Nevertheless, most of the participants have "a *very* low level of education and consequently also a very low level of comprehension. Teaching, thus, must concentrate, and be confined to what is *essentially* required by them" (Maria Carvajal).

The DESAP programme which is intended as a "business education process", mainly consists of

– a seven-week training with five evening classes a week within a training centre, by using the method of "interacting learning". The

---

120 (...continued)
from the Foundation Carvajal, by national organizations in Bolivia, Ecuador, Chile, Venezuela, El Salvador and the Dominican Republic. With reference to the – apparently less successful – "Fundación Social" set up also in Colombia by the Jesuits, the basic features of the concept are described in detail by *GRAF* (1989); especially on the Foundation Carvajal cf. also *HARPER* (1989), pp. 173–178; and *ARNOLD* (1987), pp. 85–92. Part of the information presented here was obtained from a longer talk with Maria Carvajal who currently runs the Foundation together with her husband.

121 Since mid 1990, the Foundation Carvajal offers from Cali also special training courses for smallholders with specifically developed training materials. There have been no reports yet on the initial experience.

training content is closely related to the individual experiences and the business reality and problems of the course participants, but dealing with only one core subject at a time, e.g. accounting, cost calculation, investment planning or marketing[122];
– an additional intensive specialist advice for each participant at his/her business-site by experienced business advisers familiar with the local market conditions. During this advisory period of normally about 16 hours, the specific problems and development potentials of the individual business of each participant are identified;
– a supplementary and more general business management advice by economics students who have been specifically trained for this task within the DESAP and partly also have own work experience in a small or micro-enterprise. This is to support the practical application of the imparted knowledge, and to accompany the realization of the business development plan elaborated during the training;
– the negotiation of a bank loan at usual market terms for the participants, as far as required[123], after the successful completion of the training, to support from that side the realization of the investment plan drawn up during the course. For participants interested in a credit, however, their individual entrepreneurial skills and the economic stability and development potential of their enterprises must have been proven during the training period;
– individual follow-up advice for up to two years after course completion in order to stabilize the business expansion started, which also includes to promote the set-up of procurement and marketing cooperatives.

Roughly 55 % of the normally 25 participants per training course are women, most of whom are self-employed. Joint courses for women and men reportedly are no problem. On the contrary, according to Maria Carvajal, the women are often better able than male participants to express themselves and to clearly describe their business problems and training needs.

In order to ensure that only the intended target group, i.e. small and micro-entrepreneurs and self-employed persons who are willing and

---

122 The content of the training courses and the training materials are basically the same for all participants. Special training material is provided only for entrepreneurs who trade in perishable goods, e.g. grocers or catering firms, and for the new target group of smallholders, as mentioned already.
123 Initially almost all participants decide to attend the training course only, because its successful completion is a precondition for credit assistance. Especially during the individual business advice, however, about one third of them realizes that with a more efficient business organization they will not even need credit. In the case of another third, it could be smaller or deferred for the time being.

able to expand their business, is promoted, the DESAP applies a staggered selection mechanism by which "unsuitable" participants are identified also after the training course started and, if necessary, excluded from further participation – not least in order to protect them against a cost and perhaps credit burden which would exceed their individual and business possibilities. As part of this section procedure, the participants are
– asked at the very beginning – following an introductory explanation of the programme's demands and services – to self-critically assess whether this corresponds with their own personal and business needs for training, and whether they (could) fulfil the requirements;
– encouraged through a fee of US$ 15 – to be paid for each weekly course – to constantly reassess under business aspects whether a further course attendance (still) is a useful investment;
– only admitted to the second weekly course, if they can present a positive balance sheet – to be drawn up by themselves – for their business.

Conclusion

(i) The deliberate confinement of its activities to an in every respect known local framework, the business-specific advice for each individual enterprise as part of the training course, and the "interacting learning" approach oriented to concrete business problems of the participants – these appear to be the three key success factors of the DESAP. In these aspects it is also most clearly distinguished from the countrywide and standardized Government training and advisory programmes which address the same target group. In particular, the business-specific and individual advisory assistance with accompanying regular back-up advice can undoubtedly contribute to reach in larger numbers also very small and "institution-shy" entrepreneurs and self-employed persons[124].

(ii) Although the DESAP itself, like the above mentioned Government programmes, explicitly intends to only promote the relatively

---

124 A programme for the promotion of (also rural) small and micro-enterprises through technical and entrepreneurial training, carried out by the Swiss Foundation for Technical Development Cooperation (SWISSCONTACT) in Costa Rica in cooperation with the local business association APTAMAI – which itself evolved with assistance from SWISSCONTACT – moves in a similar direction. It also shows that, through long-term measures for institution building, it may well be possible to gradually build up an organization with the same functions as the Foundation Carvajal.

small – in relation to the informal sector as a whole – target group of existing small and micro-entrepreneurs and self-employed persons with an evident economic development potential, some of its principles are definitely worth to be considered and applied also in training programmes for business stabilization and self-employment promotion for people from the informal sector, who, at first glance, may not seem to have much "development potential"[125].

These principles include
– to sell training and advice to interested small and micro-entrepreneurs and even self-employed persons as a service, in order to support instead of dampening their willingness and ability to undertake own efforts;
– to assign instructors, business experts and back-up advisers who, above and beyond their specialist qualifications, are also familiar with the local market conditions, the social and economic reality and mentality of small and micro-entrepreneurs and self-employed persons, and hence are able to realistically assess their learning opportunities and potentials as well as their business opportunities;
– to adapt the training contents in a flexible and problem-oriented way to the actual qualification needs and business development options of the course participants.

(iii) With respect to (bilateral) vocational training assistance, it is well conceivable that in cooperation with a suitable local counterpart institution a training approach resembling the DESAP – whose special feature notably is not the target group but its basic approach and design – is chosen not only to promote existing small and micro-entrepreneurs and already active self-employed business(wo)men from the urban informal sector.

With modified curricula, it might well be applied also, for example, for the promotion of
– small business or self-employment creation by lowest-income and casual workers who may have a rather low level of education, but considerable, perhaps even specialized occupational experience from many years of work;
– smallholders and subsistence farmers who, in principle, have a potential for (increased) surplus production from their farm land;
– home-tied women who have the personality and economic potential and the interest to set up a commercial home production.

---

125 An example is the initiative for business *creation* assistance to very poor target groups in Port Sudan, further described in Section 6.2.3, Point (3).

6.2.2 Assistance for Small and Micro-Business Creation

Training and advisory services to promote business creation particularly among target groups from the informal sector with no evident economic development potential, is occasionally carried out by local NGOs, but normally as one element of a more integrated development approach. As a separate measure, it is still relatively rare, especially for adults above the normal vocational training age. An extremely interesting project experience in Port Sudan, however, shows that this is, in principle, possible.

Furthermore, a critical look is taken at a concept for "New Business Creation" as developed by the GTZ, and at the Rural Trade School in Salima/Malawi, two approaches which are occasionally introduced as positive examples for the promotion of small business creation through vocational training and education accessible for people from the information sector, too.

(1) Business creation by men and women with an entrepreneurial personality

is the objective of the GTZ concept of "New Business Creation Training" (NBC)[126] and similar programmes[127]. The NBC training is a six-week course for potential small entrepreneurs. They are trained in key qualifications improving their entrepreneurial "competence", especially their capability to gather and assimilate relevant business information, and given assistance in planning their intended business creation. Successful participants who are able by the end of the course to draw up their own business plan and present it convincingly to

---

126 Under this name, the concept was first introduced by the GTZ in 1986 in Nepal. In the meantime, these business creation courses have been offered in almost 20 countries; cf. *FRENZ/KOLSHORN* (1987) and *GTZ* (year of publication unknown). Later the programme has been renamed as "Competency-based Economy through Formation of Entrepreneurs" (CEFE).

127 In cooperation with the Udon Thani Technical College (UTC) in northern Thailand, the Carl Duisberg Society (CDG) has been carrying out since 1990 the "Small Enterprises Development Training Project" as a management training programme for small business creation, like the NBC without (additional) technical training. The target groups are the students of the final class and former UTC graduates who are still unemployed. Apart from UTC staff, also employees from business and trade associations are to be trained as "part-time trainers", as well as owners of small and micro-enterprises from the area, preferably former UTC graduates who have successfully set up their own business.

A programme also similar to the NBC concept, but with greater emphasis on technical training, has been started by the "Malawian Entrepreneurs Development Institute" (MEDI). This is also referred to by *JUNG* (1989), pp. 213–216.

lenders, receive a business creation loan, provided that they themselves can contribute at least 25 % of the capital required.

The applicants for NBC training courses must already have some kind of vocational qualification or job experience. Apart from that, they are selected with particular regard to their entrepreneurial personality traits. These include the willingness to take calculated risks and the ability to identify risk factors, staying power, decision-making abilities, openness towards innovation and change, the ability to make contacts, flexibility and a sense for market opportunities. Furthermore, the ability to easily read, write and calculate is a precondition for participation. Finally, the interested potential entrepreneurs must be prepared to invest quite a substantial amount of money, first for the course fees and later for their own capital contribution to the business creation.

The NBC training comprises four distinct stages:

– "Achievement Motivation", during which each participant is encouraged and guided to realize objectively given restrictions and individually felt limitations to the planned venture, to then assess the risk, and to become clear on his/her essential objectives, hopes and motivating forces related to the business creation plan;

– "Product identification", during which each participant is supposed to develop his/her project (product) idea for the intended business creation by realistically taking into consideration existing market conditions;

– "Product development", during which the participants are trained – by simulating competitive pressure through permanent confrontation in the group – to develop the attitudes and behavioural techniques required for a successful realization of their business project idea under real terms;

– "Project elaboration", for which each participant must carry out, entirely on his/her own, a real market analysis to gather all the information required for planning and preparing the business creation, and then evaluate the information obtained in a business project proposal to be presented in a written form.

If after a successful presentation of this business project proposal to bank representatives at the end of the course, the potential entrepreneurs will be entitled to a loan. Experience shows that it will then take between three months and two years for them to translate the project idea into an actual business creation. During this period they have to rely mainly on themselves. From those who finally manage to set up their business, reportedly roughly 75 % can still be found working in their own enterprises after two years. About the reasons for the failure of a quarter of the successful course participants, nothing is known. No information could also be obtained on the number of course drop-outs and their reasons, nor on those who did not succeed or not even tried to realize their business plans after a successful course completion.

Conclusion

(i)   It is difficult to imagine that there is a significant number of potential small or micro-entrepreneurs or self-employed persons living in the informal sector, who would feel addressed by a training programme of this kind. The requirements for admittance are simply too demanding, and the way in which the courses are normally announced – in the mass media, especially newspapers – is too general and anonymous. Insofar as they (can) read about it, at all, most of these people will regard such an announcement as completely irrelevant to them.

Those who nevertheless apply and also get through the – deliberately tough – selection procedure, will probably fail later, at the latest in the project elaboration phase, for mainly three reasons:

– People who have been socialized in the poverty of an urban slum or the rural areas normally are very unlikely to develop the entrepreneurial personality required, nor to engage themselves in the desired way in group-dynamic learning processes[128];

– The inevitable loss of income during the full-time course in combination with the quite substantial training costs in terms of course fees, expenses during the market study and, finally, the 25 % own capital share required for the business creation, exceed by far the financial means of most people from the informal sector, even with family support;

– The demands made on the learning capacity – especially as regards theoretical learning, written expression, and the ability to independently gather and evaluate information relevant in connection with the business creation plan – are nowhere near fulfilled by the overwhelming majority of people from the informal sector, often not even by secondary-school graduates.

Only among the children of reasonably well-established small and micro-entrepreneurs in the informal sector, there may be few who meet the admission requirements. They may have had the choice of

---

128 The experience of an NBC (CEFE) trainer in one of these business creation courses carried out with "poverty groups" confirms this judgement.

proper school education and, at the same time, some vocational training through helping out in their parents' enterprise, and may also be able to raise within their families the financial means for both the course participation and a subsequent business creation.

(ii) There is no indication that the NBC training and similarly structured programmes do in fact reach target groups from the informal sector, in particular. This is not to say that programmes of this kind and orientation cannot be a meaningful tool for economic development assistance insofar as the promotion of qualified "middle-class" small and micro-entrepreneurs is concerned, although in this case, too, positive employment impacts depend on the general economic potential which can be activated in the respective region. It only should not be expected that NBC training participants – with a few exceptions – will come from the informal sector.

(iii) Regardless of its hitherto main field of application, it might be worth considering to use the NBC training approach in (bilateral) vocational training assistance in two other fields in which it could be more, though indirectly beneficial also to target groups from the informal sector:

– Firstly, it would probably to be a very suitable method for the advanced training of technical instructors – at Government and private vocational training institutions – as "small business advisers", with an accordingly adapted curriculum also as advisers for small and micro-entrepreneurs in the informal sector. The role game approach of the NBC training will give them – apart from the almost inevitable process of awareness creation as regards their role as advisers – within a relatively short period the experience of real market analysis and business planning, and a generally better understanding of the particular situation of small and micro-entrepreneurs and self-employed business(wo)men. This will definitely have a positive impact on the quality of their advisory services and their acceptance as advisers among small or micro-entrepreneurs;

– Secondly, the six-week NBC courses could be incorporated into the curricula of formal and non-formal training courses at vocational training institutions, in a move to extend the objectives of vocational training beyond a mere technical skill training and include a qualification in entrepreneurial skills, in addition.

(2) A programme of advisory assistance for (potential) small and micro-entrepreneurs through local "business consultants"
is carried out among the poorest people in Port Sudan. It shows that it is well possible through measures of occupation-oriented training

and advice combined with mini-loans to also reach the target group of (potential) small entrepreneurs and self-employed persons who operate in the informal sector somewhere between market and subsistence economy with no evident economic development potential.

The "Euro-Action Accord Small-Scale Enterprise Programme"[129] was started a few years ago and is now mainly sustained in local self-organization. About 35 % of its beneficiaries are women. Its objective is to strengthen the productive self-help potential of the men, women or young people who live in extreme poverty in the slum areas of Port Sudan by means of advice oriented to the individual needs and business potentials. Also credit is provided in order to help them to stabilize or start a gainful self-employment or small enterprise.

The concept and implementation of the programme shows a remarkable similarly to the DESAP of the Foundation Carvajal in Colombia. The target groups, however, are only superficially seen the same. The small and micro-entrepreneurs and self-employed persons in Port Sudan are both economically and in their technical skills and general education obviously a lot more disadvantaged and "backward" than the small and micro-entrepreneurs the DESAP intends to promote.

The main elements of the small enterprise promotion programme in Port Sudan can be summarized as follows:

– In this scheme, too, applicants for a loan or business advice are extremely carefully assessed as to whether they do in fact belong to the intended target group – here not small and micro-entrepreneurs "with development potential" as in the Latin American programmes, but extremely poor yet somehow "business-minded" people;

– No matter how poor they are, the (potential) small and micro-entrepreneurs and self-employed persons have to pay a *for them* significant fee for each service – credit, business advice or technical training – to make them realize its investive character and value.

The idea behind the concept of charging a fee for any kind of business

---

129 Cf. *HARPER* (1989a)
   On a much larger scale, the ILO has been implementing a similar approach through the "Programme to Support Urban Informal Sector Enterprises in French-speaking Africa" carried out in Togo, Rwanda and Mali since 1982. The programme is intended for the owners, workers and odd-job apprentices of (traditional) artisanal small and micro-enterprises. Here, however, there is particular emphasis on the setting up and strengthening of self-help organizations of the enterprises. Accompanying functional literacy measures are carried out in order to strengthen the ability within the target group to actively participate in the self-help process. A detailed description can be found in *MALDONADO* (1989), pp. 77–92.

or other advice as well as for the credit or technical skill training provided, is to ensure that these services are not viewed as charity, since this would undermine rather than strengthen the (potential) business(wo)men's self-help motivation. Furthermore, it helps to prevent that credit or advisory services are demanded more or longer than really necessary, which forces the (potential) entrepreneurs to push for the economic viability of their business, and also allows to offer the services to a larger group of "clients" as the participants in the programme are deliberately called.

A third parallel to the DESAP is that
– the measures and services, and accordingly the qualification of the staff are flexibly adapted to the local conditions, the environment-determined business options and the (qualification) needs of the target group.

As Euro-Action Accord initially was not familiar enough with neither the region nor the target groups, a preparatory and planning phase took place over about 18 months, *before* any measures, i.e. services were actually started, in order to explore the local living, working and market conditions, to roughly identify and then specify the target groups and finally elaborate tentative – later several times modified – assistance measures.

The entire programme as regards lending, business advisory services, client assessment and monitoring is almost exclusively carried out by roughly 20 local "business consultants", each of whom individually attends to and advises about 30 clients. For the technical training and advice of clients, already established and experienced local craftsmen could be found, who take on this task on request for a small fee.

The "business consultants" – about half of them women – were recruited among the target group and then trained for their tasks over several weeks with case studies, action learning and demonstration, all during the preparatory phase. Their back-up and further training is, in the meantime, the only main task of the expatriate adviser and programme coordinator. Induced by the programme, also a stable network of endogenous self-help activities reportedly has gradually developed within the target groups.

Conclusion

(i) The two principles of assigning all routine and service tasks to local staff recruited from the target groups themselves, and of selling these services to "clients" has apparently ensured that

– an externally initiated assistance programme has actually strengthened and not undermined self-help potentials;
– all business and advisory activities are – necessarily – geared to the optimum utilization of local resources and possibilities, and, thus, *can* actually emerge from within the target groups who regard, appreciate and maintain them as something which evolved from their own efforts;
– with the local "business consultants" a new kind of employment opportunity has been created, and also additional income-earning opportunities for the local workshops providing technical training and advisory services.
(ii) The experience from this programme shows that it is basically possible to induce an endogenous process for small business development and self-employment creation also at subsistence level among target groups which superficially appear to lack any economic development potential. This presupposes, however, a sensitive and participatory approach in the preparation as well as in the implementation of the assistance measures, in particular
– a thorough and adequately extensive planning phase on site to learn about the mentality and the environment-determined (business) development options of the target groups;
– to recruit and train the local staff required – business advisers, technical instructors and social catalysts – already during the preparatory stage, as far as possible from within or close to the target groups, and to also involve them in the planning process;
– to realize and promote the – normally existing – willingness and ability within the target groups to pay for the advisory, training and credit services desired and to assume own responsibility for their development process right from the beginning;
– accordingly, to delegate at a very early stage and to the greatest extent possible the routine implementation tasks to local staff, with the input of external planners and advisers being confined to coordinating and monitoring tasks, advisory assistance in more conceptual questions and the (advanced) training of the local staff.
(iii) Altogether, the animation-oriented "business consultants" concept as developed for Port Sudan can well be regarded as one model approach to occupation-oriented training for target groups from the informal sector, namely for the promotion of viable small business and self-employment of – at least initially – subsistence entrepreneurs.
Neither in planning nor in implementation, such programmes are necessarily bound exclusively to a *non*-government executing

organization. What is absolutely essential, however, is the creation or strengthening of self-help structures within the target groups. In many cases, this is facilitated or only possible in cooperation with a flexible and socially committed local counterpart institution which normally is more likely to be found among local NGOs than on the Government side.

(3) Vocational training and social education of rural youth for rural small business creation

is carried out at the Rural Trade School in Salima in Malawi in an approach which is widely viewed as exemplary for the promotion of business creation by young craftsmen in small rural towns and villages[130]. By setting up this school in 1974 – in technical cooperation with the GTZ – the Government reacted to the double problem of growing under- and unemployment among young rural people and, at the same time, a shortage of qualified craftsmen in the more remote parts of the country. It felt that both was jeopardizing the national strategy for the promotion of endogenous rural development.

In Salima, each year 60 young people from rural areas are admitted. They are required to have completed their service with the Malawi Young Pioneers for which there are already strict admission criteria, but primary school education is sufficient. There is, however, a deliberate attempt to select especially those youngsters whose individual potential and inclinations seem to correspond well with the training objective of the Rural Trade School – i.e. the creation of small rural workshops – to make sure that rural business creation really takes place and their training, thus, contributes in the medium run to a better supply of artisanal goods and services, appropriate (agricultural) machinery and tools in the rural areas. Hence, preference is given to applicants with noticeable technical talent and/or work experience[131].

The special features of the two-year formal vocational training for rural business creation can be summarized as follows:
— With free board and lodging and a small stipend, participation in the training is also possible for youngsters from very poor village families;
— In order to familiarize the students also with the working conditions typical in self-employment or small business, they have

130 Cf. *HARPER* (1989).
131 It is not clear from the information available whether and to what extent girls are also accepted for the training.

to produce various items for the local market, as part of their technical skill training. The material they need has to be bought at the school. The profit from selling their work-pieces tops up their stipends and allows them to buy new material for further market-oriented production during the training;
– To strengthen personal initiative and a sense of responsibility, the students also have to produce during the training the tools later needed for their own business;
– With social education – which in Malawi begins already in primary school – as part of the vocational training, self-confidence, self-discipline and self-reliance are taught as fundamental values, since they are regarded as indispensable virtues of a self-employed craftsman;
– The business location for each graduate is selected carefully and in good time by the school, by taking into consideration local demands and purchasing power and the general market situation;
– After successful graduation, the students are, in addition to the tools produced by themselves, provided by the school with a basic stock of necessary working materials to facilitate the critical start-up phase as a self-employed craftsman – which reminds of the same habit in traditional informal apprenticeship;
– Even after having set up their own small business, the graduates always have the opportunity to turn to the school for advice on any problems which may arise.

The technical training is reported to have a good quality standard, and is, at US$ 5,000 per student, relatively inexpensive. There are ten qualified instructors for the 60 students admitted each year. On average, 50 of the 60 students of each training year reportedly successfully complete the training and actually set up a small rural workshop afterwards[132].

Conclusion

(i)   The intended target group of rural youth is obviously reached by the Trade School in Salima, since there are neither financial nor excessively high formal enrolment restrictions.

---

132 There was as little information found on the training of the instructors and the fluctuation among them as on the roughly 17 % apparently unsuccessful students, the reasons for their failure and their later whereabouts.

(ii) A vocational training oriented to business creation, however, can only lead to a steadily growing number of rural workshops actually set up by the graduates, if there is an increasing demand for their products and services and enough purchasing power among the rural population. The absorptive capacity of the rural market sets also for this model the limits of positive employment impacts. The school itself, therefore, is well-advised to correlate its enrolment quota to the market-determined business opportunities of its graduates. A replication of the model in the same country can only work insofar as there is a general improvement in rural economic development.

(iii) This reservation by no means belittles the positive contribution of the Salima Trade School to precisely this rural development, and it also does not make the approach unsuitable for an adequately adapted implementation in other structurally similar rural regions.

When doing so, however, it should not be ignored that there are two specific factors which certainly have particularly contributed to the success of the Trade School in Salima:

— firstly, the concept's compatibility with the national strategy to promote an endogenous rural development, within which it even assumes an explicit role;

— secondly, the combination of a sound technical vocational training with a social education towards self-help and self-reliance, which already starts in primary school.

Both factors can hardly be overrated in their relevance for the success of this approach in terms of actually reaching the intended target group of rural youth as well as the positive impacts on rural (self-) employment generation.

6.3 *Complex Approaches to Occupation-oriented Training with Social Education for Rural Target Groups*

The work of numerous local NGOs shows that the possibility to reach the really poor and disadvantaged people, a long-term perspective in the planning and implementation of assistance measures right from the beginning, and a socio-pedagogical approach in occupation-oriented training and education for people from the informal sector all are *not necessarily* bound to the (personnel) structure of a church organization such as the congregation of the Salesians. In the meantime, projects of that kind exist – sometimes documented, sometimes hardly realized from outside – in many Third World countries[133].

Normally, however, they are neither confined to directly occupation-oriented training and education measures only, nor to just one isolated target group. The distinct features of such NGO projects or approaches are that they

– have a complex and always also social objectives orientation for their development work;
– consider social communities such as families, village communities or urban neighbourhoods as the smallest target group unit;
– consequently follow integrated development strategies with a complex set of measures, in which directly occupation-oriented training, education and advisory measures in conjunction with social education assume a central but not exclusive role;
– attach in training and education a high priority to social awareness creation and a strengthening of key qualifications required for the development of self-help potentials and personal initiative, such as self-organizational ability and "information processing" capacity, in the belief that this is the only way to achieve sustainable improvements in the living and working conditions of the majority of people from the informal sector, especially in rural areas.

What essentially contributes to the almost literal success of this kind of projects is that they actually reach their target groups from the informal sector – also in rural areas – and work with them on a genuinely participatory basis. Furthermore, their occupation-oriented training and education measures are not only (labour) market- but equally subsistence-oriented.

The approach and basic structure fairly common to this type of projects and their also rather common difficulties are outlined with exemplary reference to the work of the two local NGOs visited during the reconnaissance trip to India[134].

---

133 It definitely would be worthwhile conducting systematic field studies – instead of mere secondary analysis on the basis of available literature – to evaluate the working conditions, success factors, specific problems and "transferable", i.e. not context-bound, elements of such NGO projects in the field of occupation-oriented training and education for target groups from the informal sector. This would certainly provide useful ideas for the planning, priorities and implementation design of projects of (bilateral) vocational training assistance, too.
134 Presenting this type of NGO projects with reference to the projects visited, i.e. on the basis of direct information and on-site observations, seems more meaningful than the evaluation of secondary literature which can neither reflect the complexity of these approaches nor normally tells much about the practical difficulties occuring to such projects.

(1) Strengthening self-help potentials through education and occupation-oriented training to promote rural development

is the task which the Centre for Rural Education and Development Action (CREDA) has set itself[135]. One of CREDA's main objectives is to qualify economically and socially disadvantaged rural families – in currently 123 mostly remote villages – through simultaneous measures of social education, nutritional and health education, functional literacy education, practical occupation-oriented training and/or agricultural advisory assistance for either a directly income-generating occupation in (or near) their villages, and/or for various kinds of subsistence work which may save them expenses and enables them to improve their living conditions by own efforts[136].

The main ideas of the integrated conceptual approach on which CREDA's work in the villages is based, can be summarized as follows:

– Despite a special target group orientation to women, rural youth and bonded children[137], the village family and the village community are regarded as the unit to be helped, and to which all measures – although for individual (family) members in different ways – are geared[138];

– Rural education is perceived as an integrated combination of functional primary education for children and adults, pre-school education, occupation-oriented technical training and agricultural advice, social education, and awareness creation to strengthen self-help potentials;

---

135 CREDA is a local NGO based in Mirzapur (Uttar Pradesh) in Northeast India. It was set up in 1980 by Shamshad Khan, the son of a big landlord, after he had seen, during a field study for his doctoral thesis, the disastrous working and living conditions of the rural people who often still live in bondage.

136 The training and education activities must be seen in connection with simultaneous measures to set up village savings banks and corn banks, financial and organizational assistance for women to set up home production or small carpet-weaving mills, and the liberation of village families, especially children, from labour bondage. Other activities relate to various social services for poor families, including establishing a group insurance and emergency relief measures.

137 Bonded child labour exists – especially in Northeast India – especially in carpet-weaving, apart from in the agricultural sector. As bondage is passed on from the parents to the children, many children already work at a very young age and under absolutely wretched conditions as virtual bonded labour for big landlords or owners of carpet-weaving mills.

138 The "Thailand Institute for Rural Development" (THIRD) visited during the reconnaissance trip to Thailand, also works on the basis of this approach. Furthermore, THIRD tries – like CREDA – to professionalize the work of NGOs through target group-specific training of social multipliers in the villages. A number of noteworthy ideas in this context, especially on occupation-oriented training and education at village level in Africa, are also presented in an article by *TANNER* et al. (1989).

- In view of the situation in the villages, health, nutritional and hygiene education is regarded as indispensable part of any – also occupation-oriented – training, since this is the only way to fight at the roots the physical and mental consequences of child diseases and malnutrition which both ill-effect the ability to learn and often also to work for the rest of a life[139];
- Rural youngsters without primary school graduation have hardly any further vocational training and employment opportunities. But without pre-school education children from the villages can hardly keep up with the lessons in a normal primary school. Therefore, pre-schools are set up at village level, in which, beside basic literacy and social education, also rules of hygiene and some agricultural knowledge are taught, with accompanying counselling in the families[140];
- With the technical training and agricultural advice carried out directly in the villages, especially also for women, it is tried to create possibilities of income-earning and/or reducing spending, with village competitions as apparently effective incentive for the villagers to take up the training and advisory offers;
- Through socio-pedagogical training programmes for community development and awareness creation it is hoped that people in the villages will learn to realize their own development potential and gradually develop personal initiative, also to make better use of existing Government assistance programmes for the poor, and to free themselves – which, in principle, is possible – from bondage.

Sociological studies carried out by CREDA for its own work and also for other NGOs and Government institutions, and the continuous work experience in the villages provide the information base for the detailed design of the CREDA measures.

---

139 The implementation of a planned Rural Health Project during which women in all 123 villages are to be trained as health workers by qualified medical staff, is jeopardized because of the lack of funds to buy – not to operate – a cross-country vehicle and to organize the first "awareness creation camps" in the villages. A training programme for low-cost housing construction for poor families in Mirzapur is also planned, since most of them live in mud-huts which disappear each year during the rainy season and then have to be rebuilt, which makes it virtually impossible to observe rules of hygiene.

140 Up to now, CREDA has set up 30 such pre-schools (balwadi) for altogether 2,500 children. The CTVT of the Church of India, which was already mentioned in connection with the Community Polytechnic in Yellareddy, has also realized the importance of pre-school education for village children. The diocese of Medak has initiated the setting up of pre-schools already in 30 villages. In repeated meetings with social workers from the diocese, the women there were made aware of the relevance of pre-school education, and some of them were trained as pre-school teachers. The programme is planned to be extended to ultimately cover 300 villages.

Another objective of CREDA is the liberation and social (re)integration of bonded children. Under a special programme – the "Mirza-pur-Bhadohi Child Labour Project" – roughly 500 children aged between 5 and 12, who before worked in bonded child labour in backyard carpet-weaving mills, are given socio-psychological treatment and education in ten special schools[141]. The aim is to rehabilitate them both mentally and socially, and to bring them within three years time to an educational level equivalent to primary school. In addition, they all are trained in some direct occupation-oriented basic vocational skills. Some children who already have quite a good knowledge in this trade, receive a full training in carpet-weaving which, in principle, provides reasonable income-earning opportunities.

A striking feature is that CREDA is hardly confronted by the usual problems of staff fluctuation and inadequate staff motivation. Most of the 26 permanent and about 30 freelance employees, half of whom are women, were trained by CREDA itself. They work as teachers, agricultural advisers, health educators, social workers, doctors and sociologists. About 85 % of them, especially the social workers, agricultural advisers and health educators, were directly recruited from the villages[142] "to ensure their continued dedication for this type of work, and also because they can support themselves in case of interruption in salary payments" (Khan). They have a certain school education, and after a training by CREDA initially work as volunteers in their villages. During this period their skills and their social commitment are regularly observed and assessed with regard to a possible employment as permanent staff.

In addition, CREDA cooperates with altogether 535 unpaid volunteers in the 123 villages. Their motivation and dedication is explained, on the one hand, by the fact that they benefit also for themselves from the knowledge and skills acquired through the CREDA training. On the other hand, they are proud of the social recognition they receive in their villages for the noticeable improvements resulting from their work.

Both the permanent staff and the voluntary development workers in

---

141 CREDA bought the freedom of most of these children; some of them also managed themselves to escape.
142 The remaining 15 % of the permanent staff come from the social context of other local NGOs. They are qualified graduates of either a Teachers College or an Indian Training Institute (technician training).

the villages receive a regular training related to their assigned field of activity. This includes a training also in pedagogical skills to improve their communication and (social) education techniques.

Whereas, according to its own statements, CREDA faces hardly any major difficulties in the planning and implementation of its programmes, there were three specific problems repeatedly mentioned as regards the financing:

– The practice of foreign donor NGOs to finance a salary topping-up for local teachers and social workers for two years at most, always leads to an interruption, in more than a few cases even to a complete discontinuation of the activities carried out by the staff concerned. This not only hits the target groups hard, but also means a waste of time and money invested in the training of these development workers;

– The conditions set by donor organizations for a possible (continued) financing – often extremely detailed ideas on the programme design – are generally difficult to discuss with them. This is problematic insofar as they normally concentrate on single aspects only, without realizing neither the complexity of the approach nor the necessity for the simultaneity and equal significance of different kinds of measures as a precondition for the success of a programme as a whole;

– Like the Community Polytechnic in Yellareddy, CREDA, too, has made the experience that donors have a preference for "tangibles". Even for education and training programmes they prefer financing visible inputs, and they take the number of course participants or graduates as indicator for training success. In many cases, however, this policy and perception correspond neither to the financial assistance needs of a programme nor to the objectives orientation of the NGO.

Conclusion

(i) No critical remarks need to be added to the complex development approach and the work of CREDA towards a – gradual but, therefore, probably sustained – occupation-oriented qualification of rural target groups in the villages, and of bonded children who, in some aspects, may be compared to the urban street children. The model character for the planning and design of occupation-oriented training and education measures in other rural areas – especially those more distant to urban areas – should be realized and acknowledged.

(ii) As already stated for the CPY[143], also the case of CREDA shows how much the quality and success of the work of local NGOs depend – regardless of their concepts – on the availability and personal commitment of qualified staff *and* a leadership personality with an "urban socialization" and management capabilities or at least an intermediary with such qualities.

(iii) It sets thinking that not only CREDA but *all* the local NGOs visited – including the Don Bosco institutions – expressed discontent and an almost resigned lack of understanding as regards their experience that it is mainly the infrastructure of training institutions set up and maintained by them, and the number of training graduates which interest donor agencies – even NGO donors – in their assessment whether the measures have been successful and hence deserve (further) assistance.

The local NGOs themselves, however, do not consider these factors as the ultimate objectives and success indicators of their activities. Their measures of vocational training, social education and awareness creation are aimed at achieving sustainable learning results, and at really reaching and keeping the truly disadvantaged target groups which are neither easily nor readily accessible.

In this context, local NGOs see their task to act as "change agents" by teaching people who have been socialized in poverty, to develop social competence and occupation-oriented skills. This includes to give them ideas and information on how much endogenous development is possible through their own efforts, if they try to obtain suitable technologies *and* the know-how and skills to produce and apply them. Such processes of – a very much occupation-oriented – development education, however, take time, and are hardly visible and even less measurable within a short term.

(2) The transfer of appropriate technologies as an element of occupation-oriented qualification at village level

is the key component of a concept for rural development which was elaborated by two departments of the Institute of Engineering & Rural Technology (IERT) – the Community Development Cell (CDC) in collaboration with the Centre for Development and

---

143 Cf. Section 6.1.4, Point (3).

Rural Technology (CDRT) – in the district of Allahabad (Uttar Pradesh) in North India[144].

The basic objectives orientation, the target groups and many of the activities carried out under the management of the CDC in the so-called "Integrated Rural Development Centres" (IRDCs) are similar to those of CREDA. The concept of the IRDCs is also based on the idea of generating income and employment opportunities in the villages by strengthening the self-help potentials of the rural people through training and education including pre-school and primary school education, health and hygiene education.

What distinguishes the IERT concept is the integration of occupation-oriented training measures, social and health education into a more comprehensive strategy for the promotion of the rural economy, which is based on the transfer of appropriate technologies applicable and/or producible at village level. In this approach, the villages are viewed "as complex systems to be kept alive and tapped with local resources by translating existing technological knowledge into operation and application by the villagers themselves", says the head of the CDRT. Hence, the dissemination of appropriate technologies – devices as well as training in both technical skills and mental ability to apply them – is the central idea.

By promoting various kinds of rural small-scale industries not in each and every village but mainly in the IRDCs, and of home production and artisanal self-employment in smaller villages, the medium-term objectives are to create income and employment opportunities at village level, and to improve the local supply of goods and services by way of subsistence work as well as through the sale of local products and services. The resultant gradual increase in the purchasing power in the villages is expected to have further stimulating effects on the

---

144 The IERT and the Gohri IRDC were visited during the reconnaissance mission in June 1990. Initially set up in 1954 as a private "Civil Engineering School" and recognized in 1962 as the "Allahabad Polytechnic" for vocational training, the IERT has existed in its present form since 1981 as Government-recognized autonomous vocational training institution for formal and non-formal training and education of technicians, graduated engineers and staff of Government institutions and also private organizations working in rural development. As a so-called "Community Polytechnic", the IERT has served as a model since 1977/78 for, in the meantime, 110 other institutions of this kind in the field of rural community development and the transfer of appropriate technologies to rural areas. The varied activities of the IERT and of the IRDCs are described in greater detail in the additional volume submitted to the BMZ. A detailed description of the concept can be also found in *REHLING* (1988), pp. 109–142, although this relates to the situation in 1986 when the IRDCs were at the peak of their development.

local agricultural and artisanal production, and, thus, ultimately on the development of endogenous economic cycles in the rural areas[145].
Over a period of roughly seven years, the strategy and the activities of the CDC and CDRT included

– the setting up of four IRDCs, with 2–3 sub-centres each, concentrating the main economic activities and a social infrastructure to meet the basic needs for 10–15 villages, respectively, in realization of the fact that the economic potential and demand of just one village would be too limited to achieve – and maintain – on its own a similar level of economic development;

– non-formal vocational training and agro-technical advice as well as management and, if need be, financial support aimed at establishing a – partly interlinked – economic structure of (very) small rural industries comprising beside small-holder and subsistence farms and traditional crafts workshops also workshops for "modern" products such as shoes or matches, and commercial home production;

– the development, prototype testing and dissemination of various kinds of appropriate technologies for which there are needs and resources in the villages, including the training required for the application of these technologies by the villagers;

– the training of local "social multipliers" such as development workers, animators and (agro-)technology advisers at village level;

– at the academic level, advanced training of technical instructors and so-called mid-level extensionists[146] who should – and for quite some time did – assume the role of "bridge-heads" between the IRDCs, on the one side, and the urban institutions and markets, on the other side, to transfer information – in a wide sense – and help to establish and stabilize the structures required for the economic and technological exchange between the villages and the town of Allahabad.

After personnel changes at the CDC, almost all the emergent development including the activities in many workshops in the IRDCs and the village-based home productions – in fact, all economic activities which were (still) dependent on the existence of

---

145 The basic idea is the same as for the CPY. The IERT, however, could put in more own personnel and material resources, and a considerable know-how on the development of appropriate technologies and – to a more limited extent – on their dissemination at village level.

146 This advanced training still takes place with a two-year postgraduate study programme and short training courses at the IERT in Allahabad. The target groups are mainly rural development workers and staff of both NGOs and Government institutions engaged in rural development, especially in the fields of technology development and dissemination and management skills.

precisely those "bridge-heads" – has come to a standstill. The people in the villages have been unable to offset the consequences of the interrupted advisory services and the suddenly lacking support in the procurement of intermediate products and in the marketing of their own products in such a way as to maintain what had already been achieved. Only those economic activities and social services are still continued in the IRDCs by already trained local instructors and social workers, which do not depend on external inputs. This covers the primary school and pre-school education, the health service, and a few workshops which produce only for village needs and only from materials easy to obtain or available directly in the villages.

Conclusion

(i)   The extremely positive development in the IRDCs over a longer period has shown that it is in fact possible to externally induce an endogenous (economic) development process in rural areas, if precisely those "development ingredients" are provided which are not available in the villages and also cannot easily be obtained by the rural people's own efforts, namely
– information on technologies which they could apply or – in case of tools and devices – produce to improve their living environment and working conditions, and/or to (better) produce marketable crops, goods or services;
– the (low-cost) procurement of materials and tools, and the access to urban sales markets which from the village perspective are already far away even at a distance of only 10 km, because of lack of transportation means and/or no experience of where in town to offer their products.
A substantial requirement for a long-term self-sustaining process, however, is that during the period of assistance a sufficient number of villagers have had the opportunity to develop the ability to acquire and apply on their own the information relevant to them and their community, and to establish their own communication links and market channels to an urban trade centre and/or to a rural extension service located there.
(ii)   The unfortunate later development of the IRDCs underlines that the acquisition of such key qualifications is at least as important as a technical skill training, but that those learning processes take a long time – even if increasing economic activities indicate some visible success already. Over a very long period of stabilization

their further development remains – as much as the economic activities themselves – dependent on external support, even though to a decreasing extent[147].

Therefore, though not the permanent presence of "bridge-head" advisers or intermediaries, yet the long-term and continuous availability of advisory and support services is essential, if a sustainable rural economic development is intended to be induced. This, however, ultimately depends on the dedicated commitment of individuals, even if – as in the case of the IERT-supported IRDCs – the concept is translated into action by an established institution[148].

(iii) As an approach which is districtly oriented to the given environment-determined occupation opportunities and development options, the IRDC concept very pragmatically combines measures for the promotion of small industries and self-employment with those of occupation-oriented training for (village-based) wage-employment and for subsistence work, hence being market- and subsistence-oriented at the same time. Especially with regard to its ability of reaching rural target groups and let them actively participate in shaping their own development, and to the income and employment generating effects induced in a rural area, it would definitely be worth making a renewed attempt to implement the IRDC approach in the context of a (bilateral) assistance programme for occupation-oriented training and education of rural target groups, in particular.

In view of the IERT experience, however, a particularly thorough emphasis should be put on the selection and, if required, very long-term support of a local counterpart institution which is qualified for this task in institutional and technical as well as in social terms.

6.4 Primary School Education as First Step Towards Occupation-oriented Training and Education

For most people from the informal sector and especially for women, primary school education is the only education opportunity they may

---

147 This, by the way, also applies to the setting up or strengthening of self-help organizations, as may be seen from the long duration of projects such as the ILO programme for the promotion of artisanal self-help organizations in Rwanda, Togo and Mali, or the SWISSCONTACT project with the business association APTAMAI in Costa Rica, to mention only two already cited examples.
148 It should be mentioned that some staff members of the still very active CDRT plan to set up a new NGO named "Agro Energy and Rural Development Society" (AERDS), to resume the IRDC concept, although not necessarily in the same villages again.

ever have. Since in the meantime most developing countries provide – normally also in rural areas – education, at least the basic facilities and legal regulations for a compulsory primary school education, the primary school possesses more than any other institution the *potential* to reach a large number of people – and this at their young, i.e. most educable, age.
When discussing the significance of primary school education with regard to later employment opportunities for disadvantaged young people from the informal sector, however, a distinction should be made between
– the basic need for a sound primary school education which *de facto* is accessible to everyone, as a prerequisite for any (chance of) further vocational or – in a wider sense – occupation-oriented training and education;
– the separate need – especially in rural areas – to incorporate into primary school education also (practical) curricula which take into account the environment-determined learning opportunities and potentials of village children and their future occupational options, and which hence are subsistence-oriented, too.

6.4.1 *Improved and Generally Accessible Primary School Education to Increase Occupation Opportunities*

The reality in Third World countries is that still almost 100 million children and youngsters remain excluded from primary school education. An even greater number does not learn to master even the basic elements of educational skills during a primary school attendance which is often seasonally interrupted or completely discontinued after 3–4 years. This means that any kind of occupation-oriented and education for target groups from the informal sector remains confronted with the problem that it can normally neither build upon an existing basic knowledge of reading and writing, let alone arithmetic, nor assume the participants to be familiar with the process and techniques of learning as such.
Occupation-oriented training offers – especially if they are aimed at providing qualifications for small business creation, gainful self-employment or a reasonably paid wage-employment – however, are a real opportunity only for those who thanks to a good primary education are not only formally, but also mentally "competitive" enough to meet the requirements for vocational training and further education. Only on the basis of a sufficient primary education can

formal or non-formal vocational training for people from the informal sector be more than the makeshift attempt to compensate the problem of underqualification already developed in childhood. Otherwise, the result will be

– either "second-class" graduates of non-formal courses without a real chance on the labour market,

– or the necessity to incorporate, as far as possible, substantial elements of primary education into vocational training to give a chance of success, at all.

Therefore, the call for a good-quality and generally accessible primary school education should top the list when considering long-term effective measures of occupation-oriented training and education for young people from the informal sector. Its main functions – each of them equally important – for the children and youngsters growing up in urban slums and in the villages, are

– to provide more equal opportunities on the labour market or in self-employment as well as for a further vocational or otherwise occupation-oriented training and education;

– to give – through a generally compulsory primary school attendance – also girls an equal chance of education and employment, in view of the fact that especially in the informal sector it is mainly the women who bear the greatest burden when it comes to providing for their families;

– to develop already during childhood, when it is most easily done, a good learning capacity and certain key qualifications required for self-organization and the "intelligent handling" of innovative information[149];

– to influence their socialization – despite the daily experience of poverty – in such a way as to familiarize them with the relevant norms, the rules of social conduct and the ways of thinking prevailing in a predominantly urban-industrial culture, and help them to develop their own criteria for assessing technological, economic and social innovations and using them creatively to improve their own living and working conditions[150].

A generally raising level of basic education also in rural areas – not

---

149 Cf. also, in a similar sense, *IBRD* (1989a), p. 192.
150 In this context, it is worth mentioning the interesting but not yet fully elaborated EDEJU concept, the approach of which is to develop and strengthen precisely such social capabilities and creativity already during childhood by means of educational games and plays. It has been developed in the Ivory Coast by the "International Institute for the Promotion of Youth Development", so far explicitly only for out-of-school education; cf. *HELMETH* (no year of publication) and *ULRICH* (no year of publication).

only by improving primary school education, but also by stepping up the functional basic education of adults – does not only increase individual opportunities of further education and vocational training, gainful wage- or self-employment or successful business creation. But a larger number of younger people with a fairly good basic education also improves the chances for

– the local recruitment and advanced training of men and women in the role of social multipliers, for example, as instructors, pre-school educators or social workers in their villages or urban squatter communities;

– economic development in rural areas, since especially relatively labour-intensive medium-sized industries will be attracted by a local labour force which can comparatively easily be trained as odd-job or semi-skilled workers according to the needs of the enterprises;

A qualified and generally accessible primary school education, therefore, has substantial positive employment impacts, both directly and indirectly. It should not be overlooked, however, that a better and wider primary school education will merely shift, but not solve the fundamental problem of inadequate income and employment opportunities for a growing number of people. This can be clearly observed in countries with an already relatively low illiteracy rate and a high level of basic and secondary education.

From an individual point of view it is undoubtedly justified to see a direct link between poor education and poor employment opportunities. However, if the overall economic development fails to keep pace with a general improvement in the level of education, the individuals will simply have to compete even stronger for a more or less stagnant number of jobs available. This is not said to conclude that a good primary education for all is not that urgent, after all. It merely is to remind that all education and training measures cannot offset adverse economic frame conditions and a sluggish or recessive economic development. A generally good level of basic education will certainly contribute to improve the economic parameters.

6.4.2 *Environment-adapted Primary School Education Related to Realistic Occupation Opportunities*

Where also for the majority of people from the informal sector in the long term even a good and generally accessible primary school education will hardly improve the chances of vocational training or gainful (self-)employment, just because there are neither enough adequate training opportunities nor enough jobs or market potential for a growing number of businesses, the only remaining option is to teach children and youngsters – especially in rural areas – already in primary school also skills useful for subsistence work and/or directly income-generating occupations in their immediate environment.

Up to now, there are only a few approaches for a primary school education which is oriented to the occupational opportunities and options given in a rural environment, three of which are presented below[151]. The "Escuela Nueva" is described mainly for another reason, but also basically suitable for the adoption of such an approach.

(1) Elements of artisanal vocational school education related to the occupation opportunities in a rural environment

were integrated into the primary and post-primary stages of the formal education system in Rwanda in 1979. Based on the assumption that

– school can reach the largest possible number of people and especially in rural areas also is the only educational institution which most people – and girls generally – will ever attend;

– the majority of the pupils in rural schools will continue to live in the villages after school, and hence will have to find income-earning and occupation possibilities at least partly in the subsistence economy;

– although (primary) school is not the place for a full-fledged vocational training, it is during primary education that young people do – or do not – develop their learning capacity and a certain "technical" way of thinking,

the conventional six-year primary education was extended by a two-year stage of education called "Ruralisation I", during which in partly practical lessons the pupils should be prepared for a working life in a rural environment. The ensuing three-year post-primary stage of "Ruralisation II" is to provide a mostly practical integrated rural and technical education for those who cannot be taken on at the secondary school level. It corresponds in its objective to a broad occupation-oriented training and education rather than to a "classic"

---

151 Only brief presentations are given, without the conclusion normally drawn. The reason is that there is neither enough secondary information on the projects nor sufficient own practical experience in this field. The selected examples are rather intended to stimulate new ideas in view of the crucial role primary school education should assume as part of an occupation-oriented education suitable to improve the development opportunities of the people in the informal sector.

vocational training[152]. Realizing that this is the only way to ensure that pupils and teachers take the practical education seriously, marks are given for the practical subjects just as for the general subjects.
The practical education takes place in school training workshops. The material and operating costs are apparently kept within limits, since both the equipment and the techniques are fairly adapted to the technological level in the rural environment, and part of the facilities and the tools required are done by the teachers and pupils themselves.
The objective orientation of the "Ruralisation" programme corresponds, particularly for the second phase, to a certain extent to that of the CPY. The main difference is that thanks to its integration into the formal school system and the – in principle – compulsory primary school attendance, the "Ruralisation" programme reaches a much larger number of children and youngsters, and also the girls. Furthermore, it can make use of existing school facilities and Government-employed teachers, and also build on a certain level of general primary education.
The successful implementation of the programme decisively depends on the quality and the motivation of the school teachers, and this appears to be one of its weakest points. Therefore, an advanced training programme for teachers of the "Ruralisation" subjects is being carried out in technical cooperation with the GTZ[153]. It provides vocational training and pedagogical skills to
– already employed teachers, through mobile advisory and training units and the provision of "Ruralisation"-specific training materials;
– will-be teachers, through a special curriculum in the technical-pedagogical branch of the secondary schools where primary school teachers are educated.
Apart from teaching the necessary practical knowledge and vocational skills, the objective of these training measures which – as incentives for the teachers – also include inter-school competitions, is for the teachers to develop certain key qualifications, in particular a sense of good personal work performance and product quality, organizing and planning skills required for the preparation of the practical lessons, and a general "technical" understanding.
Nevertheless, the biggest implementation problems of the "Ruralisation" programme remain apparently that
– both the teachers already employed and the teachers in education

---

152 Cf. *REHLING* (1988), p. 182, who gives a detailed description of the "Ruralisation" programme and the implementation experience up until the year of publication; cf. pp. 178–190.
153 This is described in brief in *BERGMANN* (1990).

generally come from an urban middle-class background, so that their adaptation to a rural environment and way of life cannot be taken for granted, not even after preparation and motivation during the (advanced) teachers training;
– the standard of the teacher training and, thus, the educational and even more the technical qualification of most teachers still is very low, with 50 % of them having no formal teacher qualification, at all;
– the subject-matters of the "Ruralisation" programme are incorporated into the primary school curricula not before the seventh class, by which time a different understanding of education – more or less oriented to urban-style career patterns – has long set in the minds of most of the pupils and their parents.

With only about 70 % of the children in any one age-group in fact enrolled for primary school, and only 45 % completing the eight primary school years, well over half of any one year are not even reached by the "Ruralisation I" education. As regards the post-primary education phase, this share increases to almost four-fifths, since after primary school a further 24 % of the youngsters of one age-group drop school and return to their villages. Only about 10 % take up the post-primary rural and technical training[154].

These figures show that the Government's ambitious objective of qualifying 90 % of the children of any one school year under the "Ruralisation" programme for gainful (self-)employment and subsistence work in their rural environment, still is far from realization. The large number of children who never attend or drop out from primary school, however, proves that this nevertheless remains a definitely meaningful education policy orientation.

(2) Agricultural education at primary school as part of an integrated rural development project

was introduced in 1983 in the Tanga region in Tanzania. Following a one-year preliminary phase, the Polytechnical Education Support Programme (PESP) was started concurrently at two levels,
– first and primarily, at the Teachers College with the education and advanced training of primary school teachers in a subject deliberately called "Agricultural Science";
– second, directly in – initially 100, by 1987 altogether 635 – village

---

154 These figures are taken from *REHLING* (1989), p. 185. Although they may not be fully up-to-date, they have probably not fundamentally changed since 1988. To complete the picture, it should be added that, according to this source, roughly 4 % of any one year attend secondary school and 7 % take up a paid employment immediately after primary school.

schools to promote this newly introduced subject among teachers, pupils and parents[155].

For the advanced teacher training and for the school lessons, teaching manuals were developed in practical case studies carried out together with the teacher students at the Polytechnic. These manuals, however, are meant for the exclusive use by the teachers, not for pupils, since the intention of the PESP is not to impart theoretical knowledge but practical agricultural skills and know-how to the school children.

The major principles for teaching the subject of "Agricultural Science" in the village schools are that

– no locally still unknown equipment is used in the practical lessons, but only tools and materials available in the villages;

– no – in relation to the area's level of development – fundamental agricultural innovations are introduced, but gradual improvements which build on the existing knowledge of local crops, cultivation techniques etc.;

– no cash crops are grown in the school farmyards, but local crops for the children's school meals, which can be taken home in case of surplus production – a measure which has contributed a lot to the popularity of the PESP.

With the introduction of practical agriculture as a compulsory subject at village primary schools, the PESP aimed at familiarizing already the children with improved cultivation techniques, agricultural technologies and new crop varieties[156], and, at the same time, improving the food supply and nutrition of the children and later also the village communities as a whole. Furthermore, the agricultural innovations and the experience from both the teachers training at the Polytechnic and the introduction of "Agricultural Science" lessons at the village school are put to use in other fields of the integrated rural development project of which the PESP is a part only.

One of the main experience of the PESP which is worth being well kept in mind is that for a sustained training success and the development of sound agro-technical and pedagogical skills, the village teachers indispensably need a regular back-up tuition after the first training for another 3–4 years.

---

155 The programme is described in *RIEDMILLER* (1989).
156 In this regard, the PESP differs from the agricultural curricula normally – if at all – taught at primary schools. They are mostly confined to teaching locally already known agricultural knowledge and skills, thus duplicating – often even inadequately – what the children learn at home, anyway; cf. *BUDE* (1988), p. 37.

(3) "Farming as Vocation"
is the basic concept of a primary school curriculum oriented to the occupation opportunities and development options given in the rural areas. It was introduced as Rural Education and Agriculture Programme (REAP) in Belize in 1976 with the support from CARE and US Peace Corps volunteers, initially as a pilot project at eight rural primary schools[157].

From realizing that projects introducing agricultural subjects in primary schools worldwide normally face severe problems or even fail because
– the teachers are inadequately qualified and/or lack motivation;
– the agricultural lessons are entirely dissociated from the general school curricula,
the REAP planners drew the conclusion that agricultural subjects must be integrated into the curricula of all subjects as a kind of "red thread" from the first year of primary school onwards. For the primary school education in Belize they identified altogether nine agricultural topic areas. The pupils have to write essays on the agricultural and social situation in their villages, or arithmetic calculations is taught with reference to rural activities, such as weighing out of seeds, to give just two examples.

With a primary school education which from the very beginning and in all subjects incorporates issues related to the predominantly rural environment, it is aimed to overcome the common perception of agricultural work as an "inferior" activity by
– teaching the children who mainly come from subsistence farming families, about improved and appropriate agricultural technologies and crops, food processing and storage, thus giving them ideas and skills for gainful (self-)employment in their village after graduation from school;
– making it clear to them in all subjects that and how a lot of the theoretical knowledge acquired at school can be usefully applied in farming, too;
– above all, developing among the children and their parents a perception of "farming" – even subsistence farming – as a recognized profession which, like any other, produces better results the more knowledge and skills go into it.

During the pilot phase, the REAP curriculum was introduced first to eight rural schools where land property rights and water supply were no issues, and both parents and teachers appreciated the project.

---

157 A description of the programme can be found in *BARRY* (1984).

Further principles in the planning and implementation of the REAP were
- to have all Government institutions responsible for primary school education at whatever administrative level from the beginning participate in the curriculum development and the implementation of the programme;
- to actively integrate also the parents – most of them subsistence farmers – into the programme through social work, especially counselling on hygiene and nutrition;
- to leave the crops grown at the school farms – some of which were not yet known locally – to the children and their families, which reportedly has contributed to substantially improve the nutritional situation, and to disseminate new crops in the villages;
- after the introduction of the new curriculum at a school, to provide a long-term and intensive back-up tuition to support and further train the school teachers.

When a first evaluation of the REAP after three years revealed that the pupils at the pilot schools did much better in all subjects than the pupils at the other primary schools of the country, the programme enjoyed a wide acceptance at all levels and further expansion. The REAP curricula for primary school education then became an integral part of teacher training at all Teachers Colleges. Since 1982, the REAP has been officially adopted and decided to be successively introduced in all primary schools countrywide[158].

(4) A "one-room school" model for primary education in sparsely populated rural areas

was initially introduced by the UNESCO in Colombia already in 1967, but without any adjustments of the curriculum and subject-matters to the specific conditions and educational requirements in a rural environment, or to the learning opportunities and potentials of village children. After the programme was subsequently financed first by USAID and then by the Inter-American Development Bank, it was taken over in 1989 by the World Bank in cooperation with UNICEF. They tried to improve it mainly in three aspects[159]:

---

158 After ten years of implementation the REAP curriculum was introduced already at 65 of the country's 206 primary schools. In 1984 an evaluation of the sustained results and long-term benefits of this kind of agriculture- and also subsistence-oriented primary school education was reportedly carried out among former pupils educated under the programme. Despite several efforts, it unfortunately was not possible to obtain any information on the evaluation results.
159 Apart from some information from discussions and a short article by *COLBERT DE ARBOLEDA* (1990), unfortunately no further information could be obtained.

- In an initial training of about ten days and two back-up training courses during the same year, village school teachers are now prepared specifically for the task of teaching in one room classes of several school-years;
- The content of the teaching materials was adapted to some extent to the rural context of the village schools;
- After a revision of the teaching materials which mainly consisted of "learning cards", into a sequence of interlinked learning steps, teachers and pupils are now forced to actually critically digest the learning content of each step, whereas before teaching meant only to have the children neatly copy in hand-writing the content of the "learning cards".

According to UNICEF, roughly 900,000 pupils in 17,000 of the country's altogether 27,000 rural primary schools are being taught on the basis of this programme known as "Escuela Nueva"[160].

The striking aspect of this "one-room school" model undoubtedly is the comparatively low cost of a relatively extensive primary school education reaching also more remote and sparsely populated areas. A primary education which qualifies for a further education or vocational training, however, can hardly be expected. Therefore, it would make sense to introduce in the "one-room school" curricula also (practical) subjects related to the living conditions and occupation opportunities in a rural environment.

The approaches described above show that a primary school education with also practical and environment-adapted curricula is feasible, in principle. But the effectiveness, acceptance and sustainability of such programmes depend – apart from the political will to introduce them and their appreciation on part of the parents – decisively on the availability, qualification and motivation of the teachers.

The teachers (to be) assigned to primary schools in rural areas hence are the most crucial *intermediate* target group in vocational training assistance programmes for rural target groups. Not only an adequate advanced training but also the first training of teachers in rural areas, therefore, deserves highest priority when the objective is to improve the occupation opportunities especially of the still young rural people.

Depending on the extent to which teachers for both primary schools and the – in many countries already extremely important –

---

160 No information was available as regards the educational and social background of the teachers and the fluctuation rate.

pre-schools are (possible to be) recruited in the villages and urban squatter areas, a countryside upgraded primary education would also directly create more employment opportunities for people from the informal sector, especially for women.

As primary school education in most countries still is under the exclusive responsibility of the Government – apart from schools run by church(-related) institutions – there is normally little scope in this field for development agencies to cooperate with private local institutions as counterparts. Any reforms of primary education will depend on Government consent, and hence the cooperation with the responsible Government institutions. At this level, still numerous reservations and objections have to be overcome by means of long-term policy advisory assistance and institutional strengthening of the responsible authorities – a worthwhile task in the interest of hundreds of thousand of young people from the informal sector.

6.5 *Synopsis of the Approaches Presented as Conceptual Modules*

As already emphasized at the beginning of this chapter, there can be no such thing as the *one* concept for occupation-oriented training and education for people from the informal sector. The heterogeneity and differences within the informal sector as regards living and working conditions, learning opportunities and potentials, their environment-determined occupation opportunities and, therefore, their assistance needs and development options are simply too great.

Consequently, not one overall concept was tried to be elaborated, which with the necessary generalization could only be vague, anyhow. Instead, a number of – in concept and design partly very different – approaches and (project) experiences of different institutions and NGOs engaged in vocational training and education have been presented and assessed as regards their suitability for the promotion of target groups from the informal sector, in particular.

Some of these approaches appear to have almost a model character, whereas others only in some elements should be taken into account when designing occupation-oriented training and education measures for target groups from the informal sector within the framework of (bilateral) vocational training assistance. Nevertheless, the approaches presented should be viewed altogether as a set of *conceptual modules* to refer to for a model or just some ideas, which, of course, in any case still have to be adapted to the specific situation and qualification needs of the target groups in mind, and to the respective frame conditions.

At the end of this chapter, the most important features of the various approaches are summarized in a synoptic table. With regard to the inadequacy of such a tabular form of presentation which necessarily omits even some relevant aspects, reference should, however, also be made to the more comprehensive descriptions in the text.

The tabular summary again shows that it is not so much the objectives or the target groups, and not even a specific type of (counterpart) institution, which largely determine the suitability and success of a particular approach, but rather the kind of planning and the appropriateness of the design of the training and education measures in detail.

If the success and the suitability of an approach to occupation-oriented training and education particularly for target groups from the urban and rural informal sector are measured in terms of

– its contribution to realize the above formulated overall objectives, i.e. vocational qualification oriented to the environment-determined occupation and learning opportunities of the target group(s), strengthening their "information processing capacity" and communication skills, creating more equal opportunities for their economic and social integration, and promoting their self-help potential;

– its ability to actually reach these target groups, and – as a prerequisite for a target group-specific design of measures – to realistically assess their character, especially their learning opportunities and potentials, their (potential) occupation opportunities and their respective qualification needs;

– its impact on (self-)employment and income generation opportunities for the people from the informal sector and/or the improvement of their living and working conditions in the subsistence economy, then a critical assessment of the various approaches described reveals that a sustainable – though not necessarily easily quantifiable – success seems to be possible to be achieved only, if for the intended measures

– the problem of availability, adequate professional and pedagogical qualification and motivation of – expatriate or local – teachers, instructors and other staff, and of intermediary target groups in the role of social multipliers is resolved;

– the planning takes place at least partly on site, with a knowledge as precise as possible of the target group-specific qualification needs, occupational options and learning opportunities, and flexible adjustments in the concept, priorities, time schedule, or activities are made during the implementation, whenever the need arises;

– there is a firmly established local (counterpart) institution to cooperate with, close enough to the target group in terms of both location and social access, working with a long-term perspective and exclusively for target groups from the informal sector;
– the occupation-oriented training and advisory services are not confined to a qualification in technical skills, but put equal emphasis on social and general education, to promote personality development and facilitate the social and occupational (re)integration of people from the informal sector;
– the training and education is (largely) free, except for advisory services and advanced training for small and micro-entrepreneurs, and also actively "propagated" among the target group(s).

These "success factors" may be found in such different approaches as
– the socio-pedagogical concept of the otherwise rather "classic" vocational training at the Don Bosco Technical Schools of the Salesians, although in rural areas they are confronted by the described problems due to their biased orientation to conventional vocational profiles;
– the environment-adapted and also subsistence-oriented vocational training of rural youth as carried out by CREDA or the Community Polytechnic in Yellareddy;
– the concept of the IRDCs, in principle, apart from the specific institutional problems;
– the DESAP programme for "business education" for small and micro-entrepreneurs and self-employed business(wo)men "with development potential" on the one side, and the concept of "business consultants" for (potential) small entrepreneurs and self-employed persons in the subsistence economy of Port Sudan, on the other side;
– the different forms of non-formal or informal dual vocational training like in the Workshop Centre in Port Bouet, under the NOAS, or in the "cooperative training" at the SISD;
– last but not least, to a certain extent also in the ordinary non-regulated informal odd-job apprenticeship training.

Although their objectives, their target groups, and the type of implementing institutions or organizations partly vary considerably, all of these approaches work basically – intentionally or not – on the above mentioned "success factors". The following chapter outlines the implications which should result from this assessment for the planning and design of occupation-oriented training and education measures for target groups from the informal sector to be carried out within the framework of (bilateral) vocational training assistance.

6.1 Individual Qualification for a (Labour) Market-oriented Occupation and/or for Subsistence Work
6.1.1 Vocational Profile-oriented Training and Education in (Partly) Government-run Training Centres

	1 Priority Objective(s)	2 Target Group(s) Actually Received	3 Employment Income-generating Effects for IS–TG	4 Other Qualifications Imparted	5 Quality and Availability of Instructors/Trainers
(1) (Partly) Government-run Vocational Training Centres Latin America	(non-)formal VT ovp of skilled workers for employment in MS	secondary school graduates (mainly from urban areas, hardly IS); hardly any girls; non-formal training also for primary school pupils	limited because of access problems of IS–TG and qualification inadequate for both MS and IS employment	none	high fluctuation, esp. loss of qualified instructors because of poor pay; qualification of instructors too ovp
(2) Metal Work Training Project NRNFEC Thailand	non-formal VT ovp for rural youngsters to set up village workshops; NFEC generally (l)m–o qualification	youngsters from/near provincial capitals, 12–15 years old, primary school graduation; no girls in project because of metal trade	limited as regards setting up of village workshops limited; reasonable in urban areas as journeymen/odd-job workers in S(M)E (but only relatively few)	entrepreneurial/business skills training planned, not (yet) carried out	technically moderate, mostly little pedagogical skills; high fluctuation/poor motivation because of poor pay and low social status

6.1.2 Forms of Dual Vocational Training in Cooperation with Private (Small) Enterprises

	1 Priority Objective(s)	2 Target Group(s) Actually Received	3 Employment Income-generating Effects for IS–TG	4 Other Qualifications Imparted	5 Quality and Availability of Instructors/Trainers
(1) Dual Vocational Training Latin America	qualification ovp of skilled labourers for employment in MS, training mainly in MS enterprise	as 6.1.1(1)	limited because of access problems; as 6.1.1(1), but more dependent on labour market situations in MS	none	number and (pedagogical) qualification of instructors inadequate; not enough enterprises interested/able to carry out practical VT in their workshops
(2) "Cooperative Training Courses" SISD Thailand	sound (non-formal) qualification of rural youngsters as semi-skilled workers for employment in rural enterprises	rural IS–TG, also without school graduation as well as unemployed; apparently no women (yet)	84 % of graduates from the "Cooperative Training Courses" subsequently employed, mainly in enterprises in the southern region	none	both at SISD and in cooperating private enterprise apparently sufficient
(3) "National Open Apprenticeship Scheme" NOAS Nigeria	non-formal/informal VT in total of 81 vocational/occupational fields in enterprises of all kinds and sizes, also for s–o occupation	youngsters, also girls, from IS(u) and IS(r), with/without primary school graduation	gainful employment so far for approx. 40 % of graduates; main fields unknown	also s–o qualification for subsistence work possible; certain vocational theory training in "saturday classes"	little information, also not on training of instructors (craftsmen and technical teachers)

(4) Workshop Centre (WC) Port Bouel Ivory Coast	non-formal, customer demand-oriented technical VT for employment esp. in IS	youngsters (boys) without school education from IS(u); no girls apparently because of trades selected (men's trades)	difficult to say, but apparently good (self-) employment opportunities also as itinerant indep. service craftsmen, also in subsistence sector	basic general education and business administration skills	master craftsmen from IS with own business at WC: type and qualification of external technical instructors unknown

6.1.3 Informal Occupation-oriented Training and Education

(1) Odd-job Apprenticeship Developing Countries Worldwide	no explicit objectives; most common form of vocational training for youngsters from IS	young people (mostly boys) of all ages, normally (almost) without school education, from IS(u) and IS(r), but mainly in urban areas	basically considerable, but dependent on general economic and employment situation	through observation perhaps development of some entrepreneurial skills enabling for business creation, also in subsistence economy	only workshop training in S(M)E; qualification of workshop owners varies considerably; often no real training, but learning-by-doing (odd-job work)
(2) Traditional Guild-like Apprenticeship West Africa	guild-like organized apprenticeship in traditional crafts	youngsters from urban/rural craftsman families, not necessarily IS; normally school graduation required; traditionally no girls	limited, depending on guild-like determined quota for admission of new craftsmen/enterprises in resp. trade	to limited extent qualification for later S(M)E business creation	only workshop training according to best local craftsmanship, mainly by workshop owner (master) himself
(3) Commercial Private Training Institutions Developing Countries Worldwide	qualification mainly in business administration for employment esp. in the modern service sector	men and women of all ages with sufficient basic educational skills, mainly from IS(u)	dependent on labour demand in business administration/secretarial services in MS; little information on actual employment chances of course participants	none	unknown, definitely extremely varying

6.1.4 Training and Education with Reference to Given Environment-determined Opportunities and Options

(1) Talleres Públicos Costa Rica	Provision of publicity accessible workshops with opport. for non-formal ()m-o/s-o pract. VT close to place of residence of TG, for IS(u) and IS(r) occupation	Men and women of all ages from IS, also without school education, but as a rule with some previous technical knowledge and skills	in case of already existing technical skills pos. through use of workshop; partly qual. subsistence work after some pract. guidance; probably little as regards ()m-o employment in MS	poss. strengthening of self-organization potential for setting up of cooperatives and/or home production	apparently adequate; preparatory training of local instructors too biased towards application of ILO-developed "Modules of Employable Skills" (MES)

233

	1 Priority Objective(s)	2 Target Group(s) Actually Received	3 Employment Income-generating Effects for IS–TG	4 Other Qualifications Imparted	5 Quality and Availability of Instructors/Trainers
(2) Village Polytechnics (VP) Kenya	promotion of endogenous rural econ. development through village-based non-formal m–o/s–o skill training of youngsters as village craftsmen	primary school graduates in the villages	limited at the time because of discrepancy in objectives and application; qualification ovp de facto neither adequate for urban MS nor for IS employment	idea: entrepreneurial skills for business creation or self-employment in rural areas; in reality: none	instructors at the time unsuitable, since neither from rural areas nor prepared for training IS(r)–TG; mainly graduates from formal VTCs
(3) Yellareddy (CPY) Andhra Pradesh India	techn./soc. education of (l)m–o, esp. s–o occupation in rural areas; information and skill training on use of AT to gradually induce endogenous rural development at village level	young school drop-outs and primary school graduates from poor village families; at present only boys, girls planned for next phase with mob. training at village level	good, esp. in subsist. sector, 50 % of grad. empl. as local craftsmen (combination of ind. work for money inc. and subsist. work); 35 % stay at CPY for better qualific.	social education; basic primary education; basic business administration skills; knowledge on AT	good; local craftsmen as instructors; technically and pedagogically very skillful director; general and social education carried out by director's wife
(4) Infrastructure Programmes Developing Countries Worldwide	purpose-oriented technical training in (building) construction skills, not spec. in m–o or s–o, but to strengthen technical SH abilities for any poss. occupation	members of families included in a (building) infrastructure programme, provided that SHO exist	dependent on avail. of raw materials for indep./subsist. work, for wage labour depend. on labour market/econom. situation	poss. further strengthening of self-organization abilities; basic knowledge in small business organization	unknown; certainly very varying; instructors not necessarily trained as such; learning-by-doing the construction work for own housing

6.1.5 *Vocational Training and Education with a Social-Pedagogical Approach in the Don Bosco (DB) institutions*

	1 Priority Objective(s)	2 Target Group(s) Actually Received	3 Employment Income-generating Effects for IS–TG	4 Other Qualifications Imparted	5 Quality and Availability of Instructors/Trainers
(1) DBTI Madras Temil Nedu	excellent (non-) formal VT ovp for employment esp. in MS enterprises corresp. to qual. labour demand and technology level of these enterprises	youngsters from IS(u) with primary school graduation because of need to master basic education skills; non-formal VT also without school graduation	high for formal VT because of training quality and Salesian contacts to priv. bus./govt. inst. for empl.; only limited for non-formal VT; training and empl. of own instructors/soc. workers	social education	techn./ped. well qual., normally in DB–VTC, then 2 yrs. ped. training for instructors against commitment for 2–3 yrs.; rel. high fluct. due to in-evit. lower pay in comp. with govt./MS enterprises

(2) St. Joseph's Home Katpadi Agro Tech Polur Tamil Nadu India	Katpadi: as 6.1.5(1) Polur: non-formal, (I)m–o VT, in principle ovp	youngsters from IS(r) with or without primary school graduation (in Katpadi 10 % women); children from vicinity for primary school back-up tuition	high for formal VT (Katpadi); limited for non-formal VT in Katpadi and Polur due to lack of (I)m-o employment opportunities in rural areas and no s-o training	social education	as 6.1.5(1)
(3) Anbu Illam Madras Tamil Nadu India	social (re-)integr. of street children through gen./social education and non-formal s–o VT in spec. education centres/homes (Anbu Illam) for IS employment, poss. later sec. education or formal VT	street children in IS(u) and possibly their families	difficult to anticipate because of long-term general/social education and skill training required, (initially) mainly s–o and for employment in IS	social education	small number of staff req., but with highest soc. commitment; loc. soc. workers avail.; self-organization from TG stimulated; former street children with "paper shops" as sM among young/newly join. street child.
(4) DBYAC Ennore Tamil Nadu India	Social education and awareness creation for IS youth and families in the villages; social "leadership training" for sM and instructors working in IS(r) and IS(u)	soc. multipliers such as "school liders", social and youth workers, instructors; village families and youngsters from IS(u) + IS(r)	not intended	not intended	existing two social/youth workers with high professional competence, but not enough in numbers to meet own targets

6.2 *Training and Business Advice for Small Enterprises and Self-employment Promotion*
6.2.1 *Training for Small and Micro-Entrepreneurs "with Development Potential"*

(1) (Partly)Government-run Vocational Training Institutions Latin America	creation/stabilization of jobs through business administration training for existing S(M)E in MS and – if reachable – in IS	S(M)E owners and skilled workers from MS and IS(u)	actual contribution to stabilizing the economic basis of S(M)E difficult to assess; creation of additional employment probably limited	none	instructors for S(M)E-specific training apparently inadequately trained, but not enough information available
(2) DESAP Carvajal Foundation Cali Colombia	strengthening/expansion of existing S(M)E and one-person enterprises in MS and IS through qualification in entrepreneurial skills and business administration	S(M)E owners and self-employed persons from MS and IS(u) in Cali; approx. 55 % women participants; actual level of education very low	significant improvement of S(M)E revenue situation; partly also expansion with more employees, esp. in MS–S(M)E and modern IS–S(M)E, but also for self-employed persons	general entrepreneurial key qualifications	good; instructors exclusively locally recruited and trained by DESAP; for long-term advice to enterprises also recruitment and training of students of economics

235

	1 Priority Objective(s)	2 Target Group(s) Actually Reached	3 Employment Income-generating Effects for IS–TG	4 Other Qualifications Imparted	5 Quality and Availability of Instructors/Trainers
6.2.2 Business Creation Assistance for Small and Micro-Enterprises and Self-Employed Persons					
(1) New Business Creation (CEFE) Developing Countries Worldwide	promotion of business creation of S(M)E in MS and IS by identifying and training sort of creative entrepreneurs	men and women with sound school education, job experience and event entrepreneurial personally	rather limited already in view of the small number of courses per country; for IS–TG even less because of de facto enrolment restrictions	especially teaching of key qualifications	good, recruited and trained in CEFE training approach by GTZ
(2) "Business consultants" Port Sudan Sudan	advisory and credit assistance for business creation/consolidation also in subsistence economy to develop local economic potential in IS(u)	very poor (potential) small and micro-entrepreneurs and self-employed persons from IS(u)	apparently considerable, esp. for securing an adequate survival income from subsistence or commercial self-employment	strengthening of self-help potential and abilities for self-organization	local "business consultants" during planning phase recruited from within the TG and trained to be respons. for "clients advisory service"; technical train./advice provided by local S(M)E against pay
(3) Rural Trade School Salima Malawi	formal VT aimed at business creation by village craftsmen, to promote (self-) employment and improve supply of goods/services in rural areas	rural youngsters, seemingly only boys	setting up of rural workshops by a good 80 % of graduates; absorption capacity of the rural markets reached at that level?	qualification to work as self-employed rural craftsmen	not known, but apparently adequate
6.3 Complex Approaches to Occupation-oriented Training with Social Education for Rural Target Groups					
(1) "Centre for Rural Education and Development Action" CREDA Mirzapur Uttar Pradesh India	social and health education, promotion of self-help, non-formal VT in remote villages, also reduction of bondage labour	village families, esp. women, (bonded) children and youngsters	varied, difficult to say in detail; esp. s–o occupation at village level improved; improvement of general employment opportunities intended in a more long-term perspective	strengthening of key qualifications required for self-help and self-organization	very good; instructors, social workers and sM mainly recruited in villages and trained by CREDA; high motiv./low fluct. also among paid staff; many long-term (CREDA-trained) volunt. workers in vill.

(2) IERT – Integrated Rural Development Centres (IRDCs) Allahabad Uttar Pradesh India	oT + E combined with transfer of AT at village level; set-up of IRDCs to induce endogenous rural economic development	village families, esp. (pot.) village craftsmen, jobless youngsters, women; advanced training for sM at IERT (technicians and extension staff from NGOs and government institutions)	considerable when IRDCs functioned, with both m-o and s-o employment creation in IRDCs, and home production also in associated villages	as 6.3(1); also transfer of knowledge and skills in AT, esp. for agriculture, crafts, low-cost building construction and transportation means	local instructors/teachers/sM still work in at IRDC; external advisers no longer available (problem at IERT, but initially available and trained from IERT in adequate qual. and number

6.4 *Primary School Education as Preparation for and Part of Occupation-oriented Training and Education*[1])

(1) "Ruralisation" Rwanda	Incorporation of practical "rural" education in prim./sec. school curric., oriented to given environment-determined options as prep./qualification for life in villages/subsistence economy	primary school children (class 7 + 5) and primary school graduates from villages; approx. 45 % of one school year in primary stage, 10 % in post-primary stage	not known; qualification primarily intended for (s-o) rural crafts and improved farm work in children's home villages	none	qualification level of teachers only moderate, therefore advanced teacher training programme (by GTZ)
(2) "Polytechnical Education Support Programme" PESP Tanga Tanzania	practical agricultural lessons in primary school to introduce new crops and cultivation methods and the like, and to improve the nutritional situation in villages in the vicinity	children from the villages	not planned as immediate affect; teaching of innovative agric. knowledge and skills in school farm. to improve food supply in villages and children's future income-earn. opp. as small-hold./subsist. farm.	none	(advanced) teacher training with long-term back-up tuition to improve their qualification and motivation
(3) "Rural Education and Agriculture Programme" REAP Belize	all subjects in primary school also related to agricultural topics to quality and motivate young rural people for "Farming as Vocation"	children from the villages (also from town ?)	long-term better employm. a. Income opport. in (subsist.) farm.; through environment rel. educat. more active interest of pupils, hence better school results, poss. also better chances of access to VT	better performance in all subjects at REAP schools in comparison with other schools	already employed primary school teachers trained to teach REAP curriculum
(4) Escuela Nueva Colombia	elementary primary school education as widespread as possible also in sparsely populated rural areas through "one-room school"	children in the villages	not intended	none	apparently limited

	6 Financing	7 Special Features in Planning, Design or Implementation	8 Suitability of Concept/ Measures esp. for oT + E for IS-TG	9 Suitability of (counterpart) institution for oT + E for IS-TG	10 Comments and Suggestions for Improvement/ Modification of oT + E for IS-IG
6.1 *Individual Qualification for a (Labour) Market-oriented Occupation and/or for Subsistence Work*					
6.1.1 *Vocational Profile-oriented Training and Education in (Partly) Government-run Training Centres*					
(1) (Partly)Government-run Vocational Training Centres Latin America	0.5–2 % of wage sum paid by MS enterprises; training fees; government subsidies	explicitly no differentiation of curricula acc. to IS–TG learning opport./potentials; new emphasis on advanced training of skilled wage-workers and S(M)E owners	limited because of T + E ovp, objectives orientation mainly to qualification for MS; because of programme design and training costs rather inadequate for IS-TG	low because of objectives orientation and (deliberate) inflexibility of institution regarding qualification needs of IS-TG	perhaps introduction of non-formal VT for semi-skilled workers courses in rural areas, similar to SISD (see 6.1.2(2))
(2) Metal Work Training Project NRNFEC Thailand	government	3rd training phase (2–3 mon.) planned as "workshop simulation"; because of shortage of (qual.) instructors not yet introduced	village craftsmen training for new workshop creation problematic as isolated measure because of limited local market potential; NFECs too far from villages to be attractive	low for rural youngsters because of distance to villages and poor training standard (in NFEC gen.); better for T + E of intermediary IS-TG	use of NFECs for oT + E of intermediary IS–TG as trainers/sM at village level (training of local trainers); development of curricula and teaching methods for that purpose
6.1.2 *Forms of Dual Vocational Training in Cooperation with Private (Small) Enterprises*					
(1) Dual Vocational Training Latin America	(private) enterprises	complete shift of practical VT to private enterprises in MS; VT theory lessons in government-run VTCs	as 6.1.1(1), apart from a small remuneration for the apprentices	presumably no interest of enterprises to accept socially difficult youngsters from IS with poor school education as apprentices	none, since implementation generally problematic; hardly accessible for IS–TG anyhow
(2) "Cooperative Training Courses" SISD Thailand	government for SISD in general; possible contributions of enterprises unknown; partly financing through GTZ Project?	only enrolment of rural youngsters/unemployed with need to subsequently earn money; training content corresp. to skill demand in local labour market	good for IS(r)–TG, provided rel. labour-intensive rural small/medium industries exist as employers and also agree to carry out practical VT	positive example for cooperation between government-run non-formal VTC and (private) enterprises	introduction of training courses especially accessible for women; corresp. "advertising" in enterprises for cooperation, poss. with assistance from local NGOs

(3) "National Open Apprenticeship Scheme" NOAS Nigeria	apparently exclusively government	use of structure of informal apprenticeship; flex. curric., thus also many small "train." workshops; use of exist. fac. for "saturday classes" with craftsmen as instructors	easy access for IS–TG (all fields?); training offers also in rural areas; in tendency nationwide and rel. low-cost VT poss. due to use of informal training structure	as govt.-run programme struggling with staff problems, but apparently politically determined; S(M)E from IS probably esp. suitable for training of IS–TG	further training for instructors in "saturday classes"; strengthening of staff and technical capacity of executing/resp. govt. inst., esp. also in rural areas
(4) Workshop Centre (WC) Port Bouet Ivory Coast	low costs; partly from municipality, partly from church-related institutions (?); (train.) enterprises in WC self-financed through external customer contracts	business stabiliz. for former IS street craftsmen through offer of WC site in exchange for their apparent. training; VT theory and social education supplem. to practical VT	good; maybe also possible in similar way in rural areas, provided that labour market potential exists	good, since socially and from the location near to IS–TG	introduction of training courses also accessible for girls, poss. in a separate centre; possibly extension into an occupational guidance and/or technology advisory centre

6.1.3 Informal Occupation-oriented Training and Education

(1) Odd-job Apprenticeship Developing Countries Worldwide	self-financing of enterprises through customer contracts	from its very character adapted to occupation opportunities in IS; often exploitation of apprentices as cheap labour; no VT theory or general education	good as evidence proves; however, purely practical skill training, very much oriented to imitation; highly varying training quality and duration	basically good, as accessible for IS–TG; income earning, often also lodging possible; low/no costs for government	careful promotion of IS–S(M)E as "training enterprises", in coop. with suitable govt. inst. through corresp. organ. dev. assist.; poss. use of S(M)E for "occupational guidance service" for IS–TG
(2) Traditional Guild-like Apprenticeship West Africa	apprenticeship fee for master; self-financing of enterprises through customer contracts	guild-like VT with limited admission; work ethic of master; comprehensive practical VT, but no VT theory or general education	limited because of "elitarian" admission rules; training is mainly in trad. craftsmenship, gen. on declin	hardly because of guild-like "closed shop" structure	none, since a relatively self-contained – and in this form gradually disappearing – VT system
(3) Commercial Private Training Institutions Developing Countries Worldwide	course fees; as a rule, purely private commercial financing	subjects oriented to labour market demand in MS, esp. tertiary sector; purely commercial course design, without further subject-related or pedagogical tuition	in principle good, esp. for IS–TG with secondary school education and/or job experience; also special courses for women; IS(u) rather than IS(r)	in principle not bad, since privately organized and commercially financed; yet too little information available	promotion as counterpart inst. type; assist. regard. qualif. of curricula and instructors; spec. courses for women; cross-country studies on function/potential of priv. train. inst.

	6 Financing	7 Special Features in Planning, Design or Implementation	8 Suitability of Concept/ Measures esp. for oT + E for IS–TG	9 Suitability of (counterpart) institution for oT + E for IS–TG	10 Comments and Suggestions for Improvement/ Modification of oT + E for IS–IG
6.1.4 *Training and Education with Reference to Given Environment-determined Opportunities and Options*					
(1) Talleres Públicos Costa Rica	government-run VT institutions which established Talleres Públicos	training on MES basis; flexible training schedules for each training module; also s–o skill training; public workshop	provision of tools in public workshops good; learning capacity of IS–TG reg. MES over-estim.; MES hardly suitable for s–o qual., esp. in IS(r), because of structure and tool/workshop requirements	as part of govt.-run VT institutions only limited suitable because of instructor problem and inflexibility; concept probably more suitable for implementation by private institutions or local NGOs	better adjustment of teaching methods to learning potentials of IS–TG; training of local technical instructors and advisers to S(M)E by using MES
(2) Village Polytechnics (VP) Kenya	idea: village community; in reality: mainly church-related institutions/ organizations	idea: environment-adapted VT in villages, with local craftsmen as addit. instructors; in reality: only (ovp) VT; not compatible with qualif. needs and situation at village level	essentially yes, esp. for more remote rural areas, though not without (additional) external financing	VP type basically yes, but only with firmly established and competent counterpart institution and adequately qualified locally required instructors	cooperation with local NGO as counterpart institution; address esp. immobile TG with strong village links and commitments, esp. women; more emphasis on an environment-adapted training of local instructors
(3) Yellareddy (CPY) Andhra Pradesh India	church-related Indian institutions (CSI–CTVT) and foreign NGO donors	thorough and long-term planning with socio-econ. study on site; local craftsmen as pract. instructors; design corr. to learn. pot./real. occ. opport. of IS(r)–TG; focus on social education and AT, too	unreservedly positive	CP type very suitable; but better link with AT institutions needed; very dependent on availability of instructors and director with technical and pedagogical competence and human qualities	girls as TG (planned with mobile training units in villages); change in criteria for assessment of success/ financing on part of foreign donors necessary

(4) Infrastructure Programmes Developing Countries Worldwide	government institution executing the infrastructure programme, normally with international financial assistance	integrated in infrastructure programme which is priority	dependent on type of infrastructure measure and on frame conditions regarding guaranteed property rights, access to credit etc.	dependent on general frame conditions and type of institution responsible for the infrastructure programme	none, since completely dependent on design of the infrastructure programme

6.1.5 *Vocational Training and Education with a Social-pedagogical Approach in the Don Bosco (DB) institutions*

(1) DBTI Madras Tamil Nadu	30–40 % of operating costs through customer contract work; otherwise donations, Salesian order and donor NGOs	VT curricula fully adjusted to skill demand and technology standard of pot. employer-enterprises; socio-ped. "preventive" educ. for personality dev., also recreational pedagogics; both sound pract. and theory VT and general educ. back-up; consid. of learning opp./pot. and poverty of TG (e.g. training largely free); also primary school tuition for children from surrounding slums/villages	good esp. due to explicit orientation to IS–TG and the socio-ped. education approach, long-term horizon and continuity of work of the DB institutions in general	good, since spatially and socially close to IS–TG; continuity of institution and personal commitment, hence good knowledge of and trust from the IS–TG	greater orientation also towards innovative technologies/fields of employment in MS and a corresp. (re-)training of instructors
(2) St. Joseph's Home Kaipadi Agro Tech Polur Tamil Nadu India	approx. 30 % of operating costs through customer contracts (Katpadi); otherwise (Agro Tech fully) Salesian order, donations and foreign donor NGOs		as 6.1.5(1)	as 6.1.5(1)	more innovative train. content, for employment in rural MS; also s–o oT + E with inclusion of AT in non-formal VT for youngsters from IS(r); corresp. (re-)training of instructors
(3) Anbu Illam Madras Tamil Nadu India	Salesian order; donations	long-term nature/flex. of programme and indiv. education; try for max. poss. oT + E + VT acc. to indiv. cap.; inclusion of family, if poss.; active approach of TG with several stages of info/contact points	as 6.1.5(1), but especially for street children	as 6.1.5(1), but to an utmost extent dependent on the availability of staff with high human and pedagogical qualities	in principle, model character; only more consideration of AT possibilities for developing income-earning/employment perspectives for street children in IS(u)
(4) DBYAC Ennore Tamil Nadu India	Salesian order; donations; course fees charged from participant institutions, e.g. schools	learning content and teaching methods oriented to learning potentials and realistic options of TG; strengthening of personality and indirect social competence	good as indirectly and long-term effective qualification of IS–TG, and for training of sM	as 6.1.5(1)	none; possibly make use of such institutions to also train sM for other projects with external donor financing

6.2 Training and Business Advice for Small Enterprises and Self-employment Promotion
6.2.1 Training for Small and Micro-Entrepreneurs "with Development Potential"

	6 Financing	7 Special Features in Planning, Design or Implementation	8 Suitability of Concept/ Measures esp. for oT + E for IS–TG	9 Suitability of (counterpart) institution for oT + E for IS–TG	10 Comments and Suggestions for Improvement/ Modification of oT + E for IS–IG
(1) (Partly)Government-run Vocational Training Institutions Latin America	government; partly course fees charged from participants	trade-specific courses, yet standardized; no offers for credit assistance; no individual business advice to enterprise	limited, since IS–S(M)E owners will have little learning success without add. advice; qualification and specific advisory needs of MS–S(M)E S(M)E and IS–S(M)E not seen differentiated	difficult to assess; in principle yes, but rather for "modern" IS–S(M)E; VTCs poss. too bureaucratic and inflexible for training of private S(M)E	develop concept for parallel indiv. enterpr. advice and more business-spec. curricula (similar to DESAP); corresp. (re-)training instructors and S(M)E advisers, poss. using MES and NBC/CEFE approach
(2) DESAP Carvajal Foundation Cali Colombia	foundation funds; course fees charged from participants	"active learning" approach; training subj. in detail oriented to bus. needs/probl.; additional indiv. advice to enterprises, long-term back-up advice after training; if necessary, credit support	good for S(M)E and self-employed persons from IS(u) with sufficient basic education skills	good due to TG proximity and exact knowledge of market situation as well as of structure and needs of local S(M)E	none, in principle model character; already often adopted by organizations outside of Colombia; Carvajel itself since 1990 also training for smallholder/subsistence farmers

6.2.2 Business Creation Assistance for Small and Micro-Enterprises and Self-employed Persons

	6 Financing	7 Special Features in Planning, Design or Implementation	8 Suitability of Concept/ Measures esp. for oT + E for IS–TG	9 Suitability of (counterpart) institution for oT + E for IS–TG	10 Comments and Suggestions for Improvement/ Modification of oT + E for IS–IG
(1) New Business Creation (CEFE) Developing Countries Worldwide	bilateral technical cooperation (GTZ); course fees charged from the participants	based essentially on group-dynamics as learning approach and sound knowledge in basic education skills; credit assist. for set-up of business with 25 % own financing	attendance impossible for majority of IS–TG because of enrolment requirements regard. personality features, level of education, and financial contribution required	no special institutional structure (course with framework of GTZ measures)	best suited for training of trainers and avisers to S(M)E; also as part of curricula of (non-)formal VT centres
(2) "Business consultants" Port Sudan Sudan	customer payments for advisory services not cost-covering, thus additional external financial support mainly from NGO donors	long-term/thorough on-site planning with recruit./ training/participation of future local staff; nominal fee for all services despite poverty of TG to maintain their SH will	good because close to TG, on-site planning, recruitment and training of predominantly local staff	institutional set-up not quite clear, coordination and advanced training done by expatriate NGO staff, routine work/advice by local staff	more information needed on implementation sucess and difficulties; model character as regards planning, concept and lay-out of implementation

Name/Location	Funding	Approach/Description	Assessment	Model character/Notes
(3) Rural Trade School Salima Malawi	government; partly through technical cooperation (e.g. GTZ)	admission quota depend. on absorpt. cap. of market; strict selection; VT oriented to real rural market and empl. opport.; social educ.; assist. in the business creation and long-term back-up support	good, esp. rural areas; detached from urbanized/industrial dev. enrolment capacity and (self-)employment opportunities dependent on rural economic power	good, but only limited chances for replication in same country because of limited market/economic potential	model character for other countries as regards concept and implementation lay-out; similarly possible for women/subsistence farmers?

6.3 Complex Approaches to Occupation-oriented Training with Social Education for Rural Target Groups

Name/Location	Funding	Approach/Description	Assessment	Model character/Notes
(1) "Centre for Rural Education and Development Action" CREDA Mirzapur Uttar Pradesh India	government (poverty alleviation schemes); external financing by NGO donors	integr. educ. approach at vill. level; mainly s–o T + E with social educ.; advanced train. of instructors/soc. workers; many women; long-term vill.-based work; reintegr. of bond. children; qualif. management	unreservedly good	as local NGO with own staff and regular activities in villages very good, since very close to TG; no problems with staff quality/fluctuation	none, in principle modal character
(2) IERT – Integrated Rural Development Centres (IRDCs) Allahabad Uttar Pradesh India	partly government via IERT; partly external financing by various donors; at times limited own economic potential (local contract work) in the IRDCs	establ. of IRDCs with advis. assist/AT transfer; "rural develop. training" in post-graduate courses and technician training at IERT; complex and integrated concept of AT and oT + E for rural development	IRDC concept in principle very good, provided that suitable/strong supporting institution and committed external advisers available	IERT only limited because of conflict with academic training/research interests; IRDCs good provided that there is suitable external institutional support	concept model character; but no IRDC establishment recommended without guaranty of long-arm committed suppl. institution and expert staff for external advice and catalysts/bridgehead function

6.4 Primary School Education as Preparation for and Part of Occupation-oriented Training and Education[1]

Name/Location	Funding	Approach/Description	Assessment	Model character/Notes
(1) "Ruralisation" Rwanda	government for school education; Technical Cooperation (GTZ) project for teacher training programme	resp. 50 % theor./pract. lessons in primary stage, 40/60 % in post-primary stage; motivation and training in key qualifications for teachers also through school competitions	in principle good, but very dependent on quality of teachers, acceptance by teachers, parents and pupils, and political will for implementation	primary school basically very suitable, since largest possible number of young people from IS reached, esp. also girls	"ruralisation" as subject not only in advanced, but also regular teacher training, measures to increase school attendance; quality of practical lessons also good i. terms of content (skill qual./adequacy)?

	6 Financing	7 Special Features in Planning, Design or Implementation	8 Suitability of Concept/ Measures esp. for oT + E for IS–TG	9 Suitability of (counterpart) institution for oT + E for IS–TG	10 Comments and Suggestions for Improvement/ Modification of oT + E for IS–IG
(2) Polytechnical Education Support Programme" PESP Tanga Tanzania	government for primary schoo; PESP within Technical Cooperation (GTZ)	teaching manual for teachers, not for pupils (purely pract. lessons); no new equipment, only use of tools avail. in fam., innovation based on existing knowl.; no cash crops, but cultiv. for school meals	in principle good, esp. because of combination of (advanced) teacher training and practical work in village primary schools	as 6.4.2(1)	not enough information for proposals for possibly meaningful modifications
(3) "Rural Education and Agriculture Programme" REAP Belize	government for primary school; external financing for curriculum development (CARE) and advanced teacher training (US Peace Corps)	REAP curric. initially only in schools where parents and teachers agreed; school farming produce left to children; participation of all responsible authorities; social work with parents	good provided that responsible government agencies/institutions are politically determined and competent to introduce such a programme	as 6.4.2(1)	none; apparently good and successful progr., since within a few years officially adopted for countrywide implementation in all primary schools (acc. to information from 1964)
(4) Escuela Nueva Colombia	apparently to a great extent external financing (first UNESCO, then inter-American Development Bank, now World Bank/ UNICEF)	"one-room school" model, i.e. teaching of several age groups by only one teacher	good compromise solution in sparsely populated and remote rural areas; but at most basic education possible	in principle as 6.4.2(1)	better/adapted qual. and local recruitment of teachers, also women; more s–o and to rural environment adapted curricula including some practical skill training/AT introduction in lessons

Legend: IS, Informal sector; IS(u), Urban informal sector; IS(r), Rural Informal sector; IS–TG, Informal sector target groups; MS, Modern sector; NFEC, Non-formal Education Centre; S(M)E, Small and micro-enterprises; sM, Various kinds of social multipliers; oT + E, Occupation-oriented training and education; VT(C), Vocational training (centres); (l)m–o, (Labour) Market-oriented; s–o, Subsistence-oriented; ovp, Oriented to (industrial) vocational profile; SH(G), Self-help (group); SHO, Self-help organization; AT, Appropriate Technologies.

[1] Point (1)–(4) refer to Chapter 6.4.2. Since Chapter 6.4.1 contains only general remarks on the occupational relevance of primary school education, it has been disregarded in this synoptical table.

7. Recommendations for the Planning and Design of Vocational Training Assistance for People from the Informal Sector

With a people-centred perception of development assistance, the ultimate objective of all promotional measures for target groups from the informal sector should be to achieve a sustained improvement in the working and living conditions of the economically and socially disadvantaged people in the slums of the big cities and in the rural areas. With respect to their occupation-related qualification needs as described in Chapter 5, the overall objectives orientation of a specific "Vocational Training Assistance for people from the Informal Sector" should, therefore, be

– a technical qualification oriented to the environment-determined occupation opportunities of the respective target groups, in terms of a reasonably paid wage-employment, small business creation or gainful self-employment, and/or a cost-saving, less hard and more effective subsistence work to improve their home and working conditions by own efforts;

– a strengthening of the "information processing capacity" and the social communication abilities of the people from the informal sector;

– the realization of more equal opportunities for them in both economic and social terms, and as regards their options for further education and vocational training, of course;

– a strengthening of their self-help potentials and their self-organization abilities.

The following recommendations reflect the implications which – in a people-centred perspective – result from this objectives orientation and from the previous descriptions and assessments for the planning and design of occupation-oriented training and education measures within the framework of (bilateral) technical cooperation and personnel assistance, and also, of course, of the supportive training measures in financial assistance.

These recommendations relate to

– a more comprehensive conceptual perspective which extends beyond the conventional objectives orientation of the "classic" vocational training assistance;

– the major principles of a flexible and integrated planning and

implementation of occupation-oriented training and education measures;
– concrete suggestions as regards the conceptual and institutional design of such measures;
– the need for a revised self-perception and new qualification profiles of (external) advisers, instructors and trainers;
– some considerations regarding the financing of training and education measures for economically poor and socially disadvantaged target groups, in particular.

7.1 Towards a More Comprehensive Conceptual Perspective in (Bilateral) Vocational Training Assistance

The need for a more comprehensive perspective in (bilateral) vocational training assistance when it comes to the discussion of suitable concepts for an – also long-term effective – occupation-oriented training and education for target groups from the informal sector has been repeatedly stressed. Without reiterating the details, the core aspects of a necessary conceptual rethinking towards a "Vocational Training Assistance for People from the Informal Sector" should, however, be highlighted again for the reader's special attention.

(1) Technical Skill Training and Social Education for Subsistence Work and Self-help

Any kind of work which is not or cannot be "marketed" – also the activities required to satisfy basic needs and secure the survival of people from the informal sector – is normally disregarded in vocational training assistance, just in line with the economists' understanding of the "non-unproductivity" of reproduction and "non-value" of utility values.

If it is true, however, that
– on the one hand, the labour markets of the modern and of the informal sector together will be unable still for a long time to absorb the growing number of people seeking wage-employment, which results not only from population growth, but also from the fact that the public sector in most countries will no longer be able to function as an "emergency employer";
– on the other hand, also self-employment and business creation are – for financial, personality-related and/or social reasons – not necessarily an alternative option for all those unable to find wage-employment, apart from the limitations set to the development of

small enterprises and self-employment by the prevailing general economic frame conditions and development potential;
– at the same time, for the majority of people in the urban and – in many more ways – in the rural informal sector, the subsistence economy is the backbone of survival, whenever they have no (sufficient) sources of cash income,
it is time to move away from the perception of the subsistence economy as an unpleasant transitional stage of socio-economic development which should be overcome as soon as possible. On the contrary, the importance and the chances of promoting and stabilizing various forms of life and work in the subsistence sector should be recognized, also in the field of vocational training and education.
For many people in the urban slums and in the villages – whether we like it or not – self-help and a (partly) subsistence-oriented skill training will be the only option throughout their lives to come to more acceptable and decent living conditions. Individual or community subsistence work to improve the living and working conditions in the informal sector, however, requires information, knowledge and technical skills, the ability to acquire and apply all this to the necessary extent, and, last but not least, the confidence that a positive development is possible to be achieved through own efforts also in the subsistence sector.
It is no more than consistent, therefore, to also perceive a subsistence-oriented technical skill training and the development of key qualifications required for self-help and self-organization as a task and field of a "Vocational Training Assistance for People from the Informal Sector". Occupation-oriented training of this kind includes social education and awareness creation for the people in urban squatter areas and in the villages to realize their own development potentials and the occupation opportunities accessible to them, and to promote their willingness to take own action for their development rather than wait for external assistance.
This will be particularly to the benefit of women who – for social and/or economic reasons – are very often unable to seek wage-employment or only a vocational training course. Consequently, they are rather immobile as regards the search for employment opportunities, and remain more or less confined to the hardest subsistence work.
Especially in rural areas, occupation-oriented training and education measures which take into realistic account the environment-determined – and hence also subsistence-oriented – occupation

opportunities, may be a vital contribution to self-help promotion, and in many cases the better alternative as compared to an only (labour) market-oriented vocational training which then cannot be put into use, anyway[161]. As regards the urban informal sector, the situation is slightly different insofar as for people living in town a certain cash income – at least the subsistence income – is indispensable, and chances to find a gainful (self-)employment maybe improved with a vocational training. Nevertheless, also in the urban areas a great deal of what is needed for the people in the slums to come to better living conditions will only be achieved through subsistence work and self-help.

(2) Training and Education to Extend Occupation Opportunities and Development Options

Extending given occupation opportunities and development options of individuals or social groups means creating more chances and enhancing the abilities for an improvement of individual or (target) group-specific working and living conditions. The more restricted the occupation opportunities and options of a target group are, and the more detached from the urban culture and the economy of the modern sector, the more difficult it hence is for that target group to be integrated, the less likely this can be achieved by means of occupation-oriented training and education alone. Additional measures will be required to create more occupation opportunities for the newly imparted knowledge and skills to be applied, at all, in wage- or self-employment or any rewarding subsistence work. Just as often, assistance measures in other fields will not be feasible or inefficient without prior or accompanying training measures for the target group(s) concerned. In many cases, therefore, integrated approaches will be the only meaningful way to really extend the target group-specific occupation opportunities and development options.

The contribution which a "Vocational Training Assistance for People from the Informal Sector" could make, relate to

161 It should be understood, however, that concepts for a "subsistence-oriented vocational training" should resist the temptation of turning the people in the informal sector into substitutes for western alternative ideals of "self-sufficiency" and culture preservation, as it appears in the proposals of *MÄRKE* (1987), pp. 301 ff. Subsistence producers normally are not self-sufficient out of their convictions, but simply under the force of circumstance. This is important to be realized and accepted as a matter of fact. Otherwise, basically meaningful approaches run the risk of developing strategies unappealing and thus ineffective for the intended target groups just because of unfamiliarity with their ideas and perceived needs.

– integrated measures for the promotion of endogenous rural (economic) development, similar to the IRDC concept, in order to increase rural employment and income opportunities in general;
– integrated measures for the promotion of small and micro-enterprises through combined (advanced) training, advisory services and credit offers for (potential) small and micro-entrepreneurs, self-employed business(wo)men, or subsistence farmers, in order to extend the scope for individual economic activities in small business and self-employment;
– qualifying training and education measures to improve the "competitiveness" of people who have many comparative disadvantages on the (labour) market, due to their low education and social background, and – in rural areas – their remote location; for example
– a good-quality and also environment-adapted primary school education for children and youngsters for whom this would still be a chance to improve their opportunities for further education, vocational training and gainful (self-)employment;
– above-average formal or non-formal vocational training adapted to the labour skills demand and the technological level of enterprises in the modern sector, and including social education to develop a "work ethic" and a self-confident social behaviour, in order to facilitate social integration and increase employment opportunities in the modern sector;
– vocational training and education in innovative technologies and industries, in which still only a few workers have the required skills, and in which hence is less competition, but a growing skilled labour demand;
– the introduction of innovative and "appropriate" technologies in "classic" vocational training as well as in environment-adapted (subsistence) occupation-oriented training and education, in order to extend the scope of technological options and hence create (partly) new occupations;
– policy advisory assistance – especially at local government level – aimed at creating training and employment opportunities for different target groups from the informal sector, namely also for women, by encouraging and advising the responsible Government administrations;
– to acknowledge and finance the tremendous need in the urban slums as well as in the villages for social services, especially in hygiene and health care and in primary and pre-school education, and,

to provide finance for these services to be carried out – at least partly – by locally recruited (pre-school) teachers or social workers;
– to officially entrust various municipal services which the municipalities do not or cannot (adequately) provide themselves, such as waste disposal – especially, but not only in squatter areas – or local passenger transportation, to cooperatives, small enterprises or self-employed individuals who in many urban areas have carried out these services since long, anyway.

(3) Primary School Education as First Stage of Occupation-oriented Training and Education

A qualified and environment-adapted primary school education which is really accessible for the children and youngsters in the villages and from the urban squatter areas, provides a better basis for a further vocational or broadly occupation-oriented training. It also helps to give some occupation and income-earning prospects for those who after primary school in any case will have to secure their survival in the rural areas or in the urban subsistence economy. For both these reasons, primary school education should be perceived and utilized as the first stage of occupation-oriented training and education.

The chances for primary school education to be improved in this sense will depend on the availability of sufficient primary and pre-school teachers who are motivated and adequately qualified in technical subjects and pedagogical skills as much as on the political will, the budget lines and staff capacity, and the competence of the responsible Government institutions.

As regards a certain school infrastructure and the availability of teaching aids, both is also undoubtedly necessary. A much greater emphasis than on the provision of a "modern" school infrastructure, however, should be placed on improving the *quality* of primary school education. Nice school buildings alone do not raise the level of education – this will be possible only with the help of good and adequately trained teachers.

For a gradual improvement of primary school education towards a better general and more environment-adapted – also more practical – education as first stage of an occupation-oriented qualification for children and youngsters from the informal sector, in particular, assistance measures are required at various levels, namely
– in policy advisory assistance including the institutional strengthening of the responsible Government institutions;

– not only for the advanced teacher training, but also – and to a greater extent than hitherto – in the first training of primary school teachers who – like pre-school teachers – should as much as possible be familiar(ized) with the social background of children from urban slums and in the villages, respectively, and possibly be recruited accordingly;
– in pre-school education which in many countries has developed to become already part of the general school education, since it is almost indispensable for later being able to keep up at primary school;
– in the development and introduction of primary school curricula which are suitable to also foster skills such as creativity and social competence, and replace the common practice of a merely repetitive teaching of fundamental education skills of reading, writing and mathematics.

In the light of past experience, advisory assistance or any programmes aimed at improving primary school education should take into account the following principles:
– With regard to the considerable differences in urban and rural living conditions and occupation opportunities, primary school curricula should not be countrywide completely standardized, but for rural schools contain a larger part of environment-adapted and occupation-oriented practical lessons;
– The discussion on suitable curricula for rural schools, however, should not get bogged down in the seeming antagonism of theoretical general education versus occupation-oriented practical training lessons, but should integrate both, for which the REAP approach described above may be taken as an example pointing in the right direction;
– Primary school education should not be confined to merely teaching a subject-related syllabus, but also take the task and opportunity of social education to foster key qualifications important for mental development and social competence already at childhood.

It should be understood that any externally induced development will become self-sustaining only, if the people addressed make the objectives their own, and make use of the opportunities provided. This presupposes understanding and ability which both can be fostered a lot through an adequate primary school education.

(4) Specific Measures for the Promotion of Women's Development
The need should again be stressed to place particular emphasis in vocational training assistance on training and education measures

specifically for girls and women, by taking into account their often particularly disadvantaged economic and social situation. More than for men, this adversely affects their learning opportunities and their occupational options, especially where they are more or less permanently tied down to their homes.

Women often complain that training, education or advisory programmes are not intended for them, or are – in the way they are designed – not accessible to them for practical and/or social reasons, while at the same time men fail to take advantages of such opportunities to acquire knowledge and skills which might help to improve their families' living conditions or income situation.

In spite of the differentiation which should be made as regards the – by no means homogenous – target group of "women in the informal sector", it is absolutely essential in many cases to adapt training and advisory services addressing women to their – at least partially – specific learning opportunities and restrictions, and to the occupation opportunities which are also and particularly accessible for women, not only in the field of household work and health care.

This may imply that it often makes more sense to offer occupation-oriented training and education measures primarily or even – maybe only in parts – exclusively for women. This is particularly important where the attendance of male participants would make it impossible for women to attend, or, if they do, would prevent them from actively participating to their full abilities, due to traditional role behaviour and social rules.

On the other hand, women-specific measures – in the sense of exclusively intended for women – should not be considered as the generally best solution. Just as frequently as this would be the better approach, gender-specific programmes will either be unnecessary – as, for example, in the DESAP programme – or may even have adverse effects. Even where women are critical against various privileges or behavioural patterns of men in the family or in the community, the majority of women are anxious to maintain social and family harmony. This, however, can easily be jeopardized, if men find themselves as formally excluded.

In any case, particularly in rural areas those approaches are normally more promising which view the farming families as a whole as the target group to be addressed. Apart from the fact that often enough only the women and children still live in the villages, anyhow, the rural people only stand a chance of improving their living conditions, if there is economic and social solidarity within the families and among the communities.

7.2 Flexible and Dovetailed Planning and Implementation

One of the probably biggest mistakes in development assistance is that the planning and implementation of programmes and projects normally are fully separate stages in terms of time, location, personnel and often also concepts.
It sets thinking that in the field of occupation-oriented training and education especially those institutions or organizations have fewer implementation problems and a maybe slower yet more sustained success, which carried out a longer and thorough on-site planning understood as the first step of project implementation, or which thanks to a long-term local presence are familiar with the local frame conditions and the specific living and working conditions of people from the informal sector. They also are least – in relative terms – troubled by the problem of the availability of instructors with the required technical and pedagogical skills and personality traits. And they are able to actually reach target groups from the informal sector, with assistance measures obviously designed with an understanding of the learning opportunities and potentials, the environment-determined (possible) occupation opportunities and development options, and the priority qualification needs of the target group(s) concerned.
So far, the approach of a dovetailed planning and implementation is found almost exclusively with local NGOs and church-related institutions. Apart perhaps from the known bureaucratic inflexibility to Government(-run) institutions, however, there is no reason, in principle, why it should not be applicable within the framework of (bi-lateral) vocational training assistance, too. Understanding and adopting the planning and implementation of occupation-oriented training and education measures for target groups from the informal sector as a dovetailed, mutually corrective and, in this sense, integrated process, would certainly increase both the chances of actually reaching the intended target groups and the impacts on their occupation opportunities, and, thus, contribute to the sustainability of such assistance measures.
It would imply to alter the process of planning and implementation in the direction of
– a participatory and iterative planning on site, perceived as the first step of programme or project implementation;
– a long-term perspective and continuity, and proximity to the target group(s) throughout the dovetailed planning and implementation process.

7.2.1 Participatory and Iterative Planning on Site

Participation as it is commonly understood and – if at all – practised in development cooperation, relates almost exclusively to the implementation phase. The views, knowledge, experience and self-help will of the target group(s) whose living environment is most directly and often heavily affected – in the positive and negative sense – by the assistance measures, however, must not be asked for the first time only when it comes to the implementation of measures which have already been bindingly decided on in an (almost) exclusively external planning[162]. The same applies to those (counterpart) institutions on whose performance and commitment the long-term success of the measures depends more than on anything else.

The participation of both – the target group(s) and the local (counterpart) institution(s) – must begin already during the planning phase, even if this means some more difficulties, "unnecessary" discussions and more time required[163]. The need for a participatory planning on site is the greater, the more the planned measures involve activities with and for people, as it is the case in the field of training and education. Here, pedagogical rather than technical skills are often the decisive factor, and the objective is to achieve learning success, though this often is identifiable only indirectly and in the long term, rather than easily tangible construction results.

The purpose of a participatory and iterative planning on site, which tries in a step by step process to get as close as possible to the given realities in the area concerned, is

– to provide information as realistic as possible for the multi-dimensional identification of target groups as outlined above, and for the conceptional and methodological design of the measures planned[164];

---

162 Cf. also, in this sense, the publication by *SCHNEIDER-BARTHOLD* (1987) with the almost programmatic title "Talking, Acting and Learning with the Poor".
163 The GTZ has carried out one such participatory project planning on site, which is described in detail by *GAGEL* (1990). Its methodology was largely based on a planning approach called "explorative project finding", first carried out and described by *LOHMAR-KUHNLE* (1984). It was modified and extended by the GTZ in Niger, also on the basis of qualitative social research and action research methods.
164 A further remark on this aspect: "A reasonably realistic picture of the frame conditions in a region, and on the specific living and working conditions of different target groups and their specific assistance needs cannot be obtained from models or secondary sources of information only. Additional first-hand experience through personal observation, everyday experience and the dialogue with the different local social groups is absolutely essential. It helps to correct own patterns of perception by comprehending the views of the local people in their complexity and contradictory character. It is important to understand that the perception of

– to prevent fallacies and wrong judgements, which helps to easier recognize hidden development potentials as well as possible obstacles for implementation, and hence also a more realistic time frame for the planned assistance;
– to increase the acceptance and the effectiveness and, thus, the sustainability of the assistance measures, since people are much more likely to perceive a development induced as their own affair and benefit, the more and sooner they are involved in its planning and design, and the more clearly they find themselves as its real beneficiaries and executing agency, respectively;
– to allow already at an early stage a realistic assessment of the strong and weak points of the – definitely responsible or intended – national and, if included, also local counterpart institutions, including the decision on possibly required measures for an institutional strengthening;
– to identify, recruit and, if required, train as early as possible local staff, instructors and other relevant intermediary target groups in the role of social multipliers and from the social environment of the ultimate target group(s).

The objectives and – so to say – terms of reference of such a partipatory and iterative planning process at least partly carried out on site must be
– the multi-dimensional identification and selection of the target group(s) to be addressed, as outlined in Chapter 4;
– the assessment of the target group-specific learning opportunities and potentials, and of the occupation opportunities (potentially) accessible to them, as a prerequisite for the identification of their qualification needs and development potentials;
– the specification of the overall objectives, the conceptual and methodological design, and the institutional set-up of the training and education measures;
– the scrutiny of needs and possibilities for some kind of integrated development approach, with training and education measures as one component;

> one and the same situation differs depending on the observer's own background of experience and socialization and also his personal concern. The argument that such a subjective perception will not allow planning on an objective basis of information has to be countered by reminding that the seemingly objective perception of external planners always entails a substantial degree of hidden subjectivity ... The attempt to understand other people's subjective perceptions of reality and their assessments as objectively given factors requires a critical distance towards one's own views and preoccupations as well as openness and empathy with other ways of thinking and lifestyles"; *LOHMAR-KUHNLE* (1984), p. 11 (translated by the author).

– the careful selection of a national and/or local counterpart institution with enough implementation capacity and competence as well as acceptance or a good reputation among the target group(s);
– the recruitment, preparatory training and, wherever meaningful, the active involvement of instructors and "social multipliers" from the immediate environment of the target group(s).

7.2.2 Long-term Perspective, Continuity and Target Group Proximity

A long-term perspective, continuity as regards the training and advisory staff as well as the institutional set-up, and, finally, the proximity to the target group in terms of location and social access are key factors for the success – both project success and individual learning success among the target groups – and the sustainability of assistance measures in the field of training and education. It is here that the most striking difference can be observed between Government-executed projects and the activities of local NGOs and church-related training institutions, probably primarily due to the latters' more people-centred and less policy-centred perception of development work.

A (bilateral) vocational training assistance which intends not only to reach but also to sustainably promote target groups from the informal sector by means of occupation-oriented training and education, however, will have to adopt these principles, too. Although this will not be easily realized in view of the specific bureaucratic character of the normally responsible counterpart institutions, it should not be ruled out as impossible.

(i) The approaches of non-governmental – which normally also means non-bureaucratic – organizations and institutions demonstrate that any assistance for occupation-oriented training and education for people from the informal sector must have a long-term perspective *from the very beginning*, the more as it normally has to be accompanied by additional primary as well as social education. This also implies a process- and not merely output-oriented perception of project success.

The long-term perspective[165] should apply to the period of time which

---

[165] Long-term does not mean a long project duration which results cumulatively from several extensions required because of an again and again still unsatisfactory realization of the project targets. Such retrospectively long-*lasting* projects are something completely different as compared to measures which are planned and designed with a long-*term* time horizon from the very beginning.

should reasonably be allocated or anticipated for
- the just described process of participatory planning;
- the development of a structure for occupation-oriented training and education and related advisory services actually accessible for the target group(s), which includes
- if necessary, the setting up of an appropriate physical infrastructure;
- indispensably, the development of a working communication structure and pattern of social interaction with both the target group(s) and the counterpart institution(s);
- if required, measures to strengthen the national/local counterpart institution(s), and to promote self-help organization among the target group(s);
- in any case, an adequately target group-specific (advanced) technical and pedagogical training of the required local staff, and of "social multipliers" from among the target group(s);
- the duration of individual and, even more so, collective learning process – which is generally under-estimated, but even longer in the case of target groups from the informal sector for whom the confrontation with innovative information and the process of cognitive learning in itself often is already the first unfamiliar stage of learning which takes time.

(ii) The need for continuity in the implementation of occupation-oriented training and education measures once they have started, has an institutional and a personnel aspect. It relates
- insofar as training institutions or advisory services are concerned, to their long-term – not necessarily indefinite – availability and accessibility for the target group(s), in view of the just described long-term character of learning and development processes;
- as regards external advisors, instructors and other required local staff, their reliable and continuous – not necessarily permanent – availability over a sufficiently long period, to ensure that individuals and the target group(s) as a whole may actually achieve *and* consolidate the intended learning results, and be able to sustain and extend on their own the information communication structures and marketing structures on which a development perspective has been based through the external assistance.

In view of the often extremely restrictive learning opportunities of people from the informal sector and their often ambivalent attitude towards training and to expert advice, finally the proximity to the target group(s) essentially determines their chances and their

willingness to make use of such offers. It refers to
- the spatial distance of training and advisory institutions or events, which is acceptable to the target group(s) in terms of time required, cost and compatibility with the prevailing social rules, and which can be wider or narrower depending on the circumstances and target group(s) concerned;
- the cognitive familiarity and social adaptation of the assistance measures as a whole as well as of the instructors or advisers personally, to be able to rightly understand the mentality, the social environment and the learning capacity of the target group(s), and to actively inform them about training or advisory offers and motivate them to participate.

A long-term perspective, continuity and target group proximity applied in the context of a dovetailed planning and implementation as outlined above, will allow to design occupation-oriented training and education measures which adequately respond to the actual needs and given occupation opportunities and development options of the target group(s), and their flexible adjustment to changing frame or target group-specific conditions at all stages of a project.

7.3 Suggestions as Regards the Conceptual and Institutional Design

Occupation-oriented training and education without any possibility in the offing of a subsequent gainful (self-)employment or some other application of the imparted knowledge and skills to improve the living conditions in subsistence work, normally is not entirely in vain, since it always contributes somehow an individual's personal development. In a situation where people are struggling for survival and for decent working and living conditions, however, an assistance measure can be called meaningful only, if it really and significantly contributes towards achieving this very objective.

This would correspond to a people-centred perception of development, and, thus, also is the touchstone for measures of "Vocational Training Assistance for People from the Informal Sector". They must be primarily *oriented to the qualification needs and the occupational options of these target groups* – not only or mainly to the skilled labour demands of modern sector enterprises, since an exclusive priority on the latter would definitely fall short of providing an occupation-oriented qualification for the majority of people from the informal sector.

7.3.1 Suitable Approaches and Instruments

To what extent and in what way the above presented "conceptual modules" of occupation-oriented training and education provide suitable approaches and instruments to be applied also in Government-supported programmes or projects of "Vocational Training Assistance for the People from the Informal Sector", was already outlined in the context of their respective descriptions. In the following, only the main conclusions and recommendations will be briefly summarized again.
(i) The way vocational training is usually carried out by the (partly) Government-run vocational training institutions in Latin America appears to be hardly suitable to reach in larger numbers target groups from the informal sector, for the reasons mentioned above, of which their formal and de facto enrolment restrictions are a major yet not the only obstacle. This applies to classroom-only training in the vocational training centres as well as to the increasingly promoted Latin American form of dual vocational training.
Furthermore, the almost exclusive focus on the "classic" vocational profiles prevailing in all – also the non-formal – training, makes the Latin American type of vocational training not very appealing and hardly meaningful for people from the informal sector, in view of the overall economic situation with its adverse effects on the labour market.
(ii) A vocational training of young people from the informal sector, in particular, must either give them comparative advantages on the labour market, or qualify them for as wide a range as possible of wage- and also self-employment opportunities in the modern sector, or – where this is not possible – in the informal sector, too. Under these aspects, the most suitable approaches for occupation-oriented training and education measures especially for young people from the informal sector – as regards the conceptual as well as the methodological and institutional design – are
– a vocational training of excellent quality, adapted to the prevailing standard of technological development, and with a socio-pedagogical approach, as carried out in the Don Bosco

Technical Schools, albeit in rural areas with the above suggested modification;
— vocational training schools like the Rural Trade School in Salima in rural areas fairly detached from urban economic development centres;
— a form of non-formal dual vocational training similar to the "cooperative training courses" at the SISD for semi-skilled workers, especially in rural areas with a certain labour-intensive industrial development;
— forms of informal dual apprenticeship training providing opportunities for both a more "classic" vocational training as well as a broader occupation-oriented qualification, introduced as countrywide programme like the NOAS, or on a much smaller dimension at local level with workshop centres similar to the one in Port Bouet – approaches which are the more attractive as they do not only provide informal training opportunities accessible to youngsters from the informal sector, but at the same time also additional income for small and micro-entrepreneurs engaged in such informal apprenticeship training.
(iii) It may be worth thinking about possibilities of an (institutional) strengthening of private commercial training institutes which especially with their offers of advanced training courses in secretarial skills, business administration and other commercial skills demanded from the modern service sector, are apparently frequented in larger numbers by certain target groups from the informal sector, too[166].
(iv) For the promotion of (potential) small and micro-entrepreneurs and self-employed business(wo)men, a kind of model character as regards both the planning and the design of training and advisory measures can be attributed – depending on the specific target groups addressed and on the general frame conditions – to
— programmes like the DESAP of the Foundation Carvajal, for already existing small and micro-enterprises and self-employed business(wo)men "with development potential";
— a "business consultant" approach like in Port Sudan, to promote small business creation or consolidation and self-employment for people who live and work – at least initially, but perhaps permanently – in the subsistence sector.
(v) Measures of non-formal occupation-oriented training and social education for the social (re)integration of target groups which are difficult to reach like urban street children and young

166 Cf. on this aspect also Chapter 7.3.2, Topic (iii).

prostitutes, and for an environment-adapted occupational qualification of young rural people with little or no primary school education will be possible within the framework of (bilateral) vocational training assistance only in close cooperation with local NGOs and other institutions with a long-term experience with these target groups. Such a cooperation is not only highly desirable, but also conceivable, especially if donor agencies would establish regional so-called "Programme Offices"[167].

As regards these particularly difficult target groups, the right direction – both conceptually and in the institutional design – is taken with approaches like
– the socio-pedagogical concept developed by the Salesians for the social and occupational (re-)integration of urban street children;
– the environment-adapted – also subsistence-oriented – non-formal vocational training with additional general and social education for rural youngsters with (almost) no school education, as carried out at the Community Polytechnic in Yellareddy;
– as far as the concept is concerned, the former Village Polytechnics in Kenya, the introduction of which – with the modifications described above – is perhaps even more feasible nowadays than twenty years ago, especially in remote and economically completely under-developed rural areas;
– the village-centred and – as regards occupational and learning opportunities and potentials – environment-adapted education and training as carried out by CREDA, including the strategy of selecting and training part of the local staff and the village development workers directly among the target group, i.e. the village people.

(vi) In all occupation-oriented training and education measures for people form the informal sector, in particular, a greater emphasis should be placed on the introduction of environment-adapted and innovative technologies suitable to increase their scope of occupation opportunities, also in the subsistence sector.

In view of its potential to create various kinds of rural occupation opportunities both at village level and in small rural centres, the IRDC approach definitely deserves to be given another chance, despite its failure in the IERT's project. The IRDC concept is regarded as a particularly promising approach for the promotion of endogenous rural development through the transfer of appropriate technologies, which, however, requires a really long-term perspective for implementation.

167 Cf. on this aspect in further detail Chapter 7.3.3.

(vii) With regard to the urgently required improvement of a generally accessible primary school education for all, special attention is drawn again to
– the environment-adapted primary school curriculum developed under the REAP, aiming at promoting the occupational perspective of "farming as vocation" already among the school children who mostly come from (subsistence) farm families;
– the basic idea of a "one-room-school" like the Escuela Nueva as a possibility to realize the objective of primary school education for all even in more remote and sparsely populated rural areas.
(viii) Neither the MES concept nor the NBC training are very likely to be successfully used to a significant extent by target groups from the informal sector, due to their normally insufficient previous vocational and even general education. For the advanced training of technical instructors at Government-run vocational training institutions as small business advisers, and perhaps also for a technical training of primary school teachers to enable them to also teach practical subjects, however, the MES may in many cases be suitable. A certain technical pre-qualification provided, they appear to be a good possibility for a relatively fast trade-specific or specialist (autodidactic) advanced technical training.

Especially for small and micro-enterprise advisers, the NBC training may be a method to acquire within a short period of time and in comparatively great depth a better understanding of the business situation and specific advisory needs of their clients. Also well conceivable is the incorporation of an NBC training into the curricula for formal and non-formal training courses at technical schools or vocational training centres, as a supplementary qualification encouraging and better enabling the students to later perhaps set up their own business.

(ix) It has already repeatedly been stressed that training and education for rural target groups, in particular must take place in or near their homes to allow them to take these opportunities, at all. Even non-formal vocational training centres located in a rural provincial town are for most villagers already too far away – both spatially and cognitively – to be actually perceived as a training opportunity for them, irrespective of enrolment requirements or the quality of the courses.

In view of this fact, it might be worth reconsidering the purpose and task of non-formal vocational training centres in rural areas – in countries where they exist like, for example, the PNFECs in Thailand –

and use them more for the training and education of intermediary target groups which could assume the role of "social multipliers". In particular, people who are relatively firmly rooted in their villages – especially women, but also village craftsmen or (retired) village school teachers – could be trained there to then take on education, training and advisory tasks at village level as technology advisers, health workers, pre-school educators, or social animators to induce or strengthen local self-help activities.

(x) Whether suitable vocational or any broader occupation-oriented training and education opportunities accessible to them do actually exist or not. Many young people from the informal sector and their parents, too, normally have no ideas about a particular career, the scope of given training opportunities, and possible – or impossible – occupation opportunities and the related qualification required. A lot of "wandering around", uncertainty, wrong training and unrealistic employment aspirations, and much of the hopelessness leading to apathy, alcohol and drug abuse, or even to gang crime could probably be prevented, if the young people – and their families, since decisions on a child's training and preferable occupation are usually a family affair – would have the opportunity to seek individual training advice and vocational guidance in the wide sense of any possible kind of occupation.

Therefore, some kind of local "Centres for Occupational Guidance and Training Advice" should be set up in urban squatter areas and in major rural towns[168], there possibly with a mobile advisory team going in regular turns directly to the villages. They could be established as independent centres, but also be affiliated to the office of a local NGO, or to a school – though, wherever possible, not to a formal vocational training institution, since this would probably bear the risk of biased advice and also be already "too far away" for many villagers.

---

168 A basically similar idea is found in *OXENHAM* (1984), there called "Livelihood Advisory Service" (LASER) concept; cf. especially pp. 197 ff.

7.3.2 Baseline and Tracer Studies

The assessment of the various approaches to occupation-oriented training and education for target groups from the informal sector repeatedly revealed that there is still a substantial information deficit in many respects.

(i) As regards the informal sector as such, this deficit does not so much refer to that kind of information which would further improve the statistical data base, but rather to a quality of information which would contribute to a better understanding of something to which most expatriate development planners and advisers – and also the overwhelming majority of their local counterparts with an urban middle-class socialization and, thus, usually quite a good formal education – never have been exposed: the culture of urban poverty and the culture of rural poverty. The more distant – in spatial and social terms – however, a target group is from the "normality" of an urbanized middle-class, the more important such an understanding becomes as a precondition for the planning of occupation-oriented training and education measures to their benefit.

It, therefore, is proposed to carry out
– a "Baseline Study on the Informal Sector" to learn more about the various forms of poverty socialization in urban slums and in rural areas, and their impact on the learning behaviour of people from the informal sector, in order to better understand their specific learning opportunities and potentials, their qualification needs, and their general and occupational development options.

(ii) Similarly worthwhile would it be to conduct for different types of (counterpart) institutions, projects and organizations – Government-run formal and non-formal vocational training institutions, projects of (bilateral) vocational training assistance as well as of local NGOs, church-related or other private vocational training and education institutions – in several countries
– a comparative "Tracer and Background Study on Trainees from the Informal Sector" including both successful graduates and also drop-outs to discover the reasons for their failure or premature withdrawal.

Apart from the provision of more precise information on the learning success and subsequent occupation opportunities of training participants from the respective institutions, this would also allow to better assess the – given or potential – suitability of different institutional set-ups as regards their ability to reach target groups from the informal sector.

(iii) The private commercial training institutes which since quite some time are mushrooming in many big cities worldwide, are hitherto given little notice, and hence are still fairly unknown as regards their structure, training contents and quality, and their clients. Apparently, however, they attract also certain target groups from mostly the urban informal sector, especially secondary school graduates who do not immediately find a job, more or less qualified persons with no or bad employment, men and women alike. It would, therefore, be worth carrying out
– a "Cross-country Study on Private Commercial Training Institutes", to obtain more detailed information on the way they work, their financing and course fees, the background and quality of their instructors, the content of their training courses and their teaching methods, and finally on the background and subsequent employment opportunities of the course participants.

These commercial training institutes might well appear – at least in some countries – to be a reasonable alternative with quite positive subsequent employment opportunities for their clients, as compared to Government-run vocational training centres which for most people from the informal sector are not accessible, or to private non-profit training institutions which may not attract them. From the point of view of (bilateral) vocational training assistance, private commercial training institutes – so they are successful – would have the advantage of being relatively independent (counterpart) institutions with a sound self-financing.

7.3.3 *Establishment of "Programme Offices"*

The following recommendation relates to an form of institutional set-up which would allow to realize the afore-mentioned principles of a flexible and dovetailed planning and implementation also within the framework of (bilateral) "Vocational Training Assistance for the People from the Informal Sector".

Instead of a conventional type of development project set up to implement in more or less close cooperation with a national counterpart institution a largely externally planned and clearly defined package of assistance measures under the responsibility of a "project manager" who is the more in charge the weaker the counterpart institution is, it is suggested to launch a pilot project for occupation-oriented training and education for target groups from the informal sector, the institutional frame of which is a "Programme Office"[169].

Such a "Programme Office" operating countrywide or – in case of several small countries – in a region, would in its structure and tasks differ from a conventional development project especially in following aspects:

– It would be set up with a long-term perspective and without an a priori defined *specific* task or operation plan, to coordinate, monitor and assist a number of projects being implemented by different counterpart institutions and for different target groups from the informal sector, at the same time;

– Apart from its specialist advisory services and the coordination and monitoring of ongoing projects, a further task would be the active project finding and advisory participation in the planning and preparation of new measures, including the conceptual design as well as the identification of the target groups to be addressed, and of possibly cooperating Government institution(s) and/or NGOs and their requirements for an institutional strengthening, whereas all of the intended measures would be carried out independent of the "Programme Office" within the framework of existing structures of Government institutions, NGOs or self-help organizations evolving from local initiatives;

– It, thus, would not have any own implementation competence, which implies that the planning and realization of all measures is only possible in a real and close cooperation with one – or more – counterpart institution(s), and only at the pace of their decision-making processes;

– vis-à-vis the national and local counterpart institutions implementing the measures, it acts as a direct "donor", with the ultimate decision on the preconditions, timing and volume of the financial input to a jointly planned project being reserved to the (expatriate) director of the "Programme Office".

The consequence of a – necessarily participatory – planning and implementation process which is adapted to the structure and time requirements of decision-making processes of the responsible (counterpart) institutions and to their priorities, is that the local partners will either view the intended measures as their own project, or there will be no project, at all. It is also foreseeable that with this kind of planning and implementation assistance measures will – in

169 This idea was prompted by a detailed discussion with the head of the "South-East Asia Project Office" (SEAPO) which the Carl Duisberg Society (CDG) set up – as the only one of its kind – some ten years ago in Thailand.

particular initially – take longer than it would normally be anticipated in a conventional project planning. Retrospectively, however, the total project duration will hardly differ. Experience shows that in most externally planned projects the time schedules are normally too tight and, thus, will eventually clash with the reality of local time horizons and decision-making processes.

The adapted and participatory planning possible within the institutional set-up of a "Programme Office", on the other side, ensures that
– the responsible (counterpart) institutions will identify themselves with the jointly planned measures much more as in the case of externally planned and controlled projects;
– in the end not a project is left behind, the achievements of which can or will hardly be maintained by the counterpart institutions, due to a lack of the required professional competence, inadequate staff capacities and/or insufficient financial endowment;
– the assistance needs of the target groups, their learning opportunities and potentials and their occupational options are indeed identified correctly.

These three factors alone would positively influence the sustainability and effectiveness of assistance measures. Additional advantages of an institutional set-up like a "Programme Office" as compared to a conventional project may be seen in
– the possibility for an integrated and flexible planning and implementation of various separate measures carried out by different (counterpart) institutions, which could perhaps even be networked with synergy effects;
– a continuous availability of a coordinator and adviser for the (counterpart) institutions and the target groups, but without a direct and permanent presence in individual projects in the role of project manager, which implies that right from the beginning, the counterpart institutions and the target groups have to be more independent and assume the responsibility for the implementation of their projects. They, thus, will not be dependent on too many external inputs which would only be provided for a limited period of time, anyhow;
– a "balance of power" between the expatriate adviser(s) and the local partners because of shared decision-making powers for the approval of project funding and for the project implementation, respectively;
– the above already mentioned distance of the director of the "Programme Office" from the individual projects, which prevents the temptation of taking over the management and the

implementation responsibility in case of a weak counterpart institution, but, however, also bears the risk of an only superficial familiarity with the different measures to be monitored and advised. Since it would not be established for just one project, but as a kind of countrywide (or regionally) operating planning and coordination office for (bilateral) "Vocational Training Assistance for the People from the Informal Sector", such a "Programme Office" can initiate, monitor and back up measures for various target groups with extremely different assistance approaches in cooperation with different types of counterpart institutions.

Apart the tasks and functions just described, it would be possible, at the same time, to affiliate special – perhaps mobile – information and advisory centres to a "Programme Office", such as, for example, an "Information Centre for Appropriate Technologies" or a "Coordination Office" for the recommended local or mobile units for "Occupational Guidance and Training Advise".

The decision to set up a "Programme Office" in a country or region where "Vocational Training Assistance for People from the Informal Sector" is (going to be) one of the donor's priority fields of development assistance, would reflect at the institutional level the understanding that the success of training and education measures should not be the assessed output- but process-oriented.

7.4 Revised Self-perception and Qualification Profile for Development and Vocational Training Experts

The afore-mentioned perception of planning and implementation, the character of the recommended approaches, and, last but not least, the nature of target groups from the informal sector also have implications as regards the qualification profile and the self-perception of external planners, advisers, instructors and trainers.

To plan and implement assistance measures with a people-centred perception requires that the experts – expatriates as well as locals – involved are personally capable and willing to take a people-centred perspective in their work. This, however, makes the demands on their professional and especially their personal qualifications different from those so far normally made in the recruitment of development experts. A revised qualification profile would include

– a not only verbally redefined understanding of the role and function of external experts, no longer regarding them as the ones "in charge" and responsible for everything including the measurable

project success, but rather as catalysts inducing learning and development processes, and in their roles as advisers being resource persons and counsellors rather than the "know-it-all" type of expert;
– beside professional competence also "social intelligence" as indispensable prerequisite for social and cultural empathy;
– the willingness to recognize and respect prevailing sociocultural values and rules of conduct as much as the given skills and the experience of the local people, understand what is worth retaining and retain it, and introduce innovations with reference to the existing knowledge, technologies, habits and the like;
– the abilities to really listen, to carefully observe, to actively participate, also to sympathize, and – very much so – to understand by intuition and comprehend with the heart;
– an understanding of the local people's notions of time, its dimension and its relevance, which in most cultures is different from the "western" perception;
– the ability to engage in inter-cultural communication with acknowledging other mentalities and preserving one's own – the trivial this may sound, since it has been demanded for so long that it should be taken for granted by now;
– the willingness and ability to communicate with people in a "human" and – which is particularly important when dealing with so-called simple people – warm and sincere way, without assuming the airs and graces of an "expert";
– finally, a professional self-image in which "Vocational Training Assistance for People from the Informal Sector" is viewed neither as charity nor as a mere job, but in the first instance as social work and educational work for both of which a lot of professional competence and pedagogical skills are required.

Although this applies to any kind of work with people in general, for the training and education of people from the informal sector it is even more true that not the type of expert is needed for whom in his work the only source of recognition from the target group and the counterpart institution is in his professional or technical competence. What is needed, instead, are instructors who are also educators and counsellors, and planners and advisers who convincingly convey the message that they are determined to work in a participatory approach together with the target groups affected and the institutions involved, in order to improve the living and working conditions of the people from the informal sector, with the understanding that everyone can and must contribute to the best of his/her knowledge, skills and experience to achieve this goal.

It is, in principle, well known that the "personality factor" is more decisive for the success of any assistance measures than commonly assumed. For measures in the field of training and education, however, it is *the* key factor.

7.5 Remarks on the Financing of Occupation-oriented Training and Education for Poor Target Groups

The question who should bear with which contributions the costs of vocational training is particularly relevant for "Vocational Training Assistance for the People from the Informal Sector", for two reasons. Firstly, vocational training often has – beside the technical training – to make up, at least partially, for a normally unsufficient primary education, and also to include some social education. Both requires longer training periods, and more and adequately qualified teachers and instructors, and maybe even the employment of local social workers for supportive measures. Secondly, it is intended for target groups which mostly can bear neither the direct nor the indirect costs of a vocational training or further education, certainly not for a longer training.

In principle, occupation-oriented training and education measures for target groups from the informal sector can be financed through

– direct financing or subsidization from Government budgets, which in most countries to a substantial extent means a financing through development assistance;

– the partial or full self-financing of private training institutions including commercial training institutes;

– an apprenticeship training – in the modern sector as well as in the informal sector – carried out (mainly) by private enterprises at their own expense in accordance with their labour demands;

– the establishment of various kinds of "production schools" which should recover at least their operating costs with contract work for external customers;

– finally, a partial cost recovery through training fees charged from the trainees, or from the enterprises benefiting from the supply of skilled labour.

When assessing the suitability of the different modes of financing, it should be taken into consideration that

– the training and education of people from the informal sector often requires more time and personnel than could be provided under cost recovery aspects, due to their restrictive learning opportunities and potentials as well as to a typically slow learning process when it comes to technical subjects and social education, the latter requiring a gradual process of learning, anyhow;

– in many cases, grants or subsidies for the trainees to cover the direct training costs – and often also the indirect costs for accommodation, food or transportation – are essential to enable people from the informal sector to participate in a training, at all;

– especially decentralized training and advisory services which are near enough for the target groups to be reached, may cause particularly high operating costs, mainly for staff payment and transportation;

– for measures of a more subsistence-oriented occupational training and social education aimed at strengthening the self-help potentials of the people in the villages and in the urban squatter areas, there is hardly any basis for a substantial self-financing by the executing institutions, often NGOs, or through fees[170];

– although both small private enterprises and private commercial training institutes may provide quite good occupation-oriented training opportunities for some target groups from the informal sector, they by far cannot meet the qualification needs of all target groups;

– production schools which under this aspect seem attractive at first glance, can recover by "training-cum-production" at best (part of) their operating costs, and also have some severe conceptual drawbacks[171], especially with respect to target groups from the informal sector;

– finally, a shift of the financing responsibility directly to the training institutions – of whatsoever type – would leave little scope for a people-centred planning and implementation of target group-specific training and education measures according to the aforementioned principles, since this would clash with the then necessary

---

[170] This can be clearly seen from the experience of the Don Bosco Technical Schools in rural areas, which – with the same approach and efforts as the Don Bosco Technical Schools in urban areas – are hardly able, with a few exceptions, to recover even part of their operating costs through external contract work. Education and training projects like the Anbu Illam for street children will even less ever be in a position to finance any of their activities by themselves, due to their priority on the social work component – although there is neither an expensive infrastructure which needs to be maintained nor high costs for personnel or transportation.

[171] Cf. on this aspect *YHR* (1990), esp. p. 7, who weighs up advantages and disadvantages of a "Production Concept in Technical Schools" with a critical – perhaps still too positive – conclusion, not even under the aspect of suitability for target groups from the informal sector; cf. also pp. 9 ff.

business management principles which must inevitably lead a standardized training for the sake of cost reduction.

A thorough consideration of these – certainly still incomplete – reasons will lead to realize that the main burden and responsibility for the financing of occupation-oriented training and education for target groups from the informal sector, in particular, must be carried by the national budgets, and hence also by financial and technical assistance from international and bilateral donor agencies. This should be accepted by the national Governments as well as by the donors as a perhaps unpleasant yet essential obligation.

This does not mean that it might not be reasonable and worthwhile to seek alternative solutions by which at least part of the financing could be provided otherwise, like, for example, in models of "dual informal apprenticeship training". Wherever this seems possible, training institutions should be encouraged to a (partial) self-financing of their operating costs[172]. Training and education tasks, however, should always take priority over the cost recovery aspect.

As regards the required high portion of financing through development assistance, it should be added that the common distinction between investment costs for physical infrastructure, equipment and teaching material which are (possible to be) financed through development assistance, and operating costs to be financed by the counterpart institutions, definitely is a very meaningful rule in many fields of development assistance. Running costs for the payment and training of instructors or "social multipliers", however, should be considered as something completely different to salary topping-up payments for regular staff of a Government counterpart institution. Without instructors in adequate number and qualification, a training project is just as impossible to be successfully implemented as is a road construction project without the required construction equipment and its largely project-financed operation.

Costs for education and occupation-oriented training indeed have an investive character, since they are an investment in the development of human resources, even if they appear as running costs in the budget. "As education and training is primarily an investment, it would be a real mistake to regard expenditures for education merely

---

172 It may also be advisable – as shown in two of the afore-mentioned approaches – to charge an at least nominal fee for training and advisory services provided for small and micro-entrepreneurs and self-employed business(wo)men, not as a substantial contribution cost recovery but primarily under educational aspects to promote a cost-conscious entrepreneurial thinking and/or to sustain the normally existing will for self-help.

as consumption"[173]. This statement of an economist applies generally, but it is particularly true with respect to "Vocational Training Assistance for People from the Informal Sector".

7.6 Conclusion

A large number of unemployed and unskilled people constitute a social problem. A large number of unemployed yet skilled people, by contrast, are a potential. "Investing in People" with the aim of putting their labour *and* their creativity to productive use for themselves and for society, therefore, is more than ever an essential requirement for a development in Third World countries, which will be to the benefit of the majority of people.

To this end, qualifying people for wage-employment, small business creation or self-employment in the modern or in the informal sector remains one of the central tasks of "Vocational Training Assistance for People from the Informal Sector". In case of broad success this may well lead first to even greater competition for a relatively – in some countries even absolutely – decreasing number of jobs and for business opportunities. This dilemma, however, can hardly be resolved through vocational training and education alone. But it also cannot mean, of course, to refrain from a (labour) market-oriented occupational qualification especially of young people from the informal sector to improve their employment opportunities. The inevitable labour selection must not happen through inferior training or no training, at all, for those who are economically and socially disadvantaged already. Also from a macro-economic point of view, it must take place directly on the labour markets, since only an evident (surplus) supply of adequately skilled labour will eventually induce economic reorientation.

Occupation-oriented training and education measures must contribute to create more equal occupation opportunities for the people from the informal sector by improving, first of all, the opportunities for good-quality and accessible primary education and vocational training for gainful (self-)employment. As regards employment generation in rural areas, the known argument especially from development banks is certainly not wrong, according

---

173 *SCHULZ* (1986), p. 18, who angle in his book "In Menschen investieren" ("Investing in People") convincingly advocates from an economic point of view to regard education and training costs macro-economically as investment costs; cf. pp. 17 f. and pp. 37 ff (quoted text translated by the author).

to which small and micro-enterprises will only develop and potential investors in labour-intensive rural industries will only be attracted, if there is sufficient number of sufficiently qualified (semi-)skilled labour.

At the same time, a fundamental reconsideration must take place in (bilateral) vocational training assistance to extend the conventional objectives orientation of the "classic" (labour) market-oriented vocational training. An environment-adapted occupational qualification for improved subsistence work and self-help in the subsistence sector must be recognized as a serious alternative – and sometimes the only possibility, at all – especially, though by far not only, for rural target groups. For very many people from the informal sector, the only possible and meaningful occupation-oriented training and education is a qualification which enables them to realize, fully use, extend or create new occupational options and opportunities accessible to them. People who can see realistic possibilities to improve their living conditions and to alleviate the burden of (subsistence) work by own efforts or in community work without a great financial burden, are more likely to (be able to) take the required initiatives for self-help.

To a certain extent, this concept of a "Vocational Training Assistance for People from the Informal Sector" – which is rooted in a people-centred perception – moves away not only in its target group orientation, but particularly in its planning and implementation principles from the idea(l)s of the "classic" vocational training assistance, in that

– the starting-point for the planning and design of occupation-oriented training and education measures is not the definition of policy-centred development objectives, but the multi-dimensional identification of the target group(s) to be promoted;

– the objectives of assistance measures and their design in detail are derived in the first instance from the identified qualification needs of the respective target group(s), by taking into account their different learning opportunities and potentials and their environment-determined (potential) occupational options;

– the subjects of occupation-oriented training and education accordingly, are related not only to the labour market and/or business opportunities in the modern or in the informal sector, but also to subsistence activities, altogether more adapted to the environment-determined actual and potential occupational options of the respective target group(s) than to "classic" vocational profiles with a clear correlation to modern industrial and artisanal trades;

– occupation-oriented training and education more often than not has also a socio-pedagogical dimension in that not only technical knowledge and possibly entrepreneurial skills are imparted, but also social education and, if required, some basic primary-level education is carried out to facilitate social and occupational (re-)integration and promote key qualifications, such as "information processing capacity", creativity, self-reliance, self-organization ability, or a sense of work quality;
– the target groups are not merely viewed for a defined period as simply receptive consumers of training, education or advisory services with a clearly specified content, but as actors shaping their own development and learning processes;
– training, education or advisory measures are not just "launched" and their mere existence then regarded as already sufficient announcement, but in particular target groups which are difficult to reach for training and education are actively approached and motivated to take up such an offer;
– the identification of the target groups as well as the conceptual and methodological design of assistance measures are not in advance bindingly determined in external planning, but are subject to a participatory process of dovetailed planning and implementation flexibly adjusted to changing conditions, to ensure that occupational options of the respective target group(s) and their related qualification needs are perceived as realistically as possible;
– the success of education training and advisory measures is defined and assessed not output- but process-oriented, and quantifiable results hence do not take priority over more qualitative criteria applied to assess learning success as indicator for the effectiveness and sustainability of a measure;
– finally, new demands are made on the technical competence, pedagogical skills, "social intelligence" and personality traits – i.e. the qualification profile – and on the motivation of local as well as expatriate experts, who should as instructors also be educators, as advisers also sincere counsellors, and as planners also observers and partners in discussion.

In order to realize a "Vocational Training Assistance for People from the Informal Sector" in this sense, a rethinking and revised (self-)perception is required in the minds of all those involved in the planning and implementation of occupation-oriented training and education measures for these target groups. In the interest of the people from the informal sector it can only be hoped that this will not be postponed to some time or other.

Bibliography

Bibliography

Part I:	Informal Sector	280
1.	Informal Sector in General	280
2.	Latin America: Informal Sector in General	281
	2.1 Latin America: Urban Informal Sector	282
	2.2 Latin America: Rural Informal Sector	284
3.	Africa: Informal Sector in General	284
	3.1 Africa: Urban Informal Sector	285
	3.2 Africa: Rural Informal Sector	287
4.	Asia: Informal Sector in General	287
	4.1 Asia: Urban Informal Sector	288
	4.2 Asia: Rural Informal Sector	288
Part II:	Occupation-oriented Training and Education	290
5.	General Approaches and Concepts	290
6.	Country-specific Programmes and Projects	297
	6.1 Latin America	297
	6.2 Africa	300
	6.3 Asia	303
7.	Technology Transfer	304
8.	Self-help Approaches	305
9.	Planning, Design and Financing of Programmes and Projects	305

Part I: Informal Sector

1. Informal Sector in General

ALMEIDA VASCONCELOS, Pedro de, "Le travail informel urbain: une évaluation de la littérature" in: Revue Canadienne d'Etudes du Développement, Vol. 6, No. 1, 1985, p. 87–124.

BHASIN, K., "Peasants in Developing Countries are Conservative and Backward: Myth or Reality?" in: Adult Education and Development, No. 30, 1988, p. 51–55.

BROMLEY, Ray, "Introduction – The Urban Informal Sector: Why Is It Worth Discussing?" in: World Development, Vol. 6, No. 9/10, 1978, p. 1033–1039.

CARVAJAL, Jaime, "Microenterprise as a Social Investment" in: LEVITSKY, Jacob, "Microenterprises in Developing Countries", Portsmouth, 1989, p. 202–207.

CHANDAVARKAR, Anand, "The Informal Sector: Empty Box or Portmanteau Concept?" in: World Development, Vol. 16, No. 10, 1988, p. 1259–1261.

CHARMES, Jacques, "Méthodes et résultats d'une meilleure évaluation des ressources humaines dans le secteur non-structuré d'une économie en voie du développement" in: O.R.S.T.O.M., Vol. XIX, No. 1, 1983, p. 93–106.

CHAUDHURI, Tamal Datta, "A Theoretical Analysis of the Informal Sector" in: World Development, Vol. 17, No. 3, 1989, p. 351–355.

DIXON-MUELLER, Ruth, "Women's Work in Third World Agriculture. Concepts and Indicators", Geneva, 1985.

ELWERT, Georg, "Überlebensökonomien und Verflechtungsanalyse" in: Zeitschrift für Wirtschaftsgeographie, Vol. 29, No. 2, 1985, p. 73–84.

ESSER, Johannes, "Der informelle Sektor", Konstanz, 1984.

HERRLE, Peter, "The Informal Sector: Survival Economy in Third World Metropolitan Cities" in: Economics, Vol. 26, 1982, p. 109–126.

JACOBI, Carola, "Frauen als neu-entdeckte Zielgruppe" in: BERNINGHAUSEN, J./KERSTAN, B., "Die unsichtbare Stärke: Frauenarbeit in der Dritten Welt, Entwicklungsprojekte und Selbsthilfe", Saarbrücken, 1984, p. 145–162.

KLINGER, W., "Die Rolle des informellen Sektors bei der Abfallbeseitigung in städtischen Regionen von Entwicklungsländern" (Diss.), Hanover, 1988.

MAZUMDAR, Dipak, "The Urban Informal Sector" in: World Development, Vol. 4, No. 8, 1976, p. 655–679.

MÖLLER, Sigrid, "Women Make Up Over Half the Workforce in the Informal Sector" in: GATE, No. 3, Eschborn, 1987, p. 3–5.

MOSER, Caroline, "The Informal Sector Reworked: Viability and Vulnerability in Urban Development" in: Regional Development Dialogue, 1984, p. 135–182.

NICKEL, Herbert J., "Probleme des informellen Sektors in Entwicklungsländern", Research Paper of the "Fachgruppe Geowissenschaften", University of Bayreuth, Vol. 11, Bayreuth, 1984.

NUNNENKAMP, Peter, "Industrialization and Urban Labour Absorption" in: KOPP, Andreas, "Scientific Positions to Meet the Challenge of Rural and Urban Poverty in Developing Countries", Hamburg, 1987, p. 237–268.

PEATTIE, Lisa, "An Idea in Good Currency and How It Grew: The Informal Sector" in: World Development, Vol. 15, No. 7, 1987, p. 851–860.

RICHARDSON, Harry W., "The Role of the Urban Informal Sector: An Overview" in: Regional Development Dialogue, 1984, p. 3–41.

SANYAL, Bishwapriya, "The Urban Informal Sector Revisited. Some Notes on the Relevance of the Concept of the 1980s" in: Third World Planning Review, Vol. 10, No. 1, 1988, p. 65–83.

SETHURAMAN, S.V. (Ed.), "The Urban Informal Sector in Developing Countries. Employment, Poverty and Environment", Geneva, 1981.

SETHURAMAN, S.V., "The Informal Sector and the Urban Poor in the Third World" in: KOPP, Andreas, "Scientific Positions to Meet the Challenge of Rural and Urban Poverty in Developing Countries, Hamburg, 1987, p. 269–284.

SOTO, Hernando de, "Structural Adjustment and the Informal Sector" in: LEVITSKY, Jacob, "Microenterprises in Developing Countries", Portsmouth, 1989, p. 3–12.

STOCKHAUSEN, Joachim von, "Der informelle Sektor als Auffangbecken für Arbeitssuchende" in: Development and Cooperation, No. 6, 1989, p. 9.

THINKER, Irène, "Street Foods as Income and Food for the Poor" in: International Foundation for Development Alternatives, 1985, p. 13–24.

VAN DIJK, Meine Pieter, "Informal Sector Policies and Programmes: An Assessment and Identification of Issues" in: VAN GELDER, P./BIJLMER, J., "About Fringes, Margins and Lucky Dips. The Informal Sector in Third World Countries: Recent Developments in Research and Policy", Amsterdam, 1989, p. 209–222.

WICHTERICH, Christa, "Frauen in der Dritten Welt", Bonn, 1984.

2. Latin America: Informal Sector in General

AMAT Y LEON, Carlos, "La familia como unidad de trabajo", Lima, 1986.

BERGER, Marguerite, "La mujer en el sector informal" in: BERGER, M./

BUVINIC, M., "La mujer en el sector informal. Trabajo femenino y microempresa en América Latina", Quito, 1988, p. 13–32.

BREUBER, B. (Ed.), "Vermittlung von Kleinkrediten für den informellen Sektor in Lateinamerika", Berlin, 1984.

DIRMOSER, Dietmar et al. (Ed.), "Aussichten auf die Zukunft", Hamburg, 1986.

INTER-AMERICAN DEVELOPMENT BANK (Ed.), "Economic and Social Progress in Latin America. Special Section: Working Women in Latin America", Washington, 1990.

JIMENEZ VEIGA, Danilo, "La Crisis, la Deuda, el Ajuste y el Desarrollo de Recursos" in: Boletín CINTERFOR, No. 99, 1987, p. 3–25.

LYCETTE, Margaret/WHITE, Karen, "Acceso de la mujer al crédito en América Latina y el Caribe" in: BERGER, M./BUVINIC, M., "La mujer en el sector informal. Trabajo femenino y microempresa en América Latina", Quito, 1988, p. 35–66.

REUTER, Rita/SPÄTH, Brigitte, "Der informelle Sektor: Eine Perspektive für Frauen ? Beispiele aus Jamaika und Sambia" in: BERNINGHAUSEN, J./ KERSTAN, B., "Die unsichtbare Stärke: Frauenarbeit in der Dritten Welt, Entwicklungsprojekte und Selbsthilfe", Saarbrücken, 1984, p. 35–75.

TOKMAN, Victor, "Micro-Level Support for the Informal Sector" in: LEVITSKY, Jacob, "Microenterprises in Developing Countries", Portsmouth, 1989, p. 13–25.

VEREDA DEL ABRIL, Antonio, "Desafío de la economía informal", Lima, 1988.

WILCHES-CHAUX, Gustavo, "Las microempresas, la participación comunitaria y el desarrollo regional" in: Boletín CINTERFOR, No. 87, 1984, p. 71–84.

2.1 Latin America: Urban Informal Sector

BROMLEY, Ray/BIRKBECK, Chris, "Researching Street Occupations of Cali: The Rationale and Methods of What Many Would Call an Informal Sector Study" in: Regional Development Dialogue, 1984, p. 184–202.

BUVINIC, M./BERGER, M./JARAMILLO, C., "Impacto de un proyecto de crédito dirigido a microempresarios" in: BERGER, M./BUVINIC, M., "La mujer en el sector informal. Trabajo femenino y microempresa en América Latina", Quito, 1988, p. 331–362.

CARBONETTO, Daniel y otros, "El sector informal urbano en los países andinos", Quito, 1985.

CARBONETTO, Daniel/BOYLE, Jenny/TUEROS, Mario, "Lima: sector informal", Tomo I y II, Lima, 1988.

CARITAS (Ed.), "Wenn die Straße zur Heimat wird. Straßenkinder in den Slums der Dritten Welt", w/o pl., w/o y.

CORVALAN VASQUEZ, O./CARIOLA, L./CERRI, M., "Empleo y capacitación en los talleres informales de Santiago", Montevideo, 1984.

DESPRES, Leo, "Industrialization, Migration and the Informal Sector in Manaus", w/o pl., 1985.

EDAPROSPO (Ed.), "Historia del área 'ambulantes' – en búsqueda de un nuevo paradigma para la promoción social", (unpublished), Lima, 1990.

ESCOBAR, Silvia, "Comercio en pequeña escala en la ciudad de la Paz, Bolivia" in: BERGER, M./BUVINIC, M., "La jujer en el sector informal. Trabajo femenino y microempresa en América Latina", Quito, 1988, p. 97–121.

FARRELL, Gilda, "Los trabajadores autónomos de Quito", 2da ed., Quito, 1983.

GILBERT, Alan, "Home Enterprises in Poor Urban Settlements: Constraints, Potentials and Policy Options" in: Regional Development Dialogue, Vol. 9, No. 4, 1988, p. 21–37.

KUGLER, Bernardo, "Estudios, programas y políticas del 'sector informal urbano' en Colombia" in: Revista de Planeación y Desarrollo, Vol. 14, No. 3, 1982, p. 53–80.

McKEAN, Cressida p., "Empresas pequeñas y microempresas. Su eficacia e implicaciones para la mujer" in: BERGER, M./BUVINIC, M., "La mujer en el sector informal. Trabajo femenino y microempresa en América Latina", Quito, 1988, p. 147–169.

MEZZERA, Jaime, "Excedente de oferta de trabajo y sector informal urbano" in: BERGER, M./BUVINIC, M., "La mujer en el sector informal. Trabajo femenino y microempresa en América Latina", Quito, 1988, p. 67–95.

MOSER, Caroline, "Surviving in the Suburbios" in: YOUNG, K./MOSER, C., "Women and the Informal Sector", Sussex Bulletin, Vol. 12, No. 3, 1981, p. 19–29.

NACIONES UNIDAS (Ed.), "La mujer en el sector popular urbano. América Latina y el Caribe", Santiago de Chile, 1984.

PREALC/OFICINA INTERNACIONAL DEL TRABAJO (Ed.), "Sector informal. Funcionamiento y políticas", Santiago de Chile, 1978.

PALMA, Diego, "La informalidad, lo popular y el cambio social", Lima, 1987.

RABANAL, César R., "Cicatrices de la pobreza", Caracas, 1989.

RODGERS, Gerry (Ed.), "Urban Poverty and the Labour Market. Access to Jobs and the Labour Market. Access to Jobs and Incomes in Asian and Latin American Cities", Geneva, 1989.

ROSSINI, Renzo G./THOMAS Jim J., "Los fundamentos estadísticos de El Otro Sendero", Lima, 1987.

SOTO, Hernando de, "El Otro Sendero. La revolución informal", Bogotá, 1987.

TOKMAN, Victor, "Informal-Formal Sector Interrelationships. An exploration into their Nature" in: CEPAL REVIEW, 1978, pp. 99–134.

2.2 Latin America: Rural Informal Sector

HARPER, Malcolm/VYAKARNAM, Shailendra, "Rural Enterprise. Case Studies from Developing Countries", London, 1988.

SCOTT, Gregory J., "Mercados, mitos e intermediarios. La comercialización de la papa en la zona central del Perú", Lima, 1985.

3. Africa: Informal Sector in General

ANHEIER, Helmut, K./SEIBEL, Hans D., "The Formal and the Informal Sector, or the Dependent and the Independent Sector ? A Reexamination of Conceptual Issues and Assumptions of Informal Sector Research in Africa", w/o pl., 1985.

ANHEIER, Helmut K./SEIBEL, Hans D., "Small-Scale Industries and Economic Development in Ghana: Business Behavior and Strategies in Informal Sector Economies", Saarbrücken/Fort Lauderdale, 1987.

BARAMPAMA, Angelo, "Secteur non-structuré en Afrique. Cacophonie de la survie et leur espoir" in: Genève-Afrique, Vol. 22, No. 1, 1984, p. 37–54.

CHARMES, Jacques, "Les contradictions du développement du secteur non-structuré" in: Revue du Tiers Monde, Vol. XXI, No. 82, 1980, p. 321–335.

CHARMES, Jacques, "Le secteur non-structuré en Tunisie: son importance, ses charactéristiques et ses possibilités de promotion" in: O.R.S.T.O.M., Vol. XIX, No. 1, 1983, p. 107–117.

DEUTSCHE STIFTUNG FÜR INTERNATIONALE ENTWICKLUNG (Ed.), "Report of the ARCT-DSE-ECA Workshop/Metal Working Branch of the Informal Sector of African Economies", Dakar, 1983.

GREENSTREET, Miranda, "Education and Reproductive Choices in Ghana: Gender Issues in Population Policy" in: Development (Journal of the Society for International Development), No. 1, 1990, p. 40–47.

HERWEGEN, Sabine, "Teufelskreis der Armut oder Verteufelung der Armen ?", Kölner Beiträge zur Entwicklungsländerforschung, Vol. 4, Saarbrücken, 1987.

INTERNATIONAL BANK FOR RECONSTRUCTION AND DEVELOPMENT (Ed.), "Women in the Informal Sector in Zimbabwe", Washington D.C., 1989.

INTERNATIONAL BANK FOR RECONSTRUCTION AND DEVELOPMENT (Ed.), "Sub-Saharan Africa. From Crisis to Sustainable Growth. A Long-Term Perspective Study", Washington D.C., 1989.

INTERNATIONAL LABOUR ORGANISATION (Ed.), "Employment, Income and Equality. A Strategy for Increasing Productive Employment in Kenya", 2nd ed., Geneva, 1974.

INTERNATIONAL LABOUR ORGANISATION (Ed.), "Informal Sector in Africa", Addis Abeba, 1985.

INTERNATIONAL LABOUR ORGANISATION (Ed.), "Rapport sur l'emploi en Afrique", Genève, 1989.

LIEDHOLM, Carl/CHUTA, Enyinna, "The Economics of Rural and Urban Small-Scale Industries in Sierra Leone", Njala/Michigan, 1976.

SABAI, M.T. u.a., "Redeployment of Human Resources in Tanzania: Report on the Informal Sector: Constraints and Opportunities", w/o pl., 1989.

SIVERS, Peter von, "Life within the Informal Sector: Tunisia and Egypt in the 1970s", (Working Paper), Bielefeld, 1985.

VITTA, Paul, B., "The Informal Sector in Eastern Africa: Selected Policy-Related Issues" in: Africa Development, No. 4, 1985, p. 60–71.

WELTER, Friederike, "Der informelle Sektor in Entwicklungsländern – dargestellt an Beispielen in Africa", Bochum, 1989.

3.1 Africa: Urban Informal Sector

ARYEE, George, "Small-Scale Manufacturing Activities: A Study of the Interrelationships between the Formal and the Informal Sectors in Kumasi, Ghana", Geneva, 1977.

BERRON, H., "The Traditional Economic Functions in Abidjan, Ivory Coast" in: DRAKAKIS-SMITH, David, "Urbanisation in the Developing World", London/Sydney, 1986, p. 195–203.

CARTON, MICHEL, "Les Artisanats Urbains en Afrique" in: Genève-Afrique, Vol. XXII, No. 1, 1984.

DEMOL, Erik/NIHAN, Georges, "The Modern Informal Sector in Yaoundé" in: International Labour Review, 1982, p. 77–88.

FAPOHUNDA, Olanrewaju J., "The Informal Sector of Lagos: An Inquiry into Urban Poverty and Employment", Geneva, 1978.

GANA, Jerry, "The Role of the Informal Sector in the Development of Small- and Intermediate-Sized Cities", (Seminar Paper), Berlin, 1985.

GERRY, Chris, "Petty Production and Capitalist Production in Dakar: The Crisis of the Self-Employed" in: World Development, Vol. 6, No. 9/10, 1978, p. 1147–1160.

HART, Keith, "Informal Income Opportunities and Urban Employment in Ghana" in: Journal of Modern African Studies, Vol. 11, No. 1, 1973, p. 61–80.

HOFFMANN, Hortense, "Frauen in der Wirtschaft eines Entwicklungslandes: Yoruba Händlerinnen in Nigeria", Saarbrücken, 1983.

HOUSE, William J., "Nairobi's Informal Sector: Dynamic Entrepreneurs or Surplus Labour?" in: Economic Development and Cultural Change, Vol. 32, No. 3, 1984, p. 277–301.

HUGON, Philippe, "Le développement des petites activités à Antanana-rivo: L'exemple d'un processus involutif" in: Revue Canadienne des Etudes Africaines, Vol. 16, No. 2, 1982, p. 293–312.

LUBELL, Harold/ZAROUR, Charbel, "The Informal Sector of Dakar", Paris, 1989.

MWANGI, Meja, "Nairobi, River Road", Wuppertal, 1982.

NIHAN, G./DEMOL, E./JONDOH, C., "The Modern Informal Sector in Lomé" in: International Labour Review, Vol. 118, No. 5, 1979, p. 631–645.

OXENHAM, John, "Educational Assistance to the Urban Informal Sector" in: Prospects, Vol. XIV, No. 2, 1984, p. 189–208.

RANSONI, P., "The Non-Formal Sector in Kigali" in: IRED Forum, Vol. 15, No. I, Geneva, 1985, p. 14–22.

ROCKSLOH-PAPENDIECK, Barbara, "Frauenarbeit am Straßenrand: Kenkeyküchen in Ghana", Hamburg, 1988.

SEIBEL, Hans D./HOLLOH, Detlef, "Handwerk in Nigeria: Unternehmensorganisation, Verbandsstruktur und Förderungsansätze", Saarbrücken, 1988.

STAUTH, Georg, "Gamaliyya: Informal Economy and Social Life in a Popular Quarter of Cairo", Bielefeld, 1986.

STEEL, William F., "Development of the Urban Artisanal Sector in Ghana and Cameroon" in: The Journal of Modern African Studies, Vol. 17, No. 2, 1979, p. 287–293.

VAN DIJK, Meine Pieter, "Le secteur informel de Daker", Paris, 1986.

VAN DIJK, Meine Pieter, "Burkina-Faso. Le secteur informel de Ouaga-dougou", Paris, 1986.

WIKAN, Unni, "Life among the Poor in Cairo", London, 1980.

ZDUNNEK, Gabriele, "Frauenarbeit im informellen Sektor in Ibadan (Nigeria)", Afrika-Hefte No. 1, Bremen, 1988.

3.2 Africa: Rural Informal Sector

BARTH, Ursula, "Frauen gehen lange Wege. Transportvorgänge von Frauen in ländlichen Regionen Afrikas südlich der Sahara", Karlsruhe, 1989.

DATE-BAH, Eugenia, "Rural Women, Their Activities and Technology in Ghana: An Overview" in: INTERNATIONAL LABOUR OFFICE, "Rural Development and Women in Africa", Geneva, 1984, p. 89–98.

DHAMIJA, Jasleen, "Income-generating Activities for Rural Women in Africa: Some Successes and Failures" in: INTERNATIONAL LABOUR OFFICE, "Rural Development and Women in Africa", Geneva, 1984, p. 75–78.

HARPER, Malcolm/VYAKARNAM, Shailendra, "Rural Enterprise. Case Studies from Developing Countries", London, 1988.

HOVEN, Ingrid-Gabriela, "Traditionelles Handwerk als Überlebenssicherung? Hirsebierbrauerinnen in ländlichen Regionen Obervoltas" in: BERNING-HAUSEN, J./KERSTAN, B., "Die unsichtbare Stärke: Frauenarbeit in der Dritten Welt, Entwicklungsprojekte und Selbsthilfe", Saarbrücken, 1984, p. 89–103.

MIKKELSEN, Britha, "Conditions for Industrial Training and Rural Industrial Development in Kakamega District, Western Province, Kenya", Nairobi, 1976.

STEVENS, Yvette, "Technologies for Rural Women's Activities: Problems and Prospects in Sierra Leone" in: INTERNATIONAL LABOUR OFFICE, "Rural Development and Women in Africa", Geneva, 1984, p. 79–88.

VERSTEYLEN-LEYZER, Dorothée, "Integrating Women in Development. The Experience of Nine EDF Rural Development Projects" in: The Courier, No. 125, 1991.

4. Asia: Informal Sector in General

CHOE, Jae-Hyeon, "Die Reziprozität zwischen dem formellen und dem informellen Sektor: eine Interpretation anhand von biographischem Material aus Südkorea" in: Internationales Asienforum, Vol. 13, No. 3/4, Bonn, 1982, p. 269–286.

FÖSTE, Wolfgang, "Verkaufte Träume. Kinderarbeit und Kinderprostitution in Thailand", Munich, 1982.

GHOSH, Jayati, "Young Women in India: Livelihood and Life-Choices" in: Development (Journal of the Society for International Development), No. 1, 1990, p. 20–23.

HEYZER, Noeleen, "Recognizing Women's Productive Potential – Case Studies from Asia and the Pacific" in: Development (Journal of the Society for International Development), No. 1, 1990, p. 92–94.

HÖRNEMANN, Maria "Zwischen großen Leiden und kleinen Erfolgen" in: MISEREOR AKTUELL, No. 1, 1990, p. 10–11.

ROELOFFS, Jan, "Small Enterprise Development in Indonesia", Eschborn, 1989.

SAVARA, Mira, "Organizing the Annapurna" in: YOUNG, K./MOSER, C., "Women and the Informal Sector", Sussex Bulletin, Vol. 12, No. 3, 1981, p. 48–53.

SETHURAMAN, S.V., "The Informal Sector in Indonesia: Policies and Prospects" in: International Labour Review, No. 121, 1985, p. 719–735.

WIDYANTORO, Ninuk, "Enhancing the Quality of Young Women's Reproductive Health Care" in: Development (Journal of the Society for International Development), No. 1, 1990, p. 35–39.

4.1 Asia: Urban Informal Sector

AMIN, Nurul, "The Role of the Informal Sector in Economic Development. Some Evidence from Dhaka, Bangladesh" in: International Labour Review, Vol. 126, No. 5, 1987, p. 611–623.

BOSCO INSTITUTE OF SOCIAL WORK (Ed.), "Situational Analysis of Street Children in Madras City", Tirupattur, w/o y.

BOSCO INSTITUTE OF SOCIAL WORK (Ed.), "A Research Study on Street Children in Salem Town", Tirupattur, 1990.

EVERS, Hans-Dieter/KORFF, Rüdiger, "Subsistence Production in Bangkok" in: Development (Journal of the Society for International Development), No. 4, 1986, p. 50–55.

IGEL, Barbara, "Die Überlebensökonomie der Slumbewohner in Thailand. Territorium und Charakteristika einer eingebetteten Wirtschaft", (Diss.), Berlin, 1988.

KARUNANAYAKE, M./WANASINGHE, Y., "Generating Urban Livelihoods: A Study of the Poor in Colombo" in: Regional Development Dialogue, Vol. 9, No. 4, 1988, p. 80–104.

RODGERS, Gerry (Ed.), "Urban Poverty and the Labour Market. Access to Jobs and Incomes in Asian and Latin American Cities", Geneva, 1989.

4.2 Asia: Rural Informal Sector

BÄR, Dagmar, "Status der Frau und geschlechtsspezifische Arbeitsteilung in der Subsistenzökonomie im ländlichen Nepal" in: BERNINGHAUSEN, J./KERSTAN, B., "Die unsichtbare Stärke: Frauenarbeit in der Dritten Welt, Entwicklungsprojekte und Selbsthilfe", Saarbrücken, 1984, p. 37–52.

BERNINGHAUSEN, Jutta/KERSTAN, Birgit, "Wo die Welt noch in Ordnung ist? Besuch in einem javanischen Dorf" in: BERNINGHAUSEN, J./KERSTAN, B., "Die unsichtbare Stärke: Frauenarbeit in der Dritten Welt, Entwicklungsprojekte und Selbsthilfe", Saarbrücken, 1984, p. 25–35.

BOONTAWEE, Kampoon, "A Child of the Northeast", Bangkok, 1988.

HARPER, Malcolm/VYAKARNAM, Shailendra, "Rural Enterprise. Case Studies from Developing Countries", London, 1988.

JOSE, A.V. (Ed.), "Limited Options. Women Workers in Rural India", New Delhi, 1989.

LEE PELUSO, Nancy, "Survival Strategies of Rural Women Traders or A Woman's Place is in the Market", Jakarta, 1980.

LOHMAR-KUHNLE, Cornelia, "Socio-economic Features of Two Villages Involved in a Labour-based Road Construction Project in Lamphun Province, Thailand", (ILO), Geneva, 1987.

PHONGPAICHIT, Pasuk, "Employment, Income and the Mobilisation of Local Resources in Three Thai Villages", (ARTEP), Bangkok, 1982.

SUDHAM, Pira, "People of Esarn", 5th ed., Bangkok, 1989.

THONGYOU, Apichart, "Simplicity Amidst Complexity: Lessons from a Thai Village", Bangkok, 1988.

VARMA, Sudhir, "Policy Planning for Women's Development at Provincial Level – The Case of Rajasthan" in: Development. Journal of the Society for International Development, No. 1, 1990, p. 95–98.

VYAKARNAM, Shailendra (Ed.), "When the Harvest is in. Developing Rural Entrepreneurship", London, 1990.

Part II: Occupation-oriented Training and Education

5. General Approaches and Concepts

ANDERSON S.D.B., "Don Bosco", 3rd ed., Bombay, w/o y.

ARNOLD, Rolf u.a., "Duale Berufsausbildung in Lateinamerika", Baden-Baden, 1985.

ARNOLD, Rolf, "Vocational Training in Latin America" in: Education. A Biannual Collection of Recent German Contributions to the Field of Educational Research, Vol. 38, 1988, p. 50–68.

ARNOLD, Rolf, "Die geteilte Berufsbildung in der Dritten Welt" in: Zeitschrift für Berufs- und Wirtschaftspädagogik, Vol. 85, No. 2, Stuttgart, 1989, p. 99–119.

ARNOLD, Rolf (Ed.), "Berufliche Bildung und Entwicklung in den Ländern der Dritten Welt. Bilanz, Probleme und Perspektiven der bundesrepublikanischen Berufsbildungshilfe", Baden-Baden, 1989.

AXT, Heinz-Jürgen/KARCHER, Wolfgang/OVERWIEN, Bernd/SCHLEICH, Bernd, "Das neue Sektorkonzept für die Entwicklungszusammenarbeit in der gewerblichen Berufsbildung des BMZ. Eine kritische Würdigung" in: Zeitschrift für Berufs- und Wirtschaftspädagogik, Vol. 83, No. 6, 1987, p. 559–564.

AXT, Heinz-Jürgen/KARCHER, Wolfgang/SCHLEICH, Bernd (Ed.), "Ausbildungs- oder Beschäftigungskrise in der Dritten Welt? Kontroversen über neue Ansätze in der beruflichen Bildung", Frankfurth (Main), 1987.

BERGMANN, Herbert, "The Effects of Education on Rural Development" in: SÜLBERG, Walter, "Ländliche Entwicklung und gemeinsames Lernen", Frankfurt (Main), 1986, p. 161–178.

BERSTECHER, Dieter, "Funktionsprobleme von Bildung in der Dritten Welt – Erfahrungen aus Asien" in: SÜLBERG, Walter, "Ländliche Entwicklung und gemeinsames Lernen", Frankfurt (Main), 1986, p. 147–160.

BÖHM, Ullrich, "Konzeptionelle Überlegungen zu beschäftigungsinitiativer und selbsthilfefördernder Berufsbildung: Verbindung von Ausbildung und produktiver Arbeit" in: WALLENBORN, M., "Strategien selbsthilfefördernder und beschäftigungsinitiativer Berufsbildung in der Dritten Welt", Mannheim, 1989, p. 143–160.

BUNDESMINISTERIUM FÜR WIRTSCHAFTLICHE ZUSAMMENARBEIT (BMZ), "Armutsbekämpfung durch Selbsthilfe. Ein Prozeß zur Ausrichtung des Instrumentariums der bilateralen Entwicklungszusammenarbeit auf die Förderung von Selbsthilfe und die Erreichung armer Zielgruppen in der Dritten Welt", Bonn, 1986.

BUNDESMINISTERIUM FÜR WIRTSCHAFTLICHE ZUSAMMENARBEIT (BMZ), "Sektor-konzept für die Entwicklungszusammenarbeit in der gewerblichen Berufsbildung", Bonn, 1986 (quoted as *BMZ* (1986) from: AXT, H./KARCHER, W./ SCHLEICH, B., "Ausbildungs- oder Beschäftigungskrise in der Dritten Welt? Kontroversen über neue Ansätze in der beruflichen Bildung", Frankfurt (Main), 1987, p. 39–52.

BUNDESMINISTERIUM FÜR WIRTSCHAFTLICHE ZUSAMMENARBEIT (BMZ), "Achter Bericht zur Entwicklungspolitik der Bundesregierung", Bonn, 1990.

CARTON, Michel, "Von der Ausbildung am Arbeitsplatz zur Berufslehre – Überlegungen zu einer Strategie", Geneva, 1989.

CDU/CSU-Frankton im Deutschen Bundestag, "Argumente. Neue Wege in der Entwicklungpolitik: Berufsausbildung als Schlüssel zur Armutsbekämpfung", Bonn, 1986.

CEBALLOS NIETO, Daniel, "La empresa veredal autónoma para la educación y el desarrollo económico y social en la zona rural" (unpublished), Bogotá, 1986.

INTERFOR (Ed.), "Seminario sobre formación profesional y actores sociales: participación para la reactivación económica y el empleo. Informe", Montevideo, 1987.

CINTERFOR/OIT (Ed.), "Reunión técnica sobre determinación de necesidades de formación profesional. Informe", Montevideo, 1981.

CINTERFOR/OIT (Ed.), "Probreza, marginalidad y formación profesional", Montevideo, 1982.

CINTERFOR/OIT (Ed.), "Promoción Profesional Popular: veinte años de capacitación para el sector informal de la economía", Boletín CINTERFOR, No. 100, 1987.

CINTERFOR/OIT (Ed.), "EMBRATER. Política y Directrices de Formación Extensionista" in: Boletín CINTERFOR, No. 102, 1988, p. 57–72.

CINTERFOR/OIT (Ed.), "Regional Review of Vocational Training in Latin America", (unpublished), w/o pl., 1989.

COMBS, Philip H./AHMED, Manzoor, "Attacking Rural Poverty. How Non-Formal Education Can Help", Washington D.C., 1974.

CROSSLEY, Michael, "The Role and Limitations of Small-Scale Initiatives in Educational Innovation" in: Prospects, Vol. 14, No. 4, 1984, p. 533–540.

DEUTSCHE GESELLSCHAFT FÜR TECHNISCHE ZUSAMMENARBEIT (GTZ), "New Business Creation: The GTZ Model", Eschborn, w/o y.

DEUTSCHE GESELLSCHAFT FÜR TECHNISCHE ZUSAMMENARBEIT (GTZ), "Förderung der ländlichen Regionalentwicklung durch formale und non-formale Bildung", Eschborn, 1986.

DEUTSCHE GESELLSCHAFT FÜR TECHNISCHE ZUSAMMENARBEIT (GTZ), "Erfassung der Aktivitäten der GTZ im Informellen Sektor", Eschborn, 1988.

DIEDRICH, Hermann, "Lernen ohne Lehrer und Lobby – Der informelle Berufsbildungsbereich" in: Entwicklung und ländlicher Raum, No. 1, 1989, p. 22–24.

DUKE, Chris, "Adult Education and Poverty: What Are the Connections?" in: Adult Education and Development, No. 30, 1988, p. 39–49.

ENGELBRECHT, Beate, "Handwerksförderung aus ethnologischer Sicht" in: ANTWEILER/BARGATZKY/BLISS, "Ethnologische Beiträge zur Entwicklungspolitik", Bonn, 1987, p. 193–199.

ERNI, Stefan, "Promotion of Self-Employment in the Informal Sector – A Modern Development Concept" in: Deutscher Volkshochschulverband, "Adult Education and Development", Bonn, 1987, p. 59–68.

EVANS, David R., "The Planning of Non-Formal Education", Paris, 1981.

FALTIN, Günter, "Bildung und Einkommenserzielung. Das Defizit: Unternehmerische Qualifikationen" in: AXT, H.J./KARCHER, W./SCHLEICH, B., "Ausbildungs- oder Beschäftigungskrise in der Dritten Welt? Kontroversen über neue Ansätze in der beruflichen Bildung", Frankfurt (Main), 1987, p. 317–338.

FAPOHUNDA, Olanrewaju J., "Small Scale Industries and Training in Zambia" in: BÖHM, U./KAPPEL, R., "Kleinbetriebe des informellen Sektors und Ausbildung im sub-saharischen Afrika", Hamburg 1990, p. 75–94.

FLUITMAN, Fred (Ed.), "Training in the Urban Informal Sector of Developing Countries: Some Recent Findings of Local Observers", Geneva, 1987.

FLUITMAN, Fred, "Training for Work in the Informal Sector: In Search of a Sensible Approach" in: FLUITMAN, Fred, "Training for Work in the Informal Sector", Geneva, 1989, p. 209–224.

FLUITMAN, Fred (Ed.), "Training for Work in the Informal Sector", Geneva, 1989.

FRENZ, Alexander/KOLSHORN, Rainer, "Existenzgründungen fördern" in: GTZ Info No. 5, 1987, p. 16–19.

GAMERDINGER, George W., "The Informal Working Sector: A Resource With a Human Face" in: Deutscher Volkshochschulverband, "Adult Education and Development", Bonn, 1987, p. 69–74.

GOODALE, Gretchan, "Training for Women in the Informal Sector" in: FLUITMAN, Fred, "Training for Work in the Informal Sector", Geneva, 1989, p. 47–69.

GREINERT, Wolf-Dietrich, "Produktionsschulen als Instrument der Berufsbildungshilfe für Länder der Dritten Welt?", (Unpublished Draft), w/o pl., 1990.

HALLAK, Jacques/CAILLODS, Françoise, "Education, Training and the Traditional Sector", Paris, 1981.

HANSEN, Hans J., "Zur Kritik des MES-Systems" in: AXT, H.J./KARCHER, W./SCHLEICH, B., "Ausbildungs- oder Beschäftigungskrise in der Dritten Welt?", Frankfurt (Main), 1987, p. 163–176.

HARPER, Malcolm, "Training and Technical Assistance for Microenterprises" in: LEVITSKY, Jacob, "Microenterprises in Developing Countries", Portsmouth, 1989, p. 177–188.

HASENCLEVER, Rolf (Ed.), "Don Bosco und die Welt der Arbeit. Ursprung, Wachstum und Profil der handwerklich-technischen Ausbildung bei Don Bosco und den Salesianern", Bonn, 1989.

HERSCHBACH, Denis, "Training and the Urban Informal Sector: Some Issues and Approaches" in: FLUITMAN, Fred, "Training for Work in the Informal Sector", Geneva, 1989, p. 3–15.

HEUSSEN, Hejo, "Über die Öffnung schon geschlossener Fragen oder Wer kann von Wem Was Wozu lernen?" in: AXT, H.J./KARCHER, W./SCHLEICH, B., "Ausbildungs- oder Beschäftigungskrise in der Dritten Welt? Krontroversen über neue Ansätze in der beruflichen Bildung", Frankfurt (Main), 1987, p. 127–132.

HINZEN, Heribert/LEUMER, Wolfgang (Ed.), "Erwachsenenbildung in der Dritten Welt. Dialog über Erfahrungen", Braunschweig, 1979.

INTERNATIONAL BANK FOR RECONSTRUCTION AND DEVELOPMENT (Ed.), "Sub-Saharan Africa. From Crisis to Sustainable Growth. A Long-Term Perspective Study", Washington D.C., 1989.

INTERNATIONAL LABOUR ORGANISATION (Ed.), "Rural and Urban Training in Africa", Geneva, 1988.

JIMENEZ VEIGA, Danilo, "La crisis, la deuda, el ajuste y el desarrollo de recursos" in: Boletín CINTERFOR, No. 99, 1987, p. 3–25.

JUNG, Dirk, "Beschäftigung geht vor Bildung! – Ansatzpunkte einer beschäftigungsinitiativen Berufsbildung in Entwicklungsländern am Beispiel von Existenzgründungsprogrammen" in: ARNOLD, Rolf (Ed.), "Berufliche Bildung und Entwicklung in der Dritten Welt. Bilanz, Probleme und Perspektiven der bundesrepublikanischen Berufsbildungshilfe", Frankfurt (Main), 1988, p. 208–221.

KING, Kenneth, "Training for the Urban Informal Sector in Developing Countries: Policy Issues for Practitioners" in: FLUITMAN, Fred, "Training for Work in the Informal Sector", Geneva, 1989, p. 17–38.

KRÖNNER, Hans, "Internationale Zusammenarbeit in der beruflichen Bildung. Die Aufgaben der UNESCO müssen neu definiert werden" in: UNESCO-Dienst (3rd Quarter), 1989, p. 26–29.

LEITE, Elenice M./CAILLODS, Françoise, "Education, Training and Employment in Small-Scale Enterprises", Paris, 1987.

LENHART, Volker, "Die Ausbildung von Ausbildern für die Beschäftigten des informellen Sektors" in: ARNOLD, Rolf, "Berufliche Bildung und Entwicklung in den Ländern der Dritten Welt. Bilanz, Probleme und Perspektiven der bundesrepublikanischen Berufsbildungshilfe", Baden-Baden, 1989, p. 195–207.

LINDAU, Joachim, "Non-formale armutsorientierte Berufsbildung im Bereich kirchlicher Entwicklungsdienste" in: AXT, H.J./KARCHER, W./Schleich, B., "Ausbildungs- oder Beschäftigungskrise in der Dritten Welt?", Frankfurt (Main), 1987, p. 339–356.

Lindau, Joachim/JOESTING, Lynn, "Kritik der formalen Berufsbildung und Vorschläge für alternative Ansätze" in: AXT, H.J./KARCHER, W./SCHLEICH, B., "Ausbildungs- oder Beschäftigungskrise in der Dritten Welt?", Frankfurt (Main), 1987, p. 307–316.

LIPSMEIER, Antonius, "Ist das duale System ein brauchbares Modell zur Überwindung der Berufsbildungsprobleme in den Ländern der Dritten Welt?" in: ARNOLD, Rolf, "Berufliche Bildung und Entwicklung in den Ländern der Dritten Welt. Bilanz, Probleme und Perspektiven der bundesrepublikanischen Berufsbildungshilfe", Baden-Baden, 1989, p. 121–140.

LISOP, Ingrid, "Das Duale System – Realität und zukünftige Entwicklung im Verhältnis zur Weiterbildung" in: Drucksache 11/5349 des Deutschen Bundestags, Bonn, p. 134–141.

LOW MURTRA, Enrique, "Participación y sector informal" in: CINTERFOR, "Seminario sobre formación professional y actores sociales: participación para la reactivación económica y el empleo", Montevideo, 1987, p. 113–114.

LUSZCYK, Artur, "MES in der Praxis" in: AXT, H.J./KARCHER, W./SCHLEICH, B., "Ausbildungs- oder Beschäftigungskrise in der Dritten Welt?", Frankfurt (Main), 1987, p. 147–162.

MÄRKE, Erika, "Marktintegration oder Selbstversorgung im informellen Sektor. Orientierungsalternativen für die Berufsbildung in Entwicklungsländern" in: AXT, H.J./KARCHER, W./SCHLEICH, B., "Ausbildungs- oder Beschäftigungskrise in der Dritten Welt?", Frankfurt (Main), 1987, p. 291–305.

MASLANKOWSKI, Willi, "Berufsbildung in Teilqualifikationen. Der modulare Ansatz der Internationalen Arbeitsorganisation" in: AXT, H.J./KARCHER, W./SCHLEICH, B., "Ausbildungs- oder Beschäftigungskrise in der Dritten Welt?", Frankfurt (Main), 1987, p. 135–145.

MASLANKOWSKI, Willi, "Ohne die Betriebe geht es nicht! – Notwendigkeiten und Grenzen einer stärkeren Ausbildungsbeteiligung der nationalen Betriebe" in: ARNOLD, Rolf, "Berufliche Bildung und Entwicklung in den Ländern der Dritten Welt. Bilanz, Probleme und Perspektiven der bundesrepublikanischen Berufsbildungshilfe", Baden-Baden, 1989, p. 141–151.

MAX-NEEF, Manfred, "Capacitación Profesional y Calidad de Vida", Montevideo, 1977.

MIDDLETON, John/ZIDERMAN, Adrian/ADAMS, Arvil van, "Skills Training for Productivity: Strategies for Improved Efficiency in Developing Countries", w/o pl., 1990.

MIDDLETON, John/ZIDERMAN, Adrian/ADAMS, Arvil van, "Policy Options for Vocational and Technical Education and Training in Developing Countries", Washington D.C., 1990.

MINGAT, Alain/TAN, Jee-Peng, "Analytical Tools for Sector Work in Education", Baltimore, 1988.

MÖLLER, P./SCHLEGEL, W./SCHLEICH, B./WALLENBORN, M., "Wie kann man informelle Berufsausbildung fördern?" in: AXT, H.J./KARCHER, W./ SCHLEICH, B., "Ausbildungs- oder Beschäftigungskrise in der Dritten Welt?", Frankfurt (Main), 1987, p. 279–287.

MÖLLER, P./SCHLEGEL, W./SCHLEICH, B./WALLENBORN, M., "Wie kann man durch Berufsbildung den informellen Sektor fördern?", Mannheim, w/o y.

MOURA CASTRO, Claudio de, "Formación profesional y productividad: Alguna luz en la caja negra?" in: Boletín CINTERFOR, No. 91, 1985, p. 3–38.

OKELO, Mary E., "Support for Women in Microenterprises in Africa" in: LEVITSKY, Jacob, "Microenterprises in Developing Countries", Portsmouth, 1989, p. 240–250.

OXENHAM, John, "Educational Assistance to the Urban Informal Sector" in: Prospects, Vol. XIV, No. 2, 1984, p. 189–208.

PETERSEN, Jens, "Berufsbildung für den informellen Sektor – Grenzen und Möglichkeiten" in: Development and Cooperation, No. 3, 1987, p. 17–18.

RAMIREZ GUERRERO, Jaime, "Opciones Estratégicas para la Formación Profesional en el Sector Informal Urbano" in: CINTERFOR/OIT, Montevideo, 1988.

RATHENBERG, Erhard, "Grundbedürfnisorientierte Berufsbildung – ein Beitrag zur Lösung des Ausbildungsdilemmas in der Dritten Welt?" in: AXT, H.J./ KARCHER, W./SCHLEICH, B., "Ausbildungs- oder Beschäftigungskrise in der Dritten Welt?", Frankfurt (Main), p. 203–217.

SCHIMPF-HERKEN, Ilse, "Erziehung zur Befreiung? Paulo Freire und die Erwachsenenbildung in Lateinamerika", Berlin, 1979.

SCHLEICH, Bernd, "Berufsbildung als Komponente eines integrierten Ansatzes zur Förderung des informellen Sektors" in: AXT, H.J./KARCHER, W./SCHLEICH, B., "Ausbildung- oder Beschäftigungskrise in der Dritten Welt?", Frankfurt (Main), 1987, p. 357–369.

SCHNEIDER-BARTHOLD, Wolfgang, "Entwicklung und Förderung des Kleingewerbes in der Dritten Welt. Bestandsaufnahme, Perspektiven, Vorschläge", Forschungsberichte des Bundesministeriums für wirtschaftliche Zusammenarbeit, No. 62, Bonn, 1984.

SCHÖNFELDT, Eberhard, "Das duale System der beruflichen Bildung", Mannheim, 1986.

SCHULZE, Waltraud/SCHULZE, Heinz (Ed.), "Volkserziehung in Latein-amerika. Von der Theorie Paulo Freires zur politischen Praxis der Unterdrückten", Berlin, 1978.

SPITTLER, Anna, "Training Promotes Self-Confidence" in: GATE No. 3, 1987, p. 14-20.

STOIKOV, Gabriele, "Formación de instructores" in: Boletin CINTERFOR, No. 97, 1987, p. 49-55.

TALAVERA GOIBURU, Rubén, "Medios masivos de comunicación para la formación de la pequeña empresa rural" in: Boletín CINTERFOR, eneromarzo, 1982, p. 51-83.

THIEL, Reinhold, E., "Berufsbildung – nur für Eliten?" in: AXT, H.J./KARCHER, W./SCHLEICH, B., "Ausbildungs- oder Beschäftigungskrise in der Dritten Welt?", Frankfurt (Main), 1987, p. 231-242.

UNITED NATIONS CHILDREN'S FUND (Ed.), "Report and Ten Year Plan, Regional Conference on Non-Formal Education", Islamabad, 1987.

URDANETA FINUCCI, Carlos, "La educación sectorial" in: Boletín CINTERFOR, No. 90, 1985, p. 59-76.

WALLENBORN, Manfred, "Posibilidades de integrar le teoría y la práctica en la formación profesional", Mannheim, 1988.

WALLENBORN, Manfred, "Krise der Berufsbildungshilfe? – Die Entwicklungszusammenarbeit auf dem Gebiet der Berufsbildung zwischen dem modernen und informellen Sektor. Einige Überlegungen zu einer notwendigen Neuorientierung" in: ARNOLD, Rolf, "Berufliche Bildung und Entwicklung in den Ländern der Dritten Welt. Bilanz, Probleme und Perspektiven der bundesrepublikanischen Berufsbildungshilfe", Baden-Baden, 1989, p. 165-178.

WALLENBORN, Manfred (Ed.), "Strategien selbsthilfefördernder und beschäftigungsinitiativer Berufsbildung in der Dritten Welt", Mannheim, 1989.

WALLENBORN, Manfred (Ed.), "Die Berücksichtigung entwicklungspolitischer Grundsätze in der Weiterbildung von technischen Lehrern", Mannheim, 1990.

WEINBERG, Pedro Daniel, "Contribuciones de la formación profesional a la generación de empleo" in: Boletín CINTERFOR, No. 90, 1985, p. 3-25.

WILLIAMS, Carlton, R., "Skills Formation in the Kenyan Informal Economy", Nairobi, 1980.

WORLD CONFERENCE ON EDUCATION FOR ALL, "World Charter on Education for All and Framework for Action to Meet Basic Learning Skills" (Draft B, unpublished), Washington D.C., 1990.

YBARRA ALMADA, Agustín, "Concepto y enfoques de la capacitación rural" in: Boletín CINTERFOR, No. 87, 1984, p. 15–31.

YHR, Carsten, "The Production Training Concept in Vocational Training", (DANIDA Discussion Paper), Copenhagen, 1990.

ZENTRALSTELLE FÜR GEWERBLICHE BERUFSFÖRDERUNG (Ed.), "Ein Vierteljahrhundert gewerbliche Berufsförderung für Entwicklungsländer", Baden-Baden, 1988.

ZIEBART, Sigmund, "Erfahrungen mit der Einführung dualer Berufsausbildung in Entwicklungsländern" in: ARNOLD, Rolf, "Berufliche Bildung und Entwicklung in den Ländern der Dritten Welt. Bilanz, Probleme und Perspektiven der bundesrepublikanischen Berufsbildungshilfe", Baden-Baden, 1989, p. 152–163.

6. Country-specific Programmes and Projects

6.1 Latin America

ABREU, Luz María, "La experiencia de MUDE dominicana" in: BERGER, M./BUVINIC, M., "La mujer en el sector informal. Trabajo femenino y microempresa en América Latina", Quito, 1988, p. 227–241.

ARIAS, María Eugenia, "Un programa integrado de crédito. El Fondo de Desarrollo Rural" in: BERGER, M./BUVINIC, M., "La mujer en el sector informal. Trabajo femenino y microempresa en América Latina", Quito, 1988, p. 277–294.

ARNOLD, Rolf (Ed.), "Berufsbildung für die kleinen Betriebe des informellen Sektors", Heidelberg, 1987.

BANCO MUNDIAL DE LA MUJER, "Como mejorar el acceso de mujeres al crédito" in: BERGER, M./BUVINIC, M., "La mujer en el sector informal. Trabajo femenino y microempresa en América Latina", Quito, 1988, p. 243–253.

BARRY, Jessica, "Reaping Benefits through Education: A Programme of Educational Reform" in: Appropriate Technology, Vol. 11, 1984, p. 20–22.

BÖRGEL, Hannelore, "Evaluierung der Arbeit des Internationalen Kolpingwerkes in Brasilien", Berlin, 1985.

BUVINIC, Mayra/BERGER, Marguerite/GROSS, Stephen, "Una mano para la mujer que trabaja" in: BERGER, M./BUVINIC, M., "La mujer en el sector informal. Trabajo femenino y microempresa en América Latina", Quito, 1988, p. 297–320.

BUVINIC, Mayra/BERGER, Marguerite/JARAMILLO, Cecilia, "Impacto de un proyecto de crédito dirigido a microempresarios" in: BERGER, M./BUVINIC, M., "La mujer en el sector informal. Trabajo femenino y microempresa en América Latina", Quito, 1988, p. 331–362.

CHANG, Ligia/REUBEN, Sergio/SANCHEZ M., Ligia, "Talleres públicos de capacitación-producción del INA", San José, 1985.

CINTERFOR/OIT (Ed.), "La educación occupacional en centros educativos" in: Boletín CINTERFOR, No. 88, 1984, p. 63–75.

CINTERFOR/OIT (Ed.), "Proyecto Haciendas Didácticas" in: Boletín CINTERFOR, No. 102, 1988, p. 73–89.

COLBERT DE ARBOLEDA; Vicky, "Escuela Nueva Moves into Final Phase" in: Development Journal, No. 2, 1990, p. 29.

CORVALAN VASQUEZ, Oscar/DELORENZI, Adriana, "El programa de formación profesional acelerada en el Paraguay" in: Boletín CINTERFOR, No. 87, 1984, p. 59–69.

CORVALAN VASQUEZ, O./CARIOLA, L./CERRI, M., "Empleo y capacitación en los talleres informales de Santiago", Montevideo, 1984.

CORVALAN VASQUEZ, Oscar, "Los programas de capacitación para trabajadores del sector informal en América Latina", Paris, 1985.

DENZLER, Stefan, "Förderung von Berufsbildungsansätzen im informellen Sektor durch SWISSCONTACT in Guatemala, Nicaragua und Costa Rica", (Working Paper), Zurich, 1989.

DEUTSCHE GESELLSCHAFT FÜR TECHNISCHE ZUSAMMENARBEIT (Ed.), "National Network of Grass-Root Women's Organizations 'Todas Juntas'" in: GATE, No. 3, 1987, p. 6–9.

DEUTSCHE STIFTUNG FÜR INTERNATIONALE ENTWICKLUNG (Ed.), "La formación profesional y la pequeña empresa del sector informal", San José, 1986.

FAJARDO, Raúl E., "Die Berufsausbildung im Ausbildungszentrum PISCO-ICA des SENATI", Heidelberg, 1988.

FRÖHLINGSDORF, Michael, "El asesoramiento también se aprende. 25 años del Centro de Fomento de la Profesiones Industriales y Artesanales", in: Desarrollo y Cooperación, No. 2, 1989, p. 17–18.

GOODALE, Gretchen, "Training for Women in the Informal Sector: The Experience of the Pathfinder Fund in Latin America and the Caribbean" in: FLUITMAN, Fred, "Training for Work in the Informal Sector", Geneva, 1989, p.179–188.

GRAF, Christoph, "Die Förderung von Mikrounternehmen in Entwicklungsländern: eine Evaluierung. Förderungsprogramme in Kolumbien als Erfahrungshintergrund" (Diss.), St. Gallen, 1989.

GUZMAN, Margarita/CASTRO, Maria C., "Un banco de la microempresa. Proceso y resultados" in: BERGER, M./BUVINIC, M., "La mujer en el sector informal. Trabajo femenino y microempresa en América Latina", Quito, 1988, p. 255–275.

HAAN, Hans, "Two Examples of Training Projects for the Informal Sector in Central America" in: FLUITMAN, Fred, "Training for Work in the Informal Sector", Geneva, 1989, p. 167–171.

HARPER, Malcolm, "The Programme for the Development of Small Enterprises (DESAP) of the Carvajal Foundation in Cali, Colombia" in: FLUITMAN, Fred, "Training for Work in the Informal Sector", Geneva, 1989, p. 173–178.

INTERNATIONAL BANK FOR RECONSTRUCTION AND DEVELOPMENT (Ed.), "Informal Sector, Labor Markets and Returns to Education in Peru", LSMS Working Paper No. 32, Washington D.C., 1988.

LEQUAY, A.L., "El aprendizaje en Trinidad y Tobago" in: Boletin CINTERFOR, No. 64, 1979, p. 15–25.

LOMBARDI, María Rosa, "Correo directo: una experiencia de su uso en investigaciones tipo follow-up en el área de la formación profesional" in: Boletín CINTERFOR, No. 99, 1987, p. 61–72.

LUTZ, Peter, "Training and Technical Assistance for Micro-enterprises. A Summary of Swisscontact's Experiences", Bern, 1988.

MÖLLER, Sigrid, "Berufsbezogene Erwachsenenbildung in Venezuela – ein Beitrag zur Reduzierung von Armut und Marginalität?", (Diss.), Frankfurt (Main), 1986.

PLACENCIA, María Mercedes, "Capacitación y crédito para microempresarias" in: BERGER, M./BUVINIC, M., "La mujer en el sector informal. Trabajo femenino y microempresa en América Latina" Quito, 1988, p. 171–183.

RAMIREZ GUERRERO, Jaime, "Programas de formación para el sector informal urbano en Colombia y Venezuela", Montevideo, 1988.

RAMIREZ GUERRERO, Jaime, "Training for Informal Sector Enterprises in Latin America" in: FLUITMAN, Fred, "Training for Work in the Informal Sector", Geneva, 1989, p. 159–166.

REICHMANN, Rebecca L., "Dos programas de crédito para microempresas. Los casos de República Dominicana y Perú" in: BERGER, M./BUVINIC, M., "La mujer en el sector informal. Trabajo femenino y microempresa en América Latina", Quito, 1988, p. 187–225.

ROCHA, Luis, "La formación profesional en la Región Autónoma de los Azores" in: Boletín CINTERFOR, No. 97, 1987, p. 43–48.

SADIK, Nafis, "The UNFPA Contribution: Theory to Action Programmes" in: Development (Journal of the Society for International Development), No. 1, 1990, p. 7–12.

SAMLOWSKI, Michael, "An Integral Approach to Adult Education – Four Years Later" in: Adult Education and Development, No. 30, 1988, p. 311–327.

SCHREIBER, Barbara, "Sparen ist Silber – Reden ist Gold. Eine Spar-und Kreditgenossenschaft im ländlichen Mexiko wird fast unbemerkt zur Frauenkooperative" in: BERNINGHAUSEN, J./KERSTAN, B., "Die unsichtbare Stärke: Frauenarbeit in der Dritten Welt, Entwicklungsprojekte und Selbsthilfe", 1984, p. 214–233.

SPITTLER, I., Wolfgang, "Los primeros veinticinco años" in: Boletín CINTERFOR, No. 98, 1987, p. 5–11.

THOMAS, Jim, "Credit Programmes for the Informal Sector" in: Appropriate Technology, Vol. 16, No. 4, 1990, p. 20–23.

TIRADO R., Guillermo, "Asistencia a microtalleres y pequeños empresarios de zonas marginales" in: Boletín CINTERFOR, No. 98, 1987, p. 55–58.

6.2 Africa

ADEPOJU, Aderanti, "Non-Formal Training in Small-Scale Industries" in: DAMACKI, U./EURUSI, K., "Manpower Supply and Utilization – Ghana, Nigeria and Sierra Leone", Geneva, 1979, p. 115–139.

ARYEE, George, A., "Education and Training and Informal Sector Employment in Kumasi, Ghana" in: DAMACKI, U./DIEJOMAOH, V., "Human Resources and African Development", New York/London, 1978, p. 278–319.

BAS, Daniel, "On-the-Job Training in Africa" in: International Labour Review, Vol. 128, No. 4, 1989, p. 485–496.

BELLE-PROUTY, Diane van, "Reproducers Reproduced: Female Resistance in a Rwanda Classroom" in: Development (Journal of the Society for International Development), No. 1, 1990, p. 74–79.

BERGMANN, Herbert, "Praxisunterricht – nur Vermittlung von Techniken?" in: Development and Cooperation, No. 3, 1990, p. 10–11.

BLUMÖR, Rüdiger, "Education with Production in Zimbabwe", Frankfurt (Main), 1988.

BÖHM, Ullrich, "Lehrlingsausbildung in Kleinstbetrieben – am Beispiel Nigerias", (Seminar Paper), w/o pl., 1990.

BUDE, Udo, "Erziehung für eine eigenständige Entwicklung", w/o pl., 1980.

BUDE, Udo, "The Primary School's Role in Development: Services for the Improvement of Local Living Conditions – Facts and Fallacies from Cameroon", 2nd ed., Bonn, 1988.

DEUTSCHE GESELLSCHAFT FÜR TECHNISCHE ZUSAMMENARBEIT (Ed.), "Small-Scale Projects", GATE, No. 4, 1987.

FLUITMAN, Fred/SANGARE, A. Kader, "Some Recent Evidence of Informal Sector Apprenticeship in Abidjan, Côte d'Ivoire" in: FLUITMAN, Fred, "Training for Work in the Informal Sector", Geneva, 1989, p. 107–115.

GAGEL, Dieter, "Aktionsforschung – Methoden partizipativer Handwerksförderung" in: BÖHM, U./KAPPEL, R., "Kleinbetriebe des informellen Sektors und Ausbildung im sub-saharischen Afrika, Hamburg, 1990, p. 45–53.

GRÄN, Christine, "Bekämpfung der Landflucht durch gezielte Ausbildung" in: Entwicklung + Ländlicher Raum, No. 1, 1989, p. 18–19.

HAKAM, Ali N., " The Apprentice System in Ghana: An Instrument for Technology Transfer and Diffusion" in: WATANABE, Susumu, "Technology, Marketing and Industrialisation. Linkages between Large and Small Enterprises", Delhi/Bombay, 1983, p. 58–72.

HARPER, Malcolm, "The Rural Trade School in Salima, Malawi" in: FLUITMAN, Fred, "Training for Work in the Informal Sector", Geneva, 1989, p. 117–122.

HARPER, Malcolm/SOON, Tan Thiam, "Small Enterprises in Developing Countries. Case Studies and Conclusions", London, 1979.

HARPER, Malcolm, "The Euro-Action Accord Programme in Port Sudan, Sudan" in: FLUITMAN, Fred, "Training for Work in the Informal Sector", Geneva, 1989, p. 129–134.

HELMETH, Wolfgang, "Hilfe zur Selbsthilfe. Praktische Spielpädagogik in der Entwicklungsförderung" in: Spielmittel, w/o y., p. 14–17.

HINZEN, H./TEJAN TAMU, S.A./AMADU TURAY, E.D. (Ed.), "Interviews on Learning and Training in Traditional Arts and Crafts", Freetown, 1987.

HOPPERS, Wim, "From School to Work: Youth, Non-Formal Training and Employment in Lusaka", The Hague, 1985.

INTERNATIONAL LABOUR ORGANISATION (Ed.), "Rural and Urban Training in Africa", Geneva, 1988.

KENSOK, P., "Fitter – Entwicklung aus der Werkzeugkiste. Informelle Ausbildung von Kraftfahrzeughandwerkern in Ghana", Saarbrücken, 1987.

KING, Kenneth, "Skill Acquisition in the Informal Sector of an African Economy: The Kenya Case" in: Journal of Development Studies, Vol. 11, No. 2, 1975, p. 260–268.

LE BOTERF, Guy, "Les Apprentis dans le Projet d'Appui au Secteur Non-Structuré de Bamako" in: Genève-Afrique, Vol. 22, No. 1, 1984, p. 74–90.

MABAWONKU, Adewale F., "An Economic Evaluation of Apprenticeship Training in Western Nigerian Small-Scale Industries", Michigan, 1979.

MALDONADO, Carlos, "Self-Training in Theory and Practice: The Programme to Support Urban Informal Sector Enterprises in French-Speaking Africa" in: FLUITMAN, Fred, "Training for Work in the Informal Sector", Geneva, 1989, p. 77–92.

McLAUGHLIN, S.D., "The Wayside Mechanic: An Analysis of Skill Acquisition in Ghana", Amherst, 1979.

MIKKELSEN, Britha, "Conditions for Industrial Training and Rural Industrial Development in Kakamega District, Western Province, Kenya", Nairobi, 1976.

ODURAN, A.B., "The Training of Roadside Mechanics in Benin City, Nigeria" in: Adult Education and Development, No. 30, 1988, p. 299–310.

OYENEYE, Olatunji Y., "An Investigation into the Nature and Process of Human Resource Development in Nigeria's Informal Sector" in: Labour and Society, Vol. 5, No. 4, 1980, p. 373–384.

OYENEYE, Olatunji Y., "The Contribution of the Informal Sector to Industrial Skill Training in Nigeria" in: Genève-Afrique, Vol. 22, No. 1, 1984, p. 55–70.

REHLING, Uwe, "Entwicklung von Technik – Entwicklung durch Technik!? Exemplarische Betrachtungen zum Techniktransfer", Frankfurt (Main), 1988.

RIEDMILLER, Sibylle, "Die Primarschule als Grundlage für ländliche Entwicklung: Erfahrungen mit Schullandwirtschaft" in: Entwicklung + Ländlicher Raum, No. 1, 1989, p. 3–7.

STURMANN, Uwe, "Bildung, Berufsausbildung ... und was dann? Angepaßte Handwerkerausbildung für den ländlichen Raum – die Youth Polytechnics in Kenia", Saarbrücken, 1990.

TANNER, Frances/LEVESQUE, Françoise/ZUMSTEIN, Johanna, "Training for Life? Training in Life. Vocational Education for Rural Women in Africa" in: Entwicklung + Ländlicher Raum, No. 1, 1989, p. 12 f.

ULRICH, Stefan, "Sag mir, was Du spielst, und ich sage Dir, was Du wirst" in: Spielmittel, w/o y., p. 11–16.

UNIVERSITY OF SIERRA LEONE (Ed.), "Training and Learning in the Informal Sector of the Economy and the Social Services of Sierra Leone", Freetown, 1987.

6.3 Asia

GÖLTENBOTH, Friedhelm, "Dorforientierte Ausbildung als Notwendigkeit für die Entwicklung von Papua Neu Guinea" in: AXT, H.J./KARCHER, W./SCHLEICH, B., "Ausbildungs- oder Beschäftigungskrise in der Dritten Welt?", Frankfurt (Main), 1987, p. 243-253.

HARPER, Malcolm/SOON, Tan Thiam, "Small Enterprises in Developing Countries. Case Studies and Conclusions", London, 1979.

HOFFMANN, Dorothee/WITT, Elke, "Frauenprojekte im ländlichen Bangladesh" in: BERNINGHAUSEN, J./KERSTAN, B., "Die unsichtbare Stärke: Frauenarbeit in der Dritten Welt, Entwicklungsprojekte und Selbsthilfe", Saarbrücken, 1984, p. 163-184.

ISKANDAR, Anwas/SABAR, Abdul/MOULTON, Daniel, "Der indonesische Fonds für 'einkommensorientierte' Projekte in der nicht-formalen Bildung" in: HINZEN, H./LEUMER, W., "Erwachsenenbildung in der Dritten Welt. Dialog über Erfahrungen", Braunschweig, 1979, p. 135-146.

JUMANI, Usha, "Training for Women in the Informal Sector: The Experience of the Self-Employed Women's Association (SEWA), Ahmedabad, India" in: FLUITMAN, Fred, "Training for Work in the Informal Sector", Geneva, 1989, p. 143-148.

KAZI, Shannaz, "Employment and Skill Acquisition in the Informal Sector of Rawalpindi and Lahore, Pakistan" in: FLUITMAN, Fred, "Training for Work in the Informal Sector", Geneva, 1989, p. 149-152.

LANZET, Peter, "Das Gemeinwesen-Polytechnikum – Ein indischer Ausbildungsansatz zur Diversifizierung ländlicher Wirtschaftsformen" in: Entwicklung + ländlicher Raum, No. 1, 1989, p. 14 f.

MELLER, Georg, "Nicht formale Berufsausbildung in Thailand – Ein Pilotprojekt des Deutschen Entwicklungsdienstes" in: Entwicklung + Ländlicher Raum, No. 1, 1989, p. 20-21.

PETCHARUGSA, Suchin/MELLER, Georg, "Metalwork Training Pilot Project under the Cooperation of Northern Region Non-Formal Education Center and German Volunteer Service", Bangkok, 1988.

POTT, Detlef/MARIENFELD, Gottfried, "Kurzzeitausbildung für Unterprivilegierte. Das Beispiel PAK-GERMAN Technical Training Programme, Peschawar/Pakistan" in: GTZ Info No. 5, 1987, p. 12-13.

REHLING, Uwe, "Entwicklung von Technik – Entwicklung durch Technik!? Exemplarische Betrachtungen zum Techniktransfer", Frankfurt (Main), 1988.

ROJAHN, Dorothee, "Stärkung selbstbeschäftigter Frauen. Wie Frauen, die sich selbst Arbeit und Einkommen suchen, ihre Position verbessern. Die Erfahrung von SEWA in Indien" in: Development + Cooperation, No. 1, 1987, p. 9-10.

SELLIAH, P., "The Self-Employed Women's Association, Ahmedabad, India", Geneva, 1989.

SCHWERK, Klaus, "Berufliche Ausbildung von Baufacharbeitern in Indien. Frühe Bemühungen um eine zielgruppenorientierte integrierte Bauhandwerkerausbildung" in: AXT, H.J./KARCHER, W./SCHLEICH, B., "Ausbildungs- oder Beschäftigungskrise in der Dritten Welt?", Frankfurt (Main), 1987, p. 179–189.

7. Technology Transfer

AGARWAL, Anil, "Try Asking Women First" in: GATE No. 4, Eschborn, 1984, p. 37–39.

AHMED, Iftikhar (Ed.), "Technology and Rural Women", London, 1985.

BARWELL, Ian, "The Real Test for Technology: Can Local Manufacturers Use It?" in: CERES, 1983, p. 35–37.

GAMSER, Matthew/ALMOND, Frank, "The Role of Technology in Microenterprise Development" in: LEVITSKY, Jacob, "Microenterprises in Development Countries", Portsmouth, 1989, p. 189–201.

GAMSER/APPLETON/CARTER, "Tinker, Tiller, Technical Change: Technologies from the People", w/o pl., 1990.

KHUNDKER, Nasreen, "Technology Adaption and Innovations in the Informal Sector of Dhaka (Bangladesh)", Geneva, 1989.

KLINGER, W., "Die Rolle des Informellen Sektors bei der Abfallbeseitigung in städtischen Regionen von Entwicklungsländern", (Diss.), Hanover, 1988.

LÖWE, Peter, "Zusammenarbeit mit Handwerkern. Erfahrungen aus einem AT-Projekt", w/o pl., 1987.

LÖWE, Peter/GEBAUER, Marie-Luise, "More Aesthetics for the Third World? Product Design and Appropriate Technology" in: GATE No. 3, 1987, p. 25–26.

LOHMAR-KUHNLE, Cornelia, "Requirements and Opportunities for Technology Transfer to Small Enterprises in the North-East of Thailand", Study for the Thailand Institute for Scientific and Technological Research (TISTR), Bangkok, 1985.

NURUL AMIN, A.T.M., "Technology Adaptation in Bangkok's Informal Sector", Geneva, 1989.

REHLING, Uwe, "Entwicklung von Technik – Entwicklung durch Technik!? Exemplarische Betrachtungen zum Techniktransfer", Frankfurt (Main), 1988.

SETHURAMAN, S.V, "Technology Adaption in Micro-enterprises: The Case of Bangalore (India)", Geneva, 1989, p. 18–45.

ULLRICH, Detlev, "Recycling – Potentials, Risks and Limitations" in: GATE No. 3, 1989, p. 3–6.

8. Self-help Approaches

BRAUER, Dieter, "Selbsthilfeförderung in Pakistan" in: Development + Cooperation, No. 6, 1989, p. 4–6.

CAMRON, Gerda, "Women and Health in Suriname – Women Taking Action" in: Development (Journal of the Society for International Development), No. 1, 1990, p. 86–91.

CEBALLOS MÜLLER, Juan, "Selbsthilfeorganisationen als Erziehungsfaktor in ländlicher Entwicklung – eine Möglichkeit zur Selbsthilfe?", (Diploma Thesis), Berlin, 1988.

FISCHER, Wolfgang E., "Selbsthilfeförderung: Von den Schwierigkeiten der Umsetzung eines Entwicklungskonzepts" in: Development + Cooperation, No. 2, 1990, p. 13–15.

KÖSTER, Gerrit, "Aspekte von Partizipation und Selbsthilfe bei Einfachwohnungsbau und Stadtentwicklung", Aachen, 1988

KORTZ, Stefan, "Große Krisen als Folgen kleiner Probleme. Verdeckte Ursachen des Scheiterns von Selbsthilfeprojekten" in: Development + Cooperation, No. 2, 1990, p. 16–17.

MARIE-SCHLEI-VEREIN (Ed.), "Wir tragen eine schwere Last ...", Hamburg, 1989.

SCHÜTZ, Eike J., "Städte in Lateinamerika. Barrio-Entwicklung und Wohnbau", MISEREOR-Dialogue, 1987.

STICKER, Georg/RAMIREZ, Benjamin et al., "Kredit- und Revolving-fonds zur Förderung von Selbsthilfegruppen", Cologne, 1989.

9. Planning, Design and Financing of Programmes and Projects

ARNOLD, Rolf, "Weiterbildung von Berufspädagogen zu Berufsförderern" in: ARNOLD, Rolf, "Berufliche Bildung und Entwicklung in den Ländern der Dritten Welt. Bilanz, Probleme und Perspektiven der bundesrepublikanischen Berufsbildungshilfe", Baden-Baden, 1989, p. 222–231.

BOLLIGER, Ernst/REINHARD, Peter/ZELLWEGER, Tonino, "Landwirtschaftliche Beratung. Ein Leitfaden für Beraterinnen und Berater im ländlichen Raum", St. Gallen, 1990.

BRAUN, Gerald, "Die hilflose Überlegenheit des Experten" in: Development + Cooperation, No. 10, 1989, p. 18–21.

BRAUN, Gerald, "Gesucht: Ein Verhaltenskodex für Experten" in: Development + Cooperation, No. 10, 1990, p. 10–11.

CHAMBERS, Robert, "Rapid and Participatory Rural Appraisal" in: Appropriate Technology, Vol. 16, No. 4, 1990, p. 14 ff.

DEUTSCHE GESELLSCHAFT FÜR TECHNISCHE ZUSAMMENARBEIT (GTZ), "Die sozio-kulturelle Dimension der Entwicklungszusammenarbeit – eine Lesemappe für GTZ-Mitarbeiter", Eschborn, 1990.

EL-MINSHAWI, B./FANGMANN, C., "Auf-Bruch oder: Einen Schritt näher gekommen – Notizen eines Gesprächs nach der Rückkehr" in: BERNINGHAUSEN, J./KERSTAN, B., Entwicklungsprojekte und Selbsthilfe", Saarbrücken, 1984, p. 275–284.

GAGEL, Dieter, "Aktionsforschung – Methoden partizipativer Handwerksförderung" in: BÖHM, U./KAPPEL, R., "Kleinbetriebe des informellen Sektors und Ausbildung im sub-saharischen Afrika", Hamburg, 1990, p. 45–53.

GERDES, Klaus, "Explorative Sozialforschung. Einführende Beiträge aus "Natural Sociology" und Feldforschung in den USA", Stuttgart, 1979.

GUNNERSON, Charles G./SCOTT-STEVENS, Susan, "Community and Counterpart Participation in Development" in: Development (Journal of the Society for International Development), No. 4, 1990, p. 122–128.

HEGELHEIMER, Armin, "Finanzierung der beruflichen Ausbildung", 2nd ed., Mannheim, 1988.

INTERNATIONAL BANK FOR RECONSTRUCTION AND DEVELOPMENT (Ed.), "Vocational Education and Training in Developing Countries: Policies for Flexibility, Efficiency and Quality", (unpublished), Washington D.C., 1989 (quoted as: IBRD (1989a)).

KOIKARA S.D.B., Felix/MANNATH S.D.B. Joe, "Youth Worker's Resource Book. Tips and Quizzes for Youth Workers. Forty-five Sessions for Youth Groups", Madras, 1985.

KOIKARA, S.D.B., Felix, "Live Your Values. Teacher's Guide and Student's Workbook", Vol. 1 and 2, Madras, 1990.

LOHMAR-KUHNLE, Cornelia, "Explorative Projektfindung vor Ort", Berlin, 1984.

MAX-NEEF, Manfred, "From the Outside Looking" in: "Experiences in Bare-foot Economics", Uppsala, 1982.

MIDDLETON, John/DEMSKY, Terry, "Vocational Education and Training. A Review of World Bank Investment", Washington D.C., 1989.

MIDDLETON, John/ZIDERMAN, Adrian/ADAMS, Arvil van, "Policy Options for Vocational and Technical Education and Training in Developing Countries", Washington D.C., 1990.

NAGEL, Uwe J. et al., "Focussing Formal Surveys. The Use of Rapid Rural Appraisal for Designing a Survey in Nam Lang (Thailand)", Berlin, 1989.

OEHRING, Eckart, "Action Learning. A Methodology for Entrepreneurial Development in Small Enterprises in Costa Rica", San José, 1985.

RATHENBERG, Erhard/MIELCK, Andreas, "Wie entwickelt man Medien für die berufliche Bildung?", Mannheim, 1986.

RETUERTO, Enrique, "Determinación de necesidades de formación profesional: metodología y manual", Montevideo, 1983.

SCHNEIDER-BARTHOLD, Wolfgang, "Mit Armen sprechen, handeln und lernen. Basisentwicklung in der Dritten Welt und ihre Förderung", Berlin, 1987.

SCHULTZ, Theodore W., "In Menschen investieren. Die Ökonomie der Bevölkerungsqualität, Tübingen, 1986.

SEEMANTINEE, K./SHANTABEN, G. et al., "How to Organize Women's Groups", New Delhi, w/o y.

SEIBEL, H.D./PARHUSIP, U., "Linking Formal and Informal Financing Institutions: An Action Programme in Asia and the Pacific – With a Case Study of Indonesia", (Seminar Paper), w/o pl., 1989.

SRINIVASAN, Lyra, "Tools for Community Participation. A Manual for Training of Trainers in Participatory Techniques", New York, 1990.

STUART, Sara, "Video as a Tool in Training and Organizing: Experiences of Video SEWA" in: Development (Journal of the Society for International Development), No. 2, 1990, p. 47–50.

TAN, Jee-Peng/LEE, Kiong Hock/MINGAT, Alain, "User Charges for Education. The Ability and Willingness to Pay in Malawi", Washington D.C., 1984.

TANDON, R./SHRIVASTAVA, G. et al., "How To Communicate Effectively with Grass-Root Women", New Delhi, w/o y.

THOBANI, Mateen, "Charging User Fees for Social Services. The Case of Education in Malawi", Washington D.C., 1983.

TRANBERG HANSEN, Karen, "Planning Productive Work for Married Women in a Low-Income Settlement in Lusaka: The Case of a Small-Scale Handicraft Industry" in: African Social Research, 1982, p. 211–223.

VELLA, Jane, "Learning to Teach. Training of Trainers for Community Development", Washington D.C., 1989.

Wolf-Dietrich Greinert

Das „deutsche System" der Berufsausbildung

Geschichte, Organisation, Perspektiven

Das deutsche „duale" System der – nicht-akademischen – Berufsausbildung ist erneut Gegenstand öffentlicher Diskussionen. Aktuell geht es um die Frage, ob dieses Qualifikationssystem angesichts der Expansion von Gymnasium und Hochschulbereich überhaupt noch eine Zukunftschance hat. Die Zeichen seiner zunehmenden Erosion sind unübersehbar.

Im vorliegenden Buch wird zum erstenmal zusammenhängend die historische Entwicklung des „dualen" Berufsausbildungssystems im Hinblick auf seine Zukunftsperspektive analysiert. Seine komplexe Einbettung in kulturelle, sozio-ökonomische und politische Prozesse wird ebenso aufgezeigt wie seine ambivalenten Beziehungen zum allgemeinen Bildungssystem.

Der Autor skizziert abschließend die entwickelte Struktur des „dualen" Systems im Augenblick seiner Ausdehnung auf ganz Deutschland und konfrontiert die zahlreichen Vorschläge zu seiner Stabilisierung mit seinen Untersuchungsergebnissen.

Er liefert damit einen wichtigen Beitrag zur bildungs- und berufsbildungspolitischen Diskussion unserer Tage.

1993, 216 S., brosch., 48,– DM, 338,50 öS, 43,50 sFr,
ISBN 3-7890-3093-7
(Studien zur Vergleichenden Berufspädagogik (GTZ), Bd. 1)

NOMOS VERLAGSGESELLSCHAFT
Postfach 610 • 76484 Baden-Baden

Wolf-Dietrich Greinert/Günter Wiemann
unter Mitarbeit von Horst Biermann und Rainer Janisch

Produktionsschulprinzip und Berufsbildungshilfe

Analyse und Beschreibungen

2. Auflage

Der Begriff „Produktionsschule" steht – prinzipiell betrachtet – für die Kombination von Erziehung und produktiver Arbeit bzw. von Ausbildung und erwerbsorientierter Produktion. Markierte der Begriff lange Zeit pädagogische Vergangenheit, gewinnt das Produktionsschulprinzip heute wieder international an Bedeutung.

Die vorliegende Untersuchung setzt sich mit der Frage auseinander, ob dieses Modell für die Organisation der Berufsausbildung in Entwicklungsländern geeignet ist. Die Frage wird unter entwicklungspolitischer, organisationssoziologischer, betriebswirtschaftlicher, qualifikationstheoretischer und didaktischer Perspektive überprüft.

Ein Schlußkapitel versucht zusammenfassend die Voraussetzungen und Bedingungen zu skizzieren, unter denen die Anwendung des Produktionsschulprinzips in der Berufsbildungshilfe sinnvoll und erfolgreich zu sein verspricht. Im zweiten Teil der Untersuchung sind neun erfolgreiche Produktionsschulen in Deutschland, Dänemark, der Schweiz, in Indonesien, Indien und Singapur systematisch und sehr ausführlich dokumentiert.

1993, 287 S., brosch., 48,– DM, 338,50 öS, 43,50 sFr,
ISBN 3-7890-3129-1
(Studien zur Vergleichenden Berufspädagogik (GTZ), Bd. 2)

NOMOS VERLAGSGESELLSCHAFT
Postfach 610 • 76484 Baden-Baden